MANAGING EMERGING DATA TECHNOLOGIES

MANAGING EMERGING DATA TECHNOLOGIES

Concepts and Use

Duncan R. Shaw

Los Angeles | London | New Delhi
Singapore | Washington DC | Melbourne

Los Angeles | London | New Delhi
Singapore | Washington DC | Melbourne

SAGE Publications Ltd
1 Oliver's Yard
55 City Road
London EC1Y 1SP

SAGE Publications Inc.
2455 Teller Road
Thousand Oaks, California 91320

SAGE Publications India Pvt Ltd
B 1/I 1 Mohan Cooperative Industrial Area
Mathura Road
New Delhi 110 044

SAGE Publications Asia-Pacific Pte Ltd
3 Church Street
#10-04 Samsung Hub
Singapore 049483

Editor: Ruth Stitt
Assistant editor: Jessica Moran
Assistant editor, digital: Mandy Gao
Production editor: Sarah Cooke
Copyeditor: Thea Watson
Proofreader: Salia Nessa
Indexer: Judith Lavender
Cover design: Naomi Robinson
Typeset by: C&M Digitals (P) Ltd, Chennai, India
Printed in the UK

Library of Congress Control Number: 2022936099

British Library Cataloguing in Publication data

A catalogue record for this book is available from the British Library

ISBN 978-1-5297-6162-7
ISBN 978-1-5297-6161-0 (pbk)

At SAGE we take sustainability seriously. Most of our products are printed in the UK using responsibly sourced papers and boards. When we print overseas we ensure sustainable papers are used as measured by the PREPS grading system. We undertake an annual audit to monitor our sustainability.

To Mum and Dad
For the start of my journey

CONTENTS

ABOUT THE AUTHOR

After working in engineering and logistics, Duncan did an MBA at Manchester Business School and went into management consultancy, where he worked for clients including Xerox, Coca-Cola, Danone and Shell. He then joined Motorola's mobile phone division and was the Customer Satisfaction Manager for the Europe, Middle East and Africa (EMEA) region.

Duncan did his PhD on Network Orchestration and now teaches business strategy and data technology strategy at Alliance Manchester Business School in Hong Kong, and at Nottingham University Business School in the UK and Kuala Lumpur, Malaysia.

He researches and consults on data monetisation, data sharing, the Internet of Things and qualitative data science. Duncan consults to private companies and the UK government, and publishes in academic journals and books. He has international academic and commercial experience in Asia, Europe and North America.

Duncan writes – and more – at www.duncanrshaw.co.uk.

ONLINE RESOURCES

Lecturers can visit **study.sagepub.com/met** to access a range of online resources designed to support teaching. *Managing Emerging Data Technologies: Concepts and Use* is accompanied by:

For lecturers

- A **Teaching Guide** containing suggested activities for seminars and assignment ideas.
- **PowerPoints** for each chapter that can be adapted and edited to suit specific teaching needs.

AT A GLANCE

This book describes how organisations are responding to global forces of change like new technologies and how to play an important part in helping them.

There are three sections to the book: 1. The forces acting on organisations, 2. How organisations are responding and 3. Skills to help organisations respond.

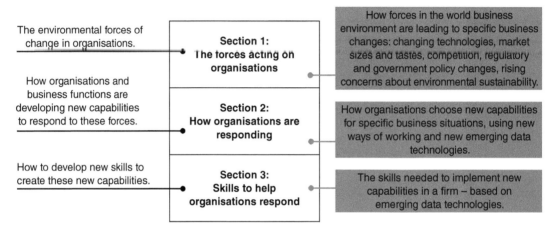

Figure 0.1   Overview of the book

Why use this book?

This book fills the gap between technical topics and pure business topics. For topics like digital business, the Internet of Things, big data, artificial intelligence, business intelligence, decision-making and analytics, it provides an overall model that explains 'why' the world is changing (Section 1) and 'how' firms are using these emerging data technologies (Section 2). This structure helps in learning and teaching the skills that firms need because knowing 'why' and 'where' show us when to apply each skill and how to evaluate the level of skill required.

The practical business implications of emerging data technologies

This book explains the practical business implications of emerging data technologies, technologies that most people will soon need to use, the forces that drive their business adoption and the skills that are required to use them. Few books focus on this subject because of the novelty of the technologies themselves. Many firms are just getting used to these emerging technologies and most education providers are only now integrating these new technological capabilities with the actual situations that businesses are in, and the specific capabilities they need.

There are books on individual technologies like **blockchain**, the **Internet of Things**, **big data** and **data analytics**, and there are many books on **artificial intelligence (AI)**. But they do not integrate different technologies together, and do not *integrate* them with old and emerging business practices. Also, most of these books are not designed to be for use in teaching. Finally, there are also many technical skills books in new digital data topics, but they rarely put things in the context of business strategy and the business skills that are required.

For learners

If you want to help organisations to transform:

- their products and services
- how they operate
- how their people work together
- how they collaborate with business partners; and even
- their fundamental purpose, then this book will help you develop the skills to do that.

Emerging data technologies are one of several forces that are changing the world. Forces like changes in markets, new types of competition, regulatory and policy changes, and rising concerns about the environment. But new data technologies are also one of the main ways that organisations are dealing with these changes.

This book connects data technologies to business operations and strategy. It will help you to commercially and strategically support the organisations that you want to work with, in areas that include the following topics:

- **Data science** – the use of software coding and mathematical tools for generating digital data, analysing it and then using insights to make decisions that help organisations and people.
- **Data** – a recording of something that happens. In words, graphs, charts or pictures; in pencil, pen, paint, in photos or digitally.
- **AI** – a group of technologies that automates and greatly increases the speed of finding patterns in very large digital datasets.
- **Data analytics** – analysing digital data.
- **Internet of Things** – a collection of electronic devices linked by the Internet.

These definitions are from this book's extensive Glossary. I hope that you will use the skills that this book teaches to take advantage of the new opportunities that these technologies bring.

For lecturers and trainers

Case studies and examples

All the ideas and skills in the book are illustrated with business examples, e.g., a step-by-step exercise on how to choose and capture the right data for an analytics problem; details of how to add the right digital services to your product or the right product to your services; or instructions on how to design and build your business ecosystem of partners. The size of examples varies from sentences to larger vignettes and small cases, as required by the span of the concepts being dealt with and novelty to the reader. Practical examples are used in all three sections, but greater detail is provided in Section 3, which deals with how to develop the skills to do specific things in work. Shorter examples and vignettes are embedded in the text, larger vignettes or cases are set out as needed. Examples, vignettes and cases come from my own research and easily available sources.

Online resources

Lecturers and trainers can access online materials, suggestions of hands-on activities using free online resources and ideas on how to teach and equip their learners with practical and up to date knowledge. This content is especially important for the skills teaching in Section 3. But the analysis skills in Section 1 (change forces) and Section 2 (organisational responses) also need hands-on type activities to support relevance, accessibility and comprehension by showing how to recognise change forces and then choose appropriate organisational responses.

Level of learners and approach

This book is written for learners who are interested in taking advantage of the changes in Section 1 that the world is dealing with. The focus is on the practicalities of helping organisations and being useful to them. So, the book is designed to be used as much by business professionals as it is for undergraduates and MBAs. All the ideas in the book have robust theoretical support, which is clearly referenced. Indeed, many of the ideas or their implications come from the author's own research with a large number of commercial and government organisations.

This research is about **Journey-based Thinking**. Journey-based Thinking comes from customer journey and customer experience ideas which are a core part of designing digital services. These ideas, and a focus on helping customers to be successful, applies just as much to all stakeholders in organisations as it does to consumers of digital services. Helping all stakeholders to mutually satisfy each other's values is the fundamental objective of a business model.

All the ideas in the book are also backed up with rich practical illustrations from the author's consultancy and research projects. These illustrations and examples breathe life into the ideas and show how many organisations are just starting to use the technologies in the book. That is why a single book can support such a wide range of learners – the whole world is just starting to learn how to profit from emerging data technologies. Newly graduated undergraduates are in a similar position to the middle level managers tasked with designing a firm's first data strategy, or its first Internet of Things product design. Few firms are as advanced as Google, Microsoft, Amazon and others, and even these firms have by no means exhausted the possibilities that readers of this book can benefit from.

SECTION I
THE FORCES ACTING ON ORGANISATIONS

I

INTRODUCTION

KEY IDEAS

- The business world is changing very fast in terms of pressures on organisations, new technologies to use and new products and services.
- Organisations are developing new capabilities to respond to these changes.
- Their responses are based on three fundamental capabilities: Understanding customers' needs, producing products and services that satisfy them, and repeating this effectively.
- These three fundamental capabilities are themselves disrupting how organisations and entire industries function.
- These capabilities frequently rely on emerging data technologies, which the skills in this book will help you use.

LEARNING OBJECTIVES

After reading this chapter you will be able to:

- Explain why emerging data technologies are important for organisations and the people that work in them.
- Explain which new capabilities organisations are using to respond to a changing world.
- Describe which skills this book has taught you.
- Describe how these skills can help your career.

Introduction

This chapter introduces the main topic of the book, emerging data technologies. It explains how business and government organisations are quickly transforming in response to forces of change by developing new capabilities. Capabilities that help them to better understand their customers' needs, produce a much fuller customer experience, and then keep on doing this in the face of continued changes in society. These capabilities frequently rely on using emerging data technologies, which requires a particular mix of skills. Chapter 1 explains how to use this book to gain those skills so that you can help organisations all over the world to do this.

Emerging data technologies are changing everything

Using emerging data technologies to respond to change

Markets are globalising, resources are diminishing, and firms are having to deal with competitors from completely different sectors. A range of forces are changing the demand for products and services and how they are produced and supplied. Organisations in different sectors and countries are confronted with different situations and different challenges. Choosing how to respond is as important as executing that choice.

Some organisations are developing new capabilities, whilst others are still trying to figure out how to use big data. Some people are worried that artificial intelligence (AI) might take their jobs, although others see massive opportunities. To get the capabilities they require, many organisations are responding to change by upskilling large parts of their workforce. Organisations need new capabilities to respond to the forces of change, and these capabilities are enabled by new skills and new resources (Figure 1.1).

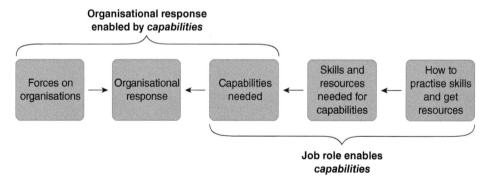

Figure 1.1   New organisational capabilities are needed to respond to the forces of change.

This book explains how businesses and other organisations are starting to use emerging data technologies like big data, the Internet of Things, AI and **machine learning techniques**, and how readers can take advantage of this in their careers. For example, AI is being used to help us shop and play, to suggest what we post and what we read on social media, as well as to diagnose illnesses and suggest medical treatments. **Robot Process Automation** is using several new technologies to reinvent whole areas of working. Firms are starting to work together in **digital ecosystems**, which are wholly different to old-style supply chains. Digital services are providing individually personalised help to people on a huge scale, for free. And **business models** are being rebalanced and reengineered to produce completely new ways of creating value.

Strategies, like **agile working** and **Minimum Viable Product** (MVP) approaches are changing how staff in organisations work together. **Platform strategies**, flywheel models, **network effects** and other feedback loops are helping organisations to grow very fast. Also, fast-moving new **start-ups** are regularly outcompeting older and slower rival firms.

Skills needed to take advantage of these changes

This book gives readers a 'big picture' view of the environmental forces that are changing organisations; and a precise understanding of how organisations and business functions are responding. It helps readers to understand the new capabilities that firms are developing, and how readers can learn the new skills that enable these capabilities.

It is still early; you can still take advantage

Many of these emerging data technologies and new business practices are still very new. What to use them for, how to use them and where to use them are still being worked out. More and more are being developed every day. The story is still unfolding and there is a huge opportunity to be the person who brings these capabilities to a firm or to use them whilst starting a company. The key is to understand how to pick the right ones to use, where to use them and how to do it. This book will help develop understanding in three key areas:

1   *Why* specific new technologies and practices are reaching into every area of business, government and society.
2   *Where* different technologies and practices fit different organisational needs.
3   *How* to use them in your career.

Digital data, qualitative data and quantitative data

The book sets out a clear framework for studying and working with emerging data technologies. It teaches you the skills to take advantage of the above changes. Sections 1 and 2 help you to choose the right skills to apply in the right situation, then Section 3 shows you how to do it.

All sections of the book deal with how digital **data** is being used in innovative new ways. Section 1 is about data for analysing change forces and deciding how an organisation should respond; Section 2 explains how data is used to support different types of responses; and Section 3 explains how to do this yourself in terms of customer relationships, product and service innovation, and finally data analytics strategies.

Sections 1 and 2 are designed to give learners a new toolbox of concepts for generating data and finding data sources by asking the right questions. Questioning is a method that can be used as a way of specifying the data that is required to solve a problem and get things done, and also a method of analysing it.

This applies to qualitative data as well as quantitative data. Before you count something, you must decide what to count. It also applies whether an analyst is using digital data or non-digital data because data is a recording of anything that has happened. It could be a digital **dataset**, an oil painting, or a stone carving. Any record of any occurrence is data; text, spreadsheets, audio, video and X-ray pictures are all data. Data technologies search through digital data records looking for patterns. There may be a useful pattern in the data, which can then be used to make decisions and to act. We will cover this in Section 3 and especially in Chapter 10 where I will explain the process of problem solving using digital data to make decisions in organisations.

Generating data and using data analytics are golden threads that run through this book. All the topics and organisational examples in Sections 1 and 2 depend on using digital data and data analytics. Sections 1 and 2 also provide the conceptual tools for generating digital data when using the analysis methods in Section 3 (see Figure 1.2: The overall layout of this book).

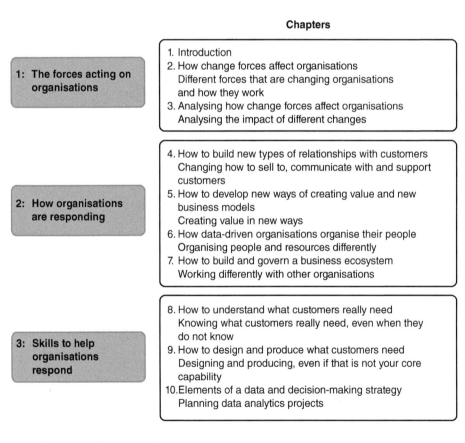

Chapters

1: The forces acting on organisations
1. Introduction
2. How change forces affect organisations
   Different forces that are changing organisations and how they work
3. Analysing how change forces affect organisations
   Analysing the impact of different changes

2: How organisations are responding
4. How to build new types of relationships with customers
   Changing how to sell to, communicate with and support customers
5. How to develop new ways of creating value and new business models
   Creating value in new ways
6. How data-driven organisations organise their people
   Organising people and resources differently
7. How to build and govern a business ecosystem
   Working differently with other organisations

3: Skills to help organisations respond
8. How to understand what customers really need
   Knowing what customers really need, even when they do not know
9. How to design and produce what customers need
   Designing and producing, even if that is not your core capability
10. Elements of a data and decision-making strategy
    Planning data analytics projects

Figure 1.2   The overall layout of this book

Tools for using data to analyse organisations

This book contains a toolset of conceptual models for using data to analyse organisations, their business models, their customers, their organisational structures and their business processes. Most importantly, it explains the strategy of how to get the right data to do this, and how to use it. All of these tools and techniques are fully explained with practical and thought-provoking examples for a range of industries and countries. The models come in the form of clearly packaged collections of useful concepts to give new viewpoints to an analysis, and in the form of step-by-step practical methods for helping and understanding organisations in a digital world. The book is written for readers who are not currently working in the roles that are dealt with here, as well as readers who are. Similar methods are being used all around the world in many organisations, and the ultimate aim is that readers will use them in future careers to amplify their success.

Section detail and the chapters of this book

Many books teach the pure 'digital skills' that organisations demand but there is rarely an overall model of how these skills fit together and no road map for developing them. The three sections of this book are designed to work together. Sections 1 and 2 explain why these skills are needed and where to apply them; this helps in choosing which skills to use, and also provides a way of evaluating that learning. Section 3 teaches the skills (Figure 1.3).

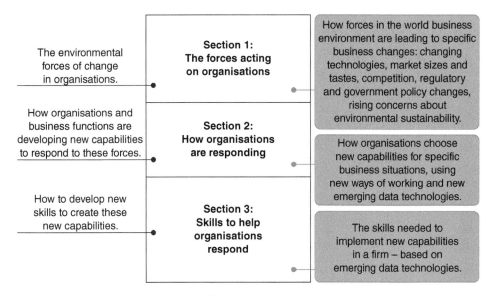

Figure 1.3 The book's three sections: 1. The forces acting on organisations, 2. How organisations are responding and 3. Skills to help organisations respond

Section 1: The forces acting on organisations

Section 1 explains *why* fundamental business changes are happening right now and what environmental forces of change mean for organisations. This section describes the forces that are changing public and private sector organisations, including companies and governments. It also looks at how organisations in different sectors and countries are responding in their own ways.

Different forces of change include new technologies, changes in market size and market tastes, changes in how firms compete with each other, regulatory changes and rising concerns about environmental sustainability. All these forces drive changes in organisations' business models and how they execute them.

This section also explains how interactions between different change forces combine with each other to alter their effect, which then produces different choices for firms. For example, changes in new technologies and their use produces changes in market size and new government regulations.

Chapter 1: Introduction

This chapter is an overall introduction to the book and how it helps readers to help organisations, and provides an overview of the book.

Chapter 2: How change forces affect organisations

This chapter describes the different forces that are changing how organisations around the world are structured, how they operate and what they aim to do. These forces include technological changes (using WhatsApp not Skype; using digital news and e-books not paper newspapers), market changes (changes in market size and market tastes), new types of competition (new competitive strategies; globalisation; competition from out-of-sector firms), regulatory and policy changes (political changes; cultural changes) and rising concerns about environmental sustainability (carbon footprints; plastics).

Chapter 3: Analysing how change forces affect organisations

This chapter explains how to watch out for and analyse how different change forces are transforming firms and other organisations. It explains how multiple change forces – especially new technologies – come together and change organisations. It looks at how change forces intermingle to affect each other as well as organisations. For example, when changes in business and government organisations alter how we use technologies or redefine how organisations compete. Lastly, this chapter explains how change forces work together with each organisation's local situation to affect it in different ways. Organisations in different sectors and countries are confronted with different situations. Choosing how to respond is different for different organisations, and critical for business success. Every organisation operates in a different community of partners and suppliers, and in a different regulatory and cultural climate. This section uses ideas from ecology to show how the individual situation of an organisation will affect its response to change forces.

Section 2: How organisations are responding

Section 2 shows you how real organisations are making changes in response to the forces in Section 1. It explains where and when organisations are using new capabilities. Organisations in different sectors and countries are confronted with different situations. Choosing specifically how to respond is very important. Many businesses' responses are enabled by using digital data in new ways. Organisations are using data to communicate with customers very differently. They are changing how they work with customers and with other organisations, they are changing their business models and creating new types of value for customers and other stakeholders and they are changing how their staff work together and how they work in new business ecosystems. This section also explains some of the new working practices, for example, agile working and MVP strategies. Businesses are changing themselves by developing three fundamental capabilities, which you can help with. These three fundamental capabilities are:

1   Understanding customers better than they understand themselves and helping them to choose what they need – because customers do not always know what is best for them, or what is possible, and they are frequently overwhelmed by choices.
2   Producing the full experience of what customers need – because your customers need more than your core product or service to be successful and satisfied.
3   Understanding how to continue doing this – because organisations need to be efficient and effective, and the forces of change keep on and on.

Chapter 4: How to build new types of relationships with customers

This chapter explains how organisations are changing the ways that they sell to, communicate with and support customers. The relationships between organisations and their customers are upgrading from discrete transactions to giving customers personalised guidance along their whole life journeys. All in return for firms harvesting rich customer data.

Chapter 5: How to develop new ways of creating value and new business models

This chapter describes how organisations are using digital capabilities to innovate how they create value for customers and other stakeholders. This means new types of value for new stakeholders and different ways of creating it. It is the business model of an organisation that creates value for customers and all its stakeholders. Many business models are being disrupted and consciously reengineered. Tangible products are being turned into digital services and vice versa. Firms are using new business models like platform strategies and business ecosystems to generate value in new ways.

Chapter 6: How data-driven organisations organise their people

This chapter describes how organisations are organising their people and their resources differently. When it's not just top management who have all the information, should organisational structures radically change to let other people make decisions? In addition to decision-making, the ways that people work together in teams and departments are also changing. The uptake of new management techniques and digital collaboration technologies is redefining who we work with and how – both inside and outside organisations.

Chapter 7: How to build and govern a business ecosystem

This chapter describes how organisations are working differently with other organisations, and how groups of firms are organising themselves into business ecosystems. Supply chains, networks and business ecosystems are different ways of organising. Business ecosystems provide new sources of resources and capabilities, new markets, new partners and new ways of connecting these all together. This has important strategic implications for how organisations set and achieve their goals.

Section 3: Skills to help organisations respond

Section 3 teaches you the new skills that firms need to make the organisational changes described in Section 2. This section is a 'how to' section, with detailed examples. It teaches the skills needed to help organisations to gain the three fundamental capabilities set out in Section 2. Different skills are needed to develop different organisational capabilities. These capabilities cover the traditional departments in a firm such as sales, marketing, customer service, HR, finance, manufacturing, distribution and strategy. This section teaches the skills needed by non-technical and technical staff at all stages of their careers for creating the three organisational capabilities; skills that complement specialist professional training in areas such as accountancy, engineering and computer science.

Chapter 8: How to understand what customers really need

This chapter explains how to understand what customers really need, even when they do not know themselves. This includes how to find the best customers for your firm and then contact them, and then how to grow and enrich the relationship. It describes how to start new and lasting customer relationships for mutual benefit, not just one-off transactions. It explains how **customer journey** models can be used to give customers a much more personalised experience by guiding them through the decisions that make up their individual customer journeys.

Chapter 9: How to design and produce what customers need

This chapter explains what production journey models are and how to model two types of production journeys – product design journeys and product manufacturing journeys. It explains how both types of production journeys can be improved by using data feedback techniques like **A/B testing** and MVP strategies, and it describes some of the many data sources that can be used to do this. Then it explains how production journey models can be used to help workers and machines in their job roles and give staff a better experience.

Chapter 10: Elements of a data and decision-making strategy

This chapter describes the elements of a data analysis and decision-making strategy including the definition of an **Analysis Question** to focus the start of a data analytics project, the role of data patterns in analytics projects and how data patterns help to answer the Analysis Question. Then it explains the types of patterns that can be found in data and the overall types of machine learning techniques that are used to search for them.

Chapter summary

The business world is changing very fast in terms of pressures on organisations, new technologies to use and new products and services. Business and government organisations are quickly transforming in response to forces of change by developing three new fundamental capabilities: new capabilities for understanding customers' needs, producing customer experiences, and continuing to do this. These three fundamental capabilities are themselves disrupting how organisations and entire industries function. But they frequently rely on emerging data technologies, which the skills in this book will help you use.

Further reading

My blog (https://duncanrshaw.co.uk), my LinkedIn posts (www.linkedin.com/in/duncan-r-shaw) and my longer articles on Medium (https://medium.com/@duncanshaw_1) contain many articles related to managing emerging data technologies. They provide further ideas, new perspectives on the subjects in this book and links to additional readings. My students find these additional articles interesting and useful. I frequently update and add to these as I continue my research.

2

HOW CHANGE FORCES AFFECT ORGANISATIONS

KEY IDEAS

- Changes to technology, markets, competition, legal regulations, and concerns about environmental sustainability and other parts of society produce forces that strongly affect organisations.
- These change forces affect organisations by changing the three elements of their business models: what their stakeholders value, the capabilities, and resources that stakeholders contribute to business models.
- How change forces affect each of these business model elements is different for every organisation's local situation.
- Research into natural ecosystems gives us valuable viewpoints for analysing the local situation of an organisation.

LEARNING OBJECTIVES

After reading this chapter you will be able to:

- Describe which changes in society produce forces that affect organisations and where they come from.
- Explain what a business model is and how it works.
- Explain why different change forces affect different business models in different ways.
- Describe how an organisation's local situation affects how change forces alter its business model.
- Explain what we can learn from research into natural ecosystems about analysing business ecosystems and business models.

How change forces affect organisations

This chapter introduces some of the change forces that affect organisations, including changes in technology, markets, competition, legal regulations and concerns about environmental sustainability. Then it describes how they influence an organisation by affecting the three elements of its business model. The three elements of a business model are what its stakeholders value, the capabilities, and resources that they can contribute to the business model. The ways that change forces affect these business model elements strongly depend on the organisation's local situation. The affect of the local situation of an organisation can be included in the analysis by using five viewpoints from research into natural ecosystems. What is a business model?

A business model is a description of how an organisation's stakeholders contribute resources and capabilities to an organisation's activities in return for what they value. A business model is not some small part of an organisation, or some separate thing to the organisation. It is the organisation's 'blueprint', its 'DNA', like a genome is the business model of an organism. It is a description of how its parts work together, how well its 'body' functions in different situations and how it interacts with others in its community. Change forces that affect an organisation do it by affecting the elements of its business model. If you change the inputs to an organisation, then you will change the outputs that it is able to produce and the parts that it can sustain. If you change the parts of an organisation, then you will change the inputs it requires and the outputs it is able to produce. A business model describes the balance of these three elements: the inputs, the outputs and the parts, which include internal and external **stakeholders**.

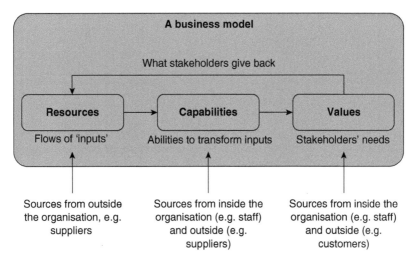

Figure 2.1   The three elements of a business model

Business models are open systems that transform inputs into outputs. They have three elements: resources, capabilities and values. These elements are the things that vary between different organisations' business models, and change as an organisation's business model changes. Business models use the capabilities of the organisation's stakeholders to transform resources into what other stakeholders value. Figure 2.1 shows how they transform inputs into outputs. The inputs depend on what the business model requires, and they vary depending on the type of organisation and what it produces. They include physical resources like raw materials and energy for factories, or information. Outputs are anything that an organisation's stakeholders value. These depend on each stakeholder: customers value products and services like delivery, credit, advice and customer support; suppliers and other partners need payments, cooperation, information and other help. An organisation's capabilities transform the resources, like when assembly lines produce cars and other finished products from raw materials. Or when websites sell tickets and answer questions by transforming potential customers and their needs into satisfied customers. These organisational capabilities can become filled up just like the resources they consume can become used up. All capabilities have a maximum capacity. For example, a bottleneck in a drainage pipe sets the maximum flow rate of water. A car assembly line has a maximum rate of car production; and a website will go down if too many people visit it.

A stakeholder is anyone with a stake in the organisation's business model, absolutely anyone with a stake. They include customers, staff, suppliers, investors, partner organisations and government regulators. They also include any person or other organisation with some connection to that organisation. Business models are based on an organisation's stakeholders because stakeholders are the source of resources and the capabilities that transform those resources (Shaw and Allen, 2017); stakeholders only do this in return for getting what they value. That's why it is very important to understand what stakeholders value, even if they do not know themselves. Different stakeholders value different things, so it depends on who the stakeholder is and what their priorities are. Roughly speaking, customers value products and services; staff and suppliers want to get paid; and government regulators want organisations to follow the rules. But they will also value other things that are less obvious. It is very difficult to completely understand what someone values. What people value is complex and subjective, as we shall see when we look at what customers value in Chapter 4. In return for getting what they value, stakeholders contribute resources back to the organisation.

Resources are any information, materials and permissions that are contributed by stakeholders, like cash payments from customers, raw materials and information from suppliers, and permissions from governments. Stakeholders also contribute capabilities to the business model. Capabilities are anything that change resources into something else. For example, data analytics and information processing capabilities transform raw data into useful patterns of knowledge; manufacturing capabilities turn raw materials into finished products. Economists and strategic management researchers have much more specific terms for resources and capabilities than the wider sense in which I use them in this book. They think of resources as sources of competitive advantage, if they are valuable, rare, impossible to copy and not substitutable (Barney, 1991); whereas here I talk about resources that are interchangeable commodities unless I talk about specific types of resources that are required to fit particular purposes. Economists and strategic management researchers also use the term 'resource' as an asset with an ability to do something – this is more like how I use the term 'capability', in its general sense in English. They also add the word 'dynamic' to make the term 'dynamic capability', by which they mean an ability to change organisational abilities (Teece et al., 1997). But in this book, I use these wider definitions of resources and capabilities to fit normal business English and to emphasise how a business model is similar to an engine, which consumes resources by using its capabilities.

Business models are open systems in the sense that they use up external resources. So, a good definition of a business model is a description of how all of an organisation's stakeholders work together to supply and transform resources into what they each individually value. Business models are just the explanation of how all stakeholders can mutually satisfy each other. That's what keeps the organisation going. Any stakeholders who do not get something out of the organisation that they value will not participate. Getting that balance, the balance between different stakeholders' priorities, can be complicated. But the three business model elements must balance in the sense that they must recirculate value to keep the business model functioning. Stakeholders must keep being satisfied, so resources must keep being consumed by capabilities.

A business model is like organising a big party with your friends. All your party guests want different things, different types of music and food. Your guests can also contribute different things to the party based on their individual capabilities and resources. If one friend is a good cook, then ask him/her to organise the food. If another friend is a massive music fan, then maybe s/he could plan the playlist? The same idea applies to other capabilities. Who is a good DJ? Who can organise all the preparation activities? Also, think about the resources that they will need. Who has a big hall or venue that you could all use? Does your business model need a mini bus for transport? And so on. But make sure that you understand what all these friends want in a good party. Maybe they want to come for the music, the food or to meet particular people? A business model describes how these elements balance together. How all the stakeholders get what they value by contributing the resources and capabilities that they have access to.

One way to analyse an organisation's business model is by using a **Value Flow Analysis (VFA) diagram** (Shaw, 2007). There are many ways of analysing business models, for example Hedman and Kalling's analysis of a business model uses a rich collection of perspectives from many different areas of business research (2003). It is a wonderful checklist of separate ideas that can help you think about a business model's 'ingredients'. Osterwalder also presents a useful list of business model ingredients (2013). Another useful overview of business model ideas is by Osterwalder et al. (2005). In contrast, a VFA diagram takes a systems approach; this helps with analysing how the ingredients work together to produce a functioning business model. A VFA analysis is focused more on how the elements of any business model work together, or do not, rather than what the elements are. I frequently use Hedman and Kalling's model to get ideas for specific business model elements and then I assemble them all together using a VFA diagram.

VFA is a simple technique that puts all the stakeholders of a business model onto one large sheet of paper and then connects them together to see if they balance, or if they could be 'rebalanced'. VFA came from my research with Manchester United Football Club, and I have used it to teach hundreds of learners (Shaw, 2007). Manchester United were one of the first football clubs to rebalance their business model so that they could sell products and services to people that were fans of the club but had no direct connection to the club. The club knew that it had millions of fans around the world, but it did not know who they were. So, the club formed partnerships with many companies around the world who helped it to contact its fans and find out which products and services they would value. These partnerships helped the club to fill up its fan **database** and earn extra revenues from partners who sold products and services to fans all around the world. I developed VFA as a way of describing how Manchester United, all its different partners and the fans could all get what they needed from the relationship.

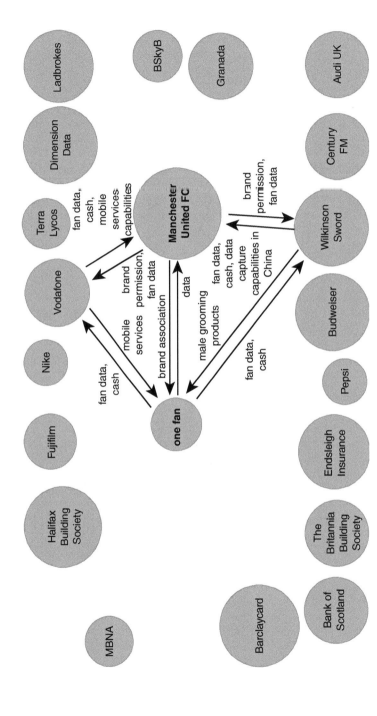

Figure 2.2 VFA diagram of Manchester United's business model, circa 2005

Case study: Analysing Manchester United's business model using VFA diagrams

Figure 2.2 shows a partial VFA diagram of Manchester United's business model around 2005, before the club was bought by the Glazer family. To make it clearer, only some of the value flows are shown. These are the ones between a fan, Manchester United, Vodafone and Wilkinson Sword. Value flows between other stakeholders are not shown and not all stakeholders are shown. Also, only one type of fan is shown. The secret to drawing VFA diagrams is to put all the flows for all the types of stakeholders into one or more VFA diagram. This is sometimes very difficult because of the sheer amount of information. So VFA diagrams are best drawn on sheets of very large flip chart paper to fit lots of business model information into one place. Many people also draw different versions of the same VFA to focus on different aspects like specific stakeholder groups or specific types of flows. It depends on what you are interested in for your VFA analysis.

How to draw VFA diagrams

Drawing VFA diagrams is an exercise in data visualisation, which is about telling a story using data. VFAs use mostly qualitative data, rather than quantitative visualisation like pie charts and histograms. VFA diagrams are made of many circles, which are joined by arrows into a huge diagram. Using online tools with a large drawing space and the ability to zoom in and out, like Prezi, Canva, Microsoft PowerPoint or whiteboard apps like Miro, will reduce some of the problems outlined below. These are problems that come from fitting large amounts of information into a single place for your analysis. The circles are the business model's stakeholders, and the arrows are what they contribute to each other. VFA diagrams are notoriously complicated because they attempt to capture as many of the main flows of resources between stakeholders as possible. These are the flows that explain how and why a business model keeps on operating. In Figure 2.2 most of the flows have been removed for clarity. Figure 2.3a has many more of the flows and is difficult to read in a book even when the text that describes the resources that flow along the arrows is removed. Also, Figure 2.3a does not contain any of the potential flows, which are directly between stakeholders who are not fans and not Manchester United. These direct flows are worth thinking about because they provide additional benefits as part of this business model's value flow system.

When drawing a VFA diagram it is crucial to add as many stakeholders (see Figure 2.3b) and as many flows between them as possible. This is because the aim of a VFA diagram is to put all the stakeholders and all the flows in one place where they can be analysed. Putting it all in one place produces a unique perspective on the business model you are analysing. If you miss out some stakeholders, then you will miss out the outflows that they contribute and the inflows that they require. If you miss out any inflows and outflows of resources or any types of stakeholders, then you will miss the opportunity to take three main insights from analysing the VFA diagram. The first main insight is spotting unmet needs – these are inflows that current stakeholders do not currently receive, but they might value. These offer possible ways to rebalance the business model. The second main insight is noticing reusable capabilities. These are current flows between one stakeholder and another that could also flow to a third stakeholder, who could be a current stakeholder or a newly recruited stakeholder. The second insight is the same as the first, but it looks in a different direction. The third main insight involves noticing that a new stakeholder needs to be recruited so that they can contribute some missing flow of a resource or a new capability.

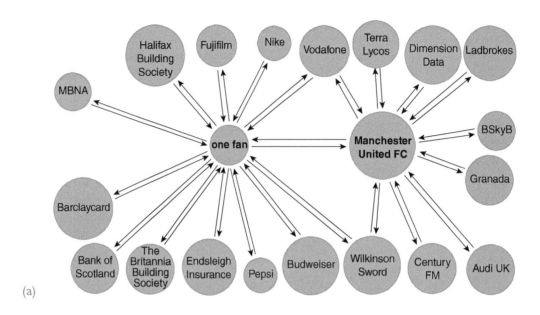

(a)

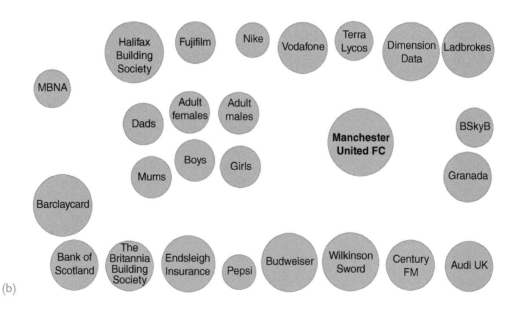

(b)

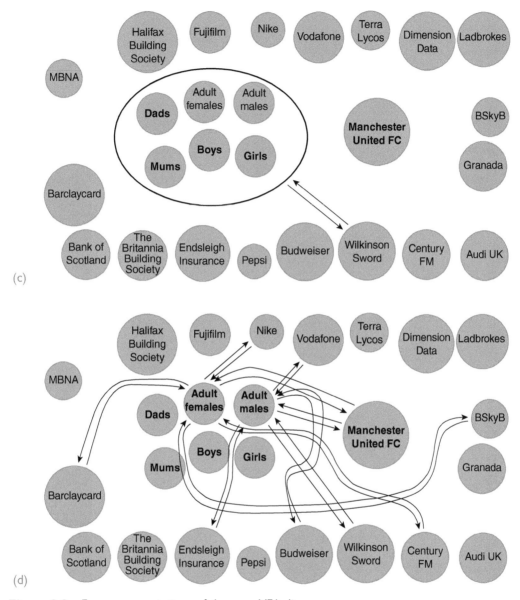

Figure 2.3   Four representations of the same VFA diagram

Panel (a) contains many more of the resource flow arrows between stakeholders, than can be shown here. There is no room to label them as you would do on a paper diagram. But there are no direct flows between stakeholders, just between fans and Manchester United. Panel (b) shows more information about stakeholders by dividing fans into sub-groups. Panel (c) shows the danger of grouping sub-groups together. It loses information from the VFA analysis. Grouping fans into a single circle will lose information about their different service-needs, e.g., boys and girls will not need shaving products from Wilkinson Sword, but other sub-groups will. Panel (d) shows that VFA diagrams should be complicated, and arrows need not be straight.

To draw a VFA, first draw a circle for every stakeholder (in this case it is the club, several partner companies and several types of fans). Use a big piece of paper and a small pen, or you will run out of room. Write a name for the stakeholder in each circle. Be as specific as you can with the stakeholder circles, name individual organisations and the precise types of stakeholder. Remember to add a circle for your own organisation, or even better, add a few circles to show your important internal stakeholders. When you start to draw a VFA, first just draw as many circles as you can; each circle can hold a single type of stakeholder. For example, Figure 2.3b presents more information on fan stakeholders by dividing fans into sub-groups. Be very careful not to group different types of stakeholders, like customer segments, together into one circle. If you group different types together, the VFA will lose information about their different service-needs. Try to be as specific as possible by separating stakeholders out into specific types and even individual companies. The reason for this is that grouping them together aggregates any information about their differences. For example, the companies in the Manchester United VFA that provide insurance, banking, building society and credit card services are all financial services companies. But they each have very different resources and capabilities to contribute, as well as very different values that need to be satisfied. Separating them out in your VFA will preserve this information so it is available for you to incorporate into your analysis and spot potential connections for rebalancing your business model.

Second, use arrows to connect as many of the stakeholder circles together as possible. These are the resource flows of a VFA and a good VFA is a tangled mess of flow arrows. They are like pipes that resources flow along. Resources are materials, energy, information, permissions, any inputs that a stakeholder circle needs, or outputs that a stakeholder contributes. Input arrows go into circles and output arrows emerge from circles. Arrows can be curved or straight to bend around circles to flow to the stakeholders that they need to get to (Figure 2.3d). VFA diagrams can get very complicated and messy. For example, Figure 2.3d only shows some of the flows between adult females, adult males and other stakeholders. When drawing a VFA it is always important to decide which stakeholders and which flows of the business model are important for your analysis. Sometimes it is best to use several VFA diagrams in the same analysis; sometimes it is best to use large flipchart paper for the early stages rather than drawing software like Microsoft PowerPoint or Visio. Online whiteboards like Miro.com also work well.

Third, explain your VFA diagram to the different people in it so that they can add more information, such as capabilities, resources and needs that you were not aware of. This third step is very important. Business models are complex, so nobody has a full picture of them. All stakeholders have more to offer than what they contribute right now. For example, suppliers always have other products that they can supply, and they have many conversations with customers like your organisation from which they pick up useful suggestions. Also, stakeholders frequently have unmet needs. Things that they would value but they are not getting from the business model right now. Going through a VFA with the people in it is great for checking it, adding more details and building consensus. It also starts the process of **business model rebalancing.** Look out for reusable resources and capabilities: anything that a stakeholder contributes to one part of a VFA could be contributed to another. Also look out for unmet stakeholders' needs. There are always more things that you could sell to customers. It is also common to sell things to suppliers, like when supermarkets sell anonymised data to their suppliers. If you make a rich VFA diagram that many of the stakeholders have checked then you can usually work on rebalancing the business model by drawing more or changing the flow arrows in the diagram. As long as the business model balances, i.e., stakeholders get what they value in return for what they contribute, then old stakeholders can be given new products and services, and new stakeholders can be connected in. The VFA also works well for analysing ecosystem business models, which we will cover in Chapter 7.

Business model rebalancing is the key to understanding how change forces affect organisations. External forces make internal changes to an organisation by forcing it to change its business model. If some change effects the resources, capabilities, or stakeholder values of a business model then they must be rebalanced, or the organisation will stop operating, just as a car engine stops if it runs out of fuel, if its ignition system fails, or if its owner does not want to use it. As we shall see later, external change forces change to what resources and capabilities are available, or they change stakeholders' values. If the supply or quality of any of these three elements change then the business model might not work to mutually satisfy its contributors. A balanced business model is a **positive feedback loop**. Satisfied stakeholders contribute more resources and capabilities, so more stakeholders can be satisfied. But it can easily become unbalanced. In an unbalanced business model, the positive feedback effects reduce, and it grinds to a halt. An example of this is when customers become dissatisfied with a brand, they buy less and complain to their friends, the company has less money for customer service and product innovation, and its business model starts to wind down.

Analysing change in organisations

There are many strategic models for analysing the forces that act on organisations and for recommending how those organisations should respond. But most of these models are 'variance models', like the Balanced Score Card (Kaplan and Norton, 1992) or the Blue Ocean Strategy (Denning, 2017). Variance models analyse organisations by measuring and comparing different aspects of an organisation and its environment. They compare 'snapshots' of an organisation like flicking between two photos to look for differences (Markus and Robey, 1988). The Balanced Score Card compares snapshots of an organisation's performance across a range of variables, and the Blue Ocean Strategy compares a snapshot of an organisation's current market with completely new markets that the organisation could create. They are powerful models for comparing different states of the organisation to check trends in performance or to decide between strategic choices. Variance methods are very good for noticing and then measuring changes or making comparisons. But they are less useful for monitoring and understanding the ongoing process of change, or for understanding its causes. Changes do not flick instantaneously from a 'before' to an 'after' state. They have many incremental stages in between: that is what a process is. A process is more like a video running from a start to an end than flicking between two photos. Processes include all the causes and effects that take us from 'before' to 'after'. Variance models are common and powerful tools for strategically analysing change, but they are better at analysing what has changed rather than how and why it happens, and in this book, I wish to explain the mechanisms of change. So, I do not provide detailed lists of the organisational characteristics that can be used to describe an organisational snapshot. These lists can be found in other books and specialised courses on subjects like Accounting and Finance, Operations Management, Strategic Management and Marketing.

Instead, this book uses a systems and process approach for analysing the interconnected elements of business models, the networked sharing of data between companies and the ecosystems of organisations and other stakeholders. A systems approach focuses on the elements of a system of organisational stakeholders at different levels of analysis and the relationships between them (Checkland, 1999). A process approach focuses on the staged nature of change unfolding over time, how change forces cause effects to business models and how organisations can respond. A process view always includes a temporal dimension, it analyses dynamic phenomena, and it views all phenomena as being made up of processes rather than of things or states (Rescher, 2000).

Most business and management approaches that come from economics tend to view what they analyse in terms of discrete things or states, rather than processes that stretch across time. A systems view, which highlights the interrelations between the parts of a whole, complements a process view, which highlights the interrelations between these parts along a timeline. A time-based viewpoint works well with **time series data**, which we will meet later. Also, a process approach has another advantage: it can be 'wound' backwards as well as forwards to avoid complexity. For example, it can be very difficult to plan ahead in business because the permutations of what might happen multiply more and more the further ahead you look. A simple way to avoid this is to start with a desired outcome and then plan backwards. Planning backwards requires a process plan divided into clear stages. This is similar to the well-known 'top-down' approach, which starts with a high-level assembly or structure and gradually works downwards to plan each supporting level. A top-down approach is a systems view version of a planning backwards approach.

Change forces that affect organisations

Change forces affect organisations by upsetting the balance of the three elements in an organisation's business model:

1   the flows of resources that sustain the business model
2   the capabilities that transform these resources
3   the values of the stakeholders that the business model satisfies and the reasons that they
     contribute resources and capabilities.

Supplies of available resources might change. They might increase or reduce, which will change their costs, or even make it impossible to get them at all. For example, during the initial lockdown of the 2020 COVID-19 pandemic, the amount of car travel reduced in many countries. This led to a huge price reduction in petrol for cars. In some countries there was also panic buying as families stocked up on things that they thought they would need. This surprised the supermarkets and, in the UK, led to a shortage of toilet roll and bread flour. People did not use any more of these items than they did normally, but supermarket supply chains could not keep up with the huge short-term increase in buying. The cost of personal protective equipment (PPE) like gloves, aprons and masks also increased massively because of a mismatch between supply and demand. Some governments spent hundreds of millions of pounds buying PPE stocks for medics and care home workers.

An organisation's capabilities might become better at transforming resources, resources might become easier or harder to find, or they might change in what they can be used for. For example, electricity generated from solar power has consistently reduced in cost and in some places, it is cheaper than any other energy source (IEA, 2020). Also, stakeholders' values might change. The number of stakeholders who value what your organisation does might change. What they value might change, e.g., fashions and public sentiment. How much they value these things might change as well, e.g., people's values change as they grow older, adolescents value excitement more than older people (Markman, 2015). A business model sustains itself by satisfying its stakeholders' values. They are an input flow – if the flow halts, then so does the business model.

Next, we will look at some specific change forces and since this book is about using emerging data technologies, I will start with technological change forces.

The technology change force

What is a technology?

Humans have developed thousands of different technologies including drawing, writing, mathematics, pottery, engineering, economics and even languages themselves. **Technologies** are ways of getting things done, and we always use them with other technologies. For example, computer hardware technology works with software, writing and language to enable you to use this book to learn how to take advantage of emerging data technologies. Together, these three technologies, and others, record my knowledge and the knowledge of other people in the form of a book. You can then access this knowledge in a way that hopefully helps you learn how to use it yourself.

The force of technological change comes from what a technology can do, and what this can be applied to. Figure 2.4 gives examples of different technologies, their **capabilities** and their common applications. Individual technologies have different capabilities that make them useful for specific applications. For example, the technology of making and bending small lengths of steel wire gives us the capability to group sheets of paper or fabric together. The application of this is a paper clip. The technology of knowing that it is worth making the tip of a screwdriver into a cross rather than a flat blade gives us the capability to stop the screwdriver slipping off the screw. The application of this is the Phillips screwdriver.

The most important thing about a technology is what it can do. Batteries can store electrical energy, and some can be recharged. Rubber is flexible and waterproof. Technologies come in the form of methods and effective ways of doing things, as well as physical things like materials and machines. It is the capabilities of these things, what they can do, that matter and that is why we use them.

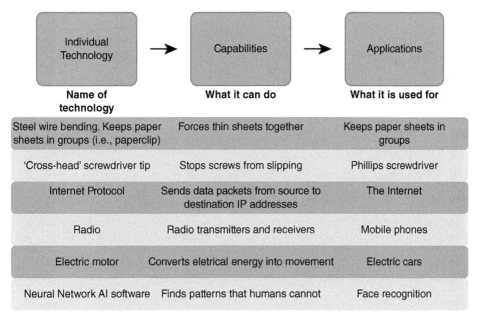

Individual Technology	Capabilities	Applications
Name of technology	**What it can do**	**What it is used for**
Steel wire bending. Keeps paper sheets in groups (i.e., paperclip)	Forces thin sheets together	Keeps paper sheets in groups
'Cross-head' screwdriver tip	Stops screws from slipping	Phillips screwdriver
Internet Protocol	Sends data packets from source to destination IP addresses	The Internet
Radio	Radio transmitters and receivers	Mobile phones
Electric motor	Converts eletrical energy into movement	Electric cars
Neural Network AI software	Finds patterns that humans cannot	Face recognition

Figure 2.4   Examples of technologies with different capabilities that make them useful for specific applications

How do technologies change?

Every tablet or laptop is made up of individual technologies that make up a hard drive, the chips, the screen, the keyboard, the battery and many other parts. All three elements in Figure 2.4 change over time: the mixtures of individual technologies, their combined capabilities and the applications that they are used for. As new technologies are developed and added, old ones are swapped out.

The capabilities of any single technology improve over time in an 'S' curve called the Technology Life Cycle. New technologies start by improving slowly, but this accelerates in an upward curve towards the middle of their life cycle. Then the rate of improvement starts to decelerate as they start to improve at a slower and slower rate. Together the periods of acceleration and then deceleration make the shape of an 'S' (see Figure 2.5).

Moore's Law is a well-known example of an improving capability that has led to huge changes in our society. Gordon Moore famously observed that the number of transistors on a microchip doubled every two years (Rotman, 2020). The capability to fit more transistors in a smaller space was roughly doubling, so the power and costs of data processing were reducing very fast. At the start, a technology's capabilities are meagre; whatever it is that makes the technology useful is minor compared to what it could be later. A Cray-2 Supercomputer in the mid-1980s was slower at processing data than a modern smartphone (Nunez, 2020). In the 1960s a mainframe computer took up a whole room. Lots of effort will go into improving a new technology to make it smaller, cheaper, more reliable and better at whatever its main capability is. This capability will only improve slowly at first. But then the rate of improvement accelerates, it will improve very fast over a short time, and for relatively less effort. Finally, the acceleration reduces, and the rate of improvement begins to flatten again. You can see this with steam engines. James Watt improved an earlier steam engine design by adding an additional cylinder to condense the steam. Steam needs to be cooled so it condenses and creates a partial vacuum that moves a piston. But cooling it in the piston cylinder means that the piston cylinder then needs reheating. Adding a separate condensing cylinder avoids wasting heat and makes the engine much more efficient. But large improvements like this became harder and harder to discover. Eventually diesel and petrol engine technologies were used for transportation when their 'S' curves became better than the steam 'S' curve at things like fuel efficiency or the lightness of the engine. Nowadays researchers only work on improving steam technology in different areas than transport, like safety and reliability for nuclear and other power generating systems.

Another example is the 'S' curve of artificial intelligence (AI). Look at how AI technologies were relatively ineffective until recently. Many people have worked on developing different AI technologies since the last century and the idea has been written about for much longer. For a short history of AI, see Gil Press' article in Forbes in the Further Reading section (Press, 2016). It was only around 2014 when several individual technologies came together to create the group of technologies that we call 'AI'. The rise of big data had produced a vast increase in data sources so there was much more data now available to be analysed, and cheap data storage and processing was available for anyone who wanted to rent it from cloud computing providers. The power of computer hardware was greatly increased by the development of graphics processing units (GPUs) – these were originally meant for manipulating images and graphics in applications like gaming, but they also made it cheaper and faster to process very large datasets. Several different types of machine learning software also advanced at this time as well, taking advantage of the improvements in the speed, storage and cost of hardware. For example, software simulations of the brain's neural networks started to become much more sophisticated. More and more layers of network nodes were added to these simulations, which made them a lot more nuanced in how

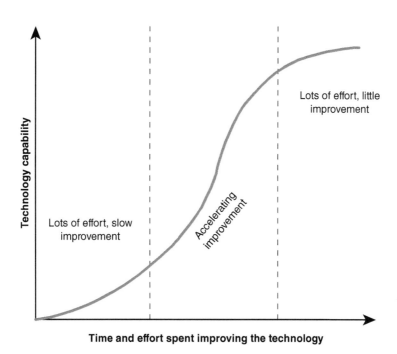

Time and effort spent improving the technology

Figure 2.5   The 'S' curve shape of the Technology Life Cycle (Christensen, 1992)

they modelled the fine distinctions in the patterns that they found in datasets, patterns that were produced when huge amounts of data were used to train the AI software (Hodjat, 2015).

Some technologies are now on the far right of the 'S' curve. They are mature, their capabilities are not really improving very quickly, but they are tried and tested. We call these 'factory technologies' and they are great for applications that need to be low cost and low risk, like petrol engines. They are nothing fancy, but they get the job done. Some technologies are at the start of the 'S' curve. They are immature, not fully developed but they have potentially valuable capabilities, like batteries for electric cars. If they could store a bit more energy and weigh less, then people could do much longer journeys on a single charge. Technologies on the left of an 'S' curve are 'experimental technologies' and they are the ones to watch. Many firms use them in pilot projects to test them, just to be ready for when they bloom.

Another example is **quantum computing**, which is an experimental technology. It has got the potential to revolutionise many business areas because of its completely new capabilities. As always it is the capabilities of a new technology that make it into a change force. The quantum world is the tiny world of electrons, photons and other quantum particles. This gives quantum computers capabilities that are potentially useful for applications in several areas including encryption, communication and data processing. Quantum computing is based on the probabilistic laws of quantum mechanics rather than the binary 1s and 0s of classical computing. This imprecision means that it is physically impossible to make an exact copy of quantum information. The main capability of quantum encryption is that messages could be encrypted and transmitted using quantum keys that would be impossible to hack. Normal keys, like your pin code or your passwords can be found if hackers have enough processing power or time to try all the combinations. But a quantum key is uncopiable no matter how much time and effort they put in. Just reading it to make a copy will change it (Giles, 2019a, 2019b; Ghose, 2020). The main capability of quantum computing is that it can do many computations at the same time. This will revolutionise data analysis that deals with complex optimisation problems. Problems like checking through millions of possible ways that different enzymes could interact with human cells in the design of drugs or the diagnosis of diseases. There are lots of business problems where the only option is to check every single permutation of a solution and pick the best. Quantum computing would also speed up searches through massive but unorganised datasets.

Quantum computing is a strong change force because its capabilities are fundamentally different to normal computing capabilities. But there are many obstacles to deal with as quantum computing moves along the start of its 'S' curve, like the instability of 'qubits', which are the counterparts of the 'bits' in classical computers. The more bits a computer uses then, generally, the more powerful it is. Qubits are currently very unstable and produce large error rates, which makes it difficult to build quantum computers with more qubits. As these barriers are dealt with, the capability to make unbreakable encryption and the capability to check many options at once will lead to some large-scale changes. For example, fundamentally secure encryption will mean that information which people are sensitive about will be more likely to be shared and therefore used differently because it will be only used as is intended. This will free up even more data for analysis projects. Also, being capable of checking many more options at once will greatly increase the sophistication of many products and services because many more aspects of their design, production, delivery and aftercare can then be personalised at low cost. Many things that we buy right now have some degree of personalisation, like product recommendations that fit customers' tastes, or delivery times that fit when they are at home. Every slight variation to a firm's standard product or service increases complexity and costs. But the capability to check through a complex set of permutations for the optimum arrangement will allow firms to find them and still increase the granularity of the product and service variations that they offer. Maybe we will be offered a much larger and finer range of options when we buy a new car or new kitchen appliances.

The market change force

What is a market?

A marketplace is where buyers come together with sellers, where customers meet suppliers. It is where people and organisations exchange things they have for things that they value, and that they want more of. A market is also the collection of people or firms that buy from your business. Individual people buy from business-to-consumer (B2C) firms, and organisations buy from business-to-business (B2B) firms. But whether you work in a B2C or B2B situation, you always sell to people. People who buy food from retailers like Walmart or Tesco, to consume themselves. Or people who work for retailers and buy food from suppliers, so they can sell it onwards to consumers. Markets are fundamentally made out of people, and it is the people in a market that change.

How do markets drive change?

A business model must give the market what it values. If this changes then the business model needs to change. The people in a market change in lots of different ways. It is important to be very precise about how you define the characteristics of your market because these definitions affect the data that you can use to analyse market changes. Change the definitions and you will change the data. For example, who is your customer? Is your customer the supermarket that buys the coffee you make or the person who drinks it? The answer is that it depends on your purpose. As we shall see in Chapter 10, the only way to start a successful data analysis project is to be very precise about what you are trying to analyse.

Here are some definitions of the characteristics of a market:

- *Customer values and interests* – this is what a customer values, what they are interested in and what they will pay for. Every customer is different: B2B or B2C customers, people, companies, or any other organisation that pays you money for something you give them. They all value different things. Even two people in the same town, in the same house, or in the same family have slightly different tastes. Every human has led a slightly different life and lives right now in a slightly different situation. Values, tastes, needs and wants are all subjective. It is the same for B2B customers because all organisations also have different backstories and different individual situations (as we shall see in Chapter 4). Finding out customers' values is the goal of many data analytics projects. If you know what a person is interested in, then maybe you can sell it to them. Customer values are not just a description of a desired product or service; they also include how each customer wants to get it and for how much. Not just how and when they want a product to be delivered but the whole experience of the customer journey of choosing, buying and then using it. Customer journeys are explained in Chapter 4, and how to use them is explained in Chapter 8.
- *Customer groups, types and segments* – these are groups of what customers value and what they are interested in, not who they are. Age, size, gender and other demographic characteristics of people are only an indirect way of understanding what they wish to buy. Who people are is related to what they need but very different people can still want similar products. An example would be when older people still buy children's toys because they collect them as a hobby. Every customer wants subtly different things. But giving everyone exactly what they want, how they want it and when they want it would be too expensive and much too complicated. But giving customers a one-size-fits-all, standardised product or service would not really fit their individual needs either. Just imagine if shoes all came in one size. Henry Ford is famous for saying customers can have any colour of his Model T car as long as it is black. But customers always prefer something that fits their individual needs, tastes and personal situations, so you must group them together in some way. If you have a few groups to satisfy rather than a whole population of individual customers, then it hugely reduces the variety of needs. That is why organisations group their customers into customer segments. If you put these groups into a pie chart, then they look like segments in an orange. Deciding how to organise customer segments is a key part of an analytical strategy (see Chapter 10).

Factors to consider when deciding market segments include:

- *Size* – this is the number of B2B or B2C customers in the market, and it is usually measured by the market population, the number of customers or the amount of money they spend. The market size can also be the number of potential paying customers or the number of actual paying customers.
- *Location* – this is the geographic footprint of the customers in the market. It could be world regions, countries, or parts of one or more countries. It could also be types of location like in towns, in the countryside or something more precise like 'within three miles of my shop'.

- *Competition* – this is a way of looking at markets to understand which other firms are offering products that compete with yours. This perspective starts with customers' values and interests and looks for anything that satisfies them. These could be similar products and services to yours or something completely different, even something that they get for free like hosting social media pages and blogs. Don't just look at your well-known competitors. Anything that is an alternative way of giving customers what they value will compete with your products and services.

The competition change force

What is competition?

Competition between organisations happens when the business models of two or more organisations conflict. For example, when two car firms try and sell their cars to the same customer, and the customer only wants to buy one car. Or when those same car firms need rechargeable batteries to manufacture electric cars but there are too few batteries available for both firms' needs. An example of this occurred in 2019 when electric vehicle firms foresaw a shortage in the materials that they made batteries from due to an increased demand for electric cars (Scheyder, 2019). Whenever organisations want to buy or sell the same things, and there are limitations, then they will come into conflict. Eventually the supplies of some resource or some capability will run out, or the needs of customers will be filled up.

How does competition drive change?

Competition changes an organisation's business model by limiting the **availability** of any of the three elements that feed its business model. Whenever there is a limited supply of the resources, capabilities, or stakeholders' values then the organisation will change its business model to use alternatives. It will try new materials, hire new staff or enter new markets. Unless there are clear rules to the contrary, organisations usually try to keep themselves going and if possible, they try to grow. People want to keep or improve their jobs, or they believe in the purpose of the organisation. Changing a business model will usually mean that the organisation starts to compete with other organisations that already use those business model elements that the first organisation wants to use. For example, biofuels like ethanol can be produced from sugar cane but where does a country find new land to grow the biofuel crop on? There are concerns that biofuel crops will compete with food crops for agricultural land (Bourguignon, 2015). Sometimes an organisation starts to find it hard to get enough of something because it has grown very large and wants to continue growing. For example, when a firm outgrows its home market and looks for international markets to enter. These new markets will usually be already serviced by other organisations.

New technologies like the **Internet** and the **World Wide Web** drive new competition by helping international trade. In 1996 Dell used the World Wide Web to start to sell PC computers directly to users (Dell, 2020). Instead of selling PCs through retailers and other third parties, it started to compete with them. The Internet and the World Wide Web enabled Dell to use a website to directly communicate with individual consumers. On a physical level, shipping containers also enabled organisations to compete with other organisations in new markets. So do the World Trade Organisation's (WTO) rules for how countries facilitate trade between each other. Shipping containers standardise how goods are transported on ships, lorries or any other mode of transport, and WTO rules help countries to agree how to align their customs checks, tariffs and regulatory barriers to trade.

The regulatory change force

What are government regulations?

Governments set laws and regulations based on their policies, which are the principles and directions that they set out to their voters. Voters decide to vote based partly on government policies, which are promises about how they will govern. Policymaking is the fundamental cycle that governments go through as they govern. First, they define a problem, then they develop a potential policy, which is a course of action to deal with it. Next, they check the potential policy to see what various stakeholders think of it, and the options and alternatives. Then they implement and enforce the policy using regulations, which can be legally enforced. Finally, they evaluate how the process went before starting the whole cycle again. The policymaking and regulation functions of government are very different to producing government services like military services, the police, education, building and maintaining basic transport infrastructure or welfare programmes. Policymaking and regulation activities are like 'steering' a boat, but delivering services is like 'rowing' a boat (Osborne and Gaebler, 1993).

Governments use regulation to influence and change the behaviours of firms, individual people, and markets to manage the economy and to meet policy goals (Khemani and Shapiro, 1993). There are many ways that a government can regulate using laws to control things like prices, production output, profits, information reported by organisations and industry standards. For example, the UK government has over 70 regulatory bodies, which cover transport, healthcare, education, financial services, utilities, the media, and environment issues (NAO, 2015).

How do regulatory forces drive change?

Regulatory changes are when governments change the rules that they require people and organisations to operate under. An example of this is how health and safety legislation requires hard hats and high visibility clothing to be worn on building sites. Another example is data protection laws like the General Data Protection Regulation (GDPR) in the EU, or the Personal Information Protection and Electronic Documents Act (PIPEDA) in Canada. Policy changes are when governments change their strategic view on national issues and how to deal with them. Policy changes drive regulatory changes. For example, in the US, Donald Trump tried to change many of the rules and laws that were made by the last administration, led by Barack Obama. Trump's strongly contrasting policies drove many extreme changes to government regulations.

Policy changes cause regulatory changes downstream, but regulatory changes can only limit what people and organisations can do. Notice that regulations only say what *cannot* be done, not what can be done. They might encourage organisations to do things like provide minimum levels of hygiene in a restaurant, but it is up to each organisation to do what the regulations say or not be allowed to operate. Regulations only stop a firm from doing something, they don't produce anything. Government services are another part of government. This means that regulations limit the resources that firms can use, the capabilities that they can use and the values of stakeholders that they can satisfy. That is how they affect business models. They describe the situations when a business model can do things, and when it cannot. Regulatory limitations are particularly fierce in the financial services industry. For example, banks must keep a minimum ratio of equity to debt. This limits the maximum probability of a bank being put out of business by bad loans or other risks. It also limits the maximum damage to other stakeholders if that were to happen. The whole financial system relies on banks, and regulations are designed to stabilise and strengthen the financial system. But when policies change, so do regulations.

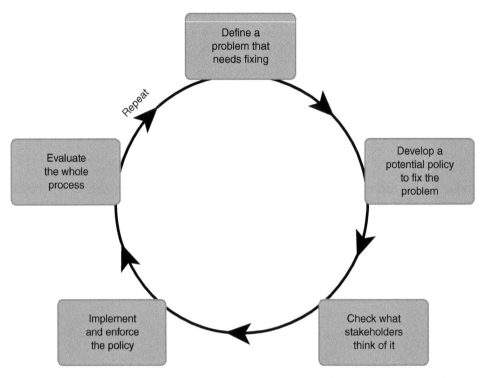

Figure 2.6   The continuous cycle of policymaking and evaluation that governments go through (adapted from Janssen and Helbig, 2018)

The change force of rising concerns about environmental sustainability

What are rising concerns about environmental sustainability?

Throughout the world there is an increasing level of concern about undesirable changes to our natural environment. Different people are concerned about different things. Some people are not concerned at all, but many people are increasingly worried about things like changes to the Earth's climate, the functioning of different ecosystems, the populations of certain species, and the levels of pollution in the atmosphere and the various landscapes that we inhabit. For example, the Intergovernmental Panel on Climate Change (IPCC) is the United Nations body charged with assessing the scientific evidence related to climate change and its effects on human and natural systems. The IPCC's work since 1988 has led to several conclusions, including:

- The climate is warming.
- It is influenced by human activities like producing green-house gases.

- Climate change has widespread impacts on human and natural systems.
- It is possible to mitigate these effects before they severely harm our economies and natural environment (IPCC, 2014).

Since the 1960s there has been a change in how the public have thought about climate change and other human activities, which have led to changes in our natural environment (Weyler, 2018). Changes like damage to the ozone layer, deforestation, reducing animal habitats, extinction of species and plastic pollution. Recently, and especially with younger people, this change in public opinion has accelerated. On 24 September 2020, the broadcaster and natural historian Sir David Attenborough started to use Instagram to publicise the need to protect our natural environment. In just 4 hours and 44 minutes, he broke the Guinness World Record for the fastest time to get one million followers (Punt, 2020).

Human business models are in competition with natural business models just as when we discussed competition change forces earlier. Human business models also depend on natural business models, as the Dasgupta Review for the UK government clearly pointed out (Dasgupta, 2021). The resources that natural organisms and ecosystems use are either being taken or used up by humans. The clean water, the space and other things that natural organisms and ecosystems rely on. For example, think about how we use plastics in food packaging, construction, cars and many other products. There are many different types of plastics but generally they are tough and they do not rot – this is a major reason why they are so useful. Another reason is that plastic is cheap to produce, which makes it easy to just throw away. Unfortunately, because most plastics do not rot, they lie around for hundreds of years without being converted into something else. In contrast, biological materials rot and break down. Worse still, some plastics emit chemicals such as phthalates: this is why you should not heat food up in a plastic container (Zanolli and Oliver, 2019). Even those plastics that do not emit chemicals can end up breaking down into microplastics. Plastics are tough polymers: wear and tear eventually breaks them down into smaller and smaller pieces, but they do not chemically change. There are huge concerns over the harm that they are doing to humans, plants and animals (Begum, 2020).

How do rising concerns about environmental sustainability drive change?

Rising concerns about the environment and changes in public attitudes have been reflected in changes in the demand for certain products and services, as well as changes to the public's expectations of how companies and governments should behave. Many firms have signed up for 'green targets' like reducing their use of fossil fuels and pledging to become carbon neutral by a certain date. Many businesses are combining a focus on environmental performance with other ethical standards that balance profit and purpose, like social and legal accountability as well as public transparency (BCorp, 2021). Also, many governments have implemented environmental legislation to do things like reduce pollution and lessen the effect of industrial processes on the natural environment. For example, the European Union's (EU) Green Deal pledged to influence its citizens to make a 40% cut in greenhouse gas emissions (based on 1990 levels) and to get at least 32% of its energy supplies from renewable sources (EC, 2020). Other targets in the EU Green Deal are in areas like healthier forms of transport, energy efficient buildings and investments in environmentally friendly technologies. These will all be supported by changes to the relevant regulations, which will cause some resources like energy from fossil fuels and certain pollutants to become harder or more expensive to get. Some alternative resources will appear as a result of new research programmes, and some new capabilities will be developed to change what can be done by firms, for example, the development of alternatives to plastic packaging produced from fungi or seaweed. New regulations will have a profound effect on the business models of organisations in energy, transport, construction, manufacturing and many other sectors. They will also affect the characteristics of the products and services that their stakeholders demand from them. As a result, many firms are increasingly changing their products, their processes, and their suppliers to align their business models with the regulatory changes. For example, China pledged to become carbon neutral by 2060, which will affect hundreds of power stations and vehicle manufacturers (Harvey, 2020).

Many organisations have already changed to business models that use alternatives to plastics or less plastics. For example, rising concerns about billions of single use nappies going into landfill every year led to a growth in the demand for an alternative. This led firms to develop reusable nappies, which were much easier to fit and wash than the cloth nappies of the past, and pretty much leak proof. Single use nappies are mostly made from plastic and wood pulp, and each one uses a cup of crude oil in the manufacturing process. Each baby will use around 5,000 to 6,000 nappies and virtually all single use nappies go into landfill or are incinerated (Shaw, J., 2018). That is a lot of wasted resources and potential pollution. So nappy makers like Baba+Boo have started to produce reusable nappies made from bamboo and a small amount of plastic that can be reused.

Five viewpoints from ecology to personalise a business analysis

This section explains how to 'personalise' your analysis of how change forces affect your organisation by taking account of the local situation that the organisation is in. Every organisation is in a different situation. It has its own market or markets; it has its own legal domain and cultural area. It might be one of a population of organisations with similar business models and purposes, or it might not. It might have worked closely for some time with a community of other organisations, or it might be only starting to work within such a community. Some organisations are strongly affected by the physical spaces that they operate in, or they have cultural and regulatory situations that they can influence by themselves or with other organisations. With every organisation its local situation has characteristics that subtly influence how change forces affect the elements of its business model. This section of Chapter 2 describes how different change forces combine with each other and with the local characteristics of a firm's location and industry sector.

Choosing how to respond to change forces is as important as the skills you need to execute that choice, and these choices are strongly affected by an organisation's local situation. To incorporate five viewpoints that bring an organisation's local situation into the analysis, I will use concepts that ecologists use to study the local situations of natural ecosystems. This personalises the businesses analysis in the sense that it considers the situation of the organisation being analysed. Multiple viewpoints are essential when analysing complex systems like organisations and their environments because different viewpoints help a reader to ask different questions. The five viewpoints here are based on two of my research projects, which looked at how ideas from natural ecosystems could be used to better understand business ecosystems. The first project was with Professor Tim Allen, a botanist and one of the main developers of Hierarchy Theory. It was my first go at using some very powerful concepts from biology, botany and ecology in the area of business and organisations, and I was very lucky to have

Tim as my guide. The second project was with Professor Judith Bronstein, the world expert on the study of **mutualism** (which we will meet later) and Professor Matt Mars whose expertise links communication, ecology and marketing.

Both of these research programmes investigated how business ecosystems can be understood better by using ideas from ecology theory. In business and in the press, it is very common to hear of terms like 'business ecosystems' or 'digital ecosystem'. These terms echo the increasing digital connections between organisations and other organisations, and between individuals and other individuals. Recently, platform business models have been used by Amazon, Google, Uber, Airbnb and other organisations to rapidly grow gigantic ecosystems of stakeholders. But for many years, email and social media also added layer upon layer of connections between people. For example, multitudes of cloud-based start-ups either have a work collaboration feature, or they are fundamentally all about collaboration, like Slack and Trello. The similarities between organisational ecosystems and natural ecosystems are their links. In natural ecosystems these links are between the living members and other living members, and between the living members and their physical environment. Similarly, in organisational ecosystems links connect human and organisational stakeholders, as well as their physical environment (Mars et al., 2012; Shaw and Allen, 2017). As we will discover next, these links make up complex systems in nature as well as in human society.

Ecology is nearly as diverse as the subject of its study but some of the most common ecosystem topics are individual organism's 'self-worlds', populations, communities, landscapes and biomes. They provide ecologists with five different ways of looking at natural ecosystems. These topics also provide us with five ways of looking at how firms change in response to change forces and the characteristics of their local environment. First, I will explain the ideas behind the perspectives of individual organisms/ businesses, populations, communities, landscapes and biomes using natural and then business examples. Then I will explain how these perspectives help us to understand how change forces change organisations. In our research, Tim and I used these ideas from his research into natural ecosystems to produce some new ways of looking at how human organisations operate (Shaw and Allen, 2017). For anyone with an interest in finding out more about complex systems or natural ecosystems, Tim's book with Thomas Hoekstra provides a fascinating read (Allen and Hoekstra, 2015). We found that natural ecosystem ideas worked as much more than a superficial metaphor for how businesses work together using digital technologies. In our research with different firms and public sector organisations, we found that there are many places where the world of natural organisms and their genomes echoes the world of organisations and their business models.

Here are five viewpoints that will help you to understand the individual situation that an organisation is in, as you analyse how to respond:

1   The 'self-world' viewpoint of an organism: how all organisations have slightly different business models, which limit their abilities to get data and to analyse it.
2   The population viewpoint: how organisations that copy the same business models affect the capacity of a single market to support them all, and how this changes the success of these organisations. Also, how the 'ancestry', or provenance, of a business model affects a situation.
3   The community viewpoint: how organisations with different business models work closely together or compete in some areas, depending on the situation.
4   The landscape viewpoint: how organisations in a single location are affected by the specific physical, legal and cultural features of that location.

5   The biome viewpoint: how organisations are affected by the cultural, regulatory and tax climates in their location. How biomes support specific communities of mixed business models, and how these can in turn influence the cultural, regulatory and tax climates that they are in (Shaw and Allen, 2017).

Other viewpoints could be taken. For example, Judie Bronstein's work on mutualism provides a complete framework for thinking about how one organisation works with another and I've included many of her ideas below (Bronstein, 2015). But I have chosen these five viewpoints because they are part of a wider research programme on business ecosystems that supports much of Section 2 of this book, which is on relationships with customers and other stakeholders, including new ways of organising the staff in an organisation and how organisations are working differently in groups of other organisations. These five viewpoints are explained in more detail next.

The 'self-world' viewpoint of an organism

Natural organisms are livings things like dogs and cats, or plants and trees. Each member of the same species has a similar genetic code, which gives them similar appearances and similar functionality. Genes are instructions for how organisms function, in a similar way to how the business models of organisations describe how they function. Several organisations might share the same business model, like supermarket chains or car manufacturers; this is similar to how organisms in the same species share a genetic code. The genetic code of a genome and the contents of a business model are both instructions for how and why they function as they do. In the living organism's case, functioning means living. In the organisation's case, functioning means operating. Natural ecosystems are made up of the linked genomes of different species. A genome is like the script of a character in a film. Each genome describes the instructions for its organism's role in an ecosystem. Similarly, business ecosystems can be built up by linking together mutually supportive business models. Again, business models are like a film script: they describe the role of an organisation together with its partners and other stakeholders.

A genome describes everything about an organism including how they sense the world and how they respond to information from those senses. Jakob von Uexküll's idea of *umwelt* helps us to understand this 'self-world'. The self-world that an organism constructs is based on its individual senses as well as its capabilities to change that world. A self-world is highly subjective, it is the world as that organism experiences it. Peter Checkland introduced the self-world idea to business, and it is used frequently in his book *Systems Thinking* (1999). A self-world is only what an organism senses in its environment, not the complete environment. It cannot sense most of its environment. Just as people see some wavelengths of light and hear some frequencies but not others. A self-world also includes what an organism can do, how it can behave and what it can accomplish. For example, a female wood tick's self-world has only three sensory inputs and three behaviours (von Uexküll, 1957; Shaw and Allen, 2017). It can sense a passing mammal, which will make it let go of the branch it perches on as it waits to pounce. It can also sense a successful landing on the mammal's fur, which will make it run around until it senses a warm membrane, such as skin, or a new branch to wait on again. If it senses a warm membrane, then it will pierce it and suck. But the senses and behaviours of a tick's self-world limit and guide what it does. It will only let go of its branch if it senses butyric acid from an animal, but it will pierce and suck at any warm membrane. Even a rubber container that holds warm glycerine will work.

An organisation's business model also gives it a self-world with limited access to external data and some very limited capabilities. Retail firms can easily get data that contains rich information about their direct interactions with their customers, for example, when customers visit the firm's website or buy goods in store. But it is much more difficult for a retailer to sense the start of a customer's shopping journey when they start to look for ideas on what to buy, for example, when they look on other retailers' websites (Hall et al., 2017). These events are not part of the retailer's self-world, so it cannot directly get that data. In order to know what customers are doing outside of its self-word a retailer must buy-in customer data from credit card companies, or data companies like Equifax and Experian. There are many retailers' websites that a shopper could look at and retailers do not directly share information. This makes it almost impossible to know when and why a shopper started the journey of looking for some beautiful item of clothing or a perfect present for a friend. These limitations on the ability to see the early stages of any customer's shopping journey lead to the problem of **attribution**. It is very difficult for advertisers to attribute any specific sale of a product to a specific advert or promotion that persuaded the shopper to buy it. Advertisers spend a huge amount of money persuading shoppers to buy from them, but they rarely know which advertisement or combination of advertisements persuaded any specific shopper to buy.

There is an old advertising saying that is attributed to John Wanamaker, 'I know that half my advertising budget is wasted, but I do not know which half' (Bradt, 2016). This was one of the main reasons for the huge decline in advertising revenue for print newspapers. Newspapers with business models that used paper newspapers could not identify who looked at the advert, for how long they looked and what they did next. But the self-worlds of digital newspapers, web advertising firms and app firms could. Other organisations have different but also very limited self-worlds. For example, the manufacturers of the products that shoppers buy have self-worlds, which do not directly include those retail customers. It sounds strange, but the manufacturers of clothes, shoes, food and other consumer goods only work directly with retailers, not with the end users of their products. So, retailers have much more shopper data than the manufacturers of the products they sell. This has led to third party firms that connect brands directly to their consumers by printing unique barcodes on the packaging of goods that shoppers buy, barcodes that shoppers can then use as proof of purchase for promotions, competitions or anything that will start a direct relationship with the manufacturer.

The self-world viewpoint helps us to understand the self-world of organisations. An organisation is a collection of interlinked human stakeholders, and an organism is a collection of interlinked physiological processes. But both have limited self-worlds, which govern what they can sense, how they analyse that sensory data and what actions they can then decide to take. Each organisation's business model is subtly different and even similar business models have different self-worlds. So, any response to change forces must be adjusted, or 'personalised' for the self-world of the specific organisation. For example, there are food retailers with similar business models, like Waitrose, Tesco and Asda in the UK. Waitrose sells higher-end goods than Tesco, and Asda aims to sell for lower prices than either Tesco or Waitrose. But all three of these retailers have slightly different business models to 'discount retailers' like Aldi and Lidl. All five retailers have retail business models, and they sell products in large shops. But Aldi and Lidl have generally lower prices because they use several techniques to reduce their costs. For example, they stock a more limited product range than the other three stores and they sell specific items that might be from less well-known brands. Just as there are grass grazing herbivores with different genomes, like sheep and cows, slightly different business models and slightly different genomes will produce slightly different self-worlds. So, these organisations and organisms will tolerate change in different ways. The balance of resources, capabilities and stakeholders' values in similar but not identical business models will be slightly different. So, they will be open to being unbalanced by changes in different ways, and they will sense changes, think and act differently.

The population viewpoint

Populations of organisms grow as they reproduce until they reach the limits of their habitat's ability to support them. Similarly, organisations split off subsidiaries, which they may not then own or control. Many organisations try to grow to consume more resources, to gain more market share or to provide more services. But there are market limits on the growth of organisations with similar business models. Longevity, growth and producing spin-offs usually mean that a business model is a success. The population viewpoint can be used to get access to ecologists' ideas of intra and inter species competition, mutuality, and **accommodation** between different species. We will look at these ideas in this section because they are useful for evaluating the success of a type of business model.

If an organism's genome is like an organisation's business model, then intra and inter species competition helps us to ask questions about the business models of competitors with similar as well as different business models. Competitors with the same business model will be under different pressures to indirect competitors with different business models. The differences in competitors' business models might provide us with answers for how to respond to change forces. This is because they will balance resources, capabilities and stakeholders' values differently, and live in a different self-world. So, they will sense, think, and act differently, and the population viewpoint can help us to measure the success of different strategies.

Thinking in terms of populations leads to questions about maximum population size, growth rates and fluctuations in populations. This has a direct business link to market saturation where firms with similar business models outgrow the demands of their current customers. Either they have manufactured too many products, or customer demand has decreased to less than what has been manufactured. In this way the population viewpoint helps us to answer questions about economic stability and cycles of boom and bust. For example, in 2020 the COVID-19 pandemic greatly reduced the global demand for oil. This caused an oversupply of crude oil and some petroleum products, whose prices fell dramatically (CNBC, 2020). In 2019 the same thing happened to memory chips (Gartner, 2020). But in 2019 and 2020, lithium, which is used in batteries for electric vehicles, was in over supply as that industry waited for car battery production to scale up. Too much lithium forced prices down but then later in 2020, Jaguar, Land Rover, Mercedes and Audi had to reduce production of some of their electric cars because they could not source enough rechargeable lithium batteries. Upstream there was a glut of lithium for battery production; downstream there were not enough batteries. In the middle, there was a bottleneck partially blocking this supply chain (Ribeiro and Zhang, 2019; Cohen, 2020).

The population viewpoint also helps us to consider the backstory of shared ancestors in a single species population. With organisations the idea of a population of shared business models can help us to analyse why technology clusters, business models and even industry standards started off and succeeded in certain locations. For example, in 'Silicon Valley', the famous location for high technology organisations near San Francisco, or in Bangalore, which is called the 'Silicon Valley of India'.

The community viewpoint

The community viewpoint involves looking at how organisations with different business models work closely together or compete. In nature, a community is a mixture of more than one species. Species mix in terms of their interlocking self-worlds, and as set out in the rules of their genomes. We can use a community viewpoint to analyse how organisations with more than one type of business model can thrive together. Like natural communities, a community of organisations is an interlocking patchwork of self-worlds, except that organisations' self-worlds are an expression of the rules of their business models. A supply chain is a type of community of linked business models. Each business model is serially linked to the next in a customer–supplier relationship. Each stage in a supply chain is linked to the next with finished products and raw materials, or with provided services and bought-in services. Ecosystems are like wheels and supply chains are like rivers. Business ecosystems are also built out of interlinked business models, but they are not a series of links like supply chains. As I will explain in Chapter 7, ecosystems are cyclic processes, not serial processes. Ecosystems thrive by recycling scarce resources, and unfortunately, supply chains do not recycle much of the materials that flow down them. Another difference between thinking in terms of a supply chains and a community viewpoint is that a community viewpoint focuses on business models and how they link together. But a supply chain perspective deals with flows of materials along it.

The interlinked self-worlds of a community are constantly changing as they respond to change forces. In nature, ecologists use the ideas of *competition, mutualism, **interference*** and *accommodation* to analyse these ongoing responses at the organism level and at the level of the whole community. These ideas give ecologists four different ways to see how different species live together. They also give us four ways to think about how organisations work together. Descriptions of these ways of viewing organizations are set out below.

Competition in the natural world is a drive to spread copies of a genome; a competition on the level of a species. But with business competition the focus is usually on the level of single organisations rather than business models competing against each other. Business growth is more commonly about growing the size of a single organisation rather than the popularity of a single business model over many organisations, although franchise business models are concerned with replicating very similar business models in different places. Businesses compete when their business models try to use the same limited resources and capabilities or when they target the same stakeholders (see the change force of competition earlier in this chapter). If customers, raw materials, or specialist staff, like data scientists are in short supply then there will be competition. You can think of competition as one end of a range of types of interactions. If two species, A and B, have a relationship and each can either be positively affected, neutrally affected, or negatively affected then there will be nine relationship combinations, although some will be repeated. Figure 2.7 shows the names that ecologists use for these relationships. The boxes are from species A's perspective unless the impact is the same for both species.

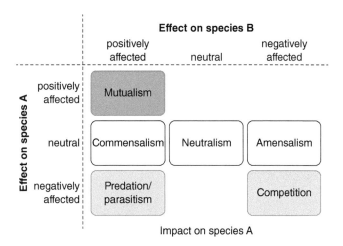

Figure 2.7   The combinations of positive, negative and neutral relationships that two species can have. Adapted from Bronstein (2015)

Mutualism is where interactions between two species benefit them both (Bronstein, 2012). It examines the relationship between one species and another. In nature mutualism is very common. Most land plants benefit from fungi, which help them to draw in water and nutrients, and virtually all mammal and insect herbivores depend on separate organisms in their guts for digesting cellulose (Bronstein, 2015). Mutualism's ideas give us a fantastic toolset for analysing how organisations interact in ways that end up benefiting them both. These interactions don't necessarily have to be altruistic, after all mutualistic relations in nature are all about maximising the benefits. For example, ants protect insects that give them sugar and bees pollinate plants because they visit flowers to get nectar. Also, mutualistic relationships always have costs. For example, the costs to the ants of producing sugar and the cost to the flowers of producing nectar. In business, it is common for organisations to look for synergies with partners; these are mutualistic interactions that lead to more success than if they had not taken place. Another concept in mutualism is called cheating, where a species takes benefits from a relationship but does not fully give back. For example, some fish that mutualistically clean parasites off larger fish will sometimes cheat by feeding on the larger fish's scales and other parts. In business, mutualism is common in outsourcing relationships, where one company has a capability that the other does not have or that is cheaper to use.

In Figure 2.7, commensalism is where interactions between two species benefit one but do not help or harm the other. Animals that track large predators and feed on their kills are examples of commensals. A business example of this is TerraCycle, which recycles waste consumer products. Amongst its many recycled products are tables made from toothpaste tubes and toothbrushes, a watering can made from crisp packets and an ashtray made from used cigarette butts (TerraCycle, 2021). Neutralism is where interactions between two species benefit neither. Amensalism is where interactions between two species harm one of the species but do not affect the other at all. Situations where one plant reduces sunlight shining onto other plants are amensal. This could also be viewed as a form of competition – a business example of this is where a forestry company harvests a large area of woodland and spoils the view for people who would have rented from a nearby Airbnb cabin. The change in the view has no effect on the forestry company but it harms the rental business of the cabin owner.

Figure 2.8   The two concentric wave patterns interfere with each other where they overlap to make a much more complicated pattern

Image: https://www.istockphoto.com/photo/water-gm185458322-27933108

Interference is one way to picture the interlocking patchwork of self-worlds for organisms as well as organisations. **Interference** is where one wave pattern merges with another, like the water waves in Figure 2.8. Two waves that coincide at high points add height to each other, two low points make a double depth low point, and a high and low point will cancel each other out. In natural ecosystems, the self-worlds of different species interfere with each other to help or hinder both species' growth across the geographical spaces and time periods where they overlap. This produces interference patterns of high points and low points of population size across space and time. The highs are points of constructive interference and the lows are points of destructive interference, like the patterns of interfering water waves in Figure 2.8. Some birds feed from conifers and some feed from deciduous trees (Shaw and Allen, 2017), but birds that feed from conifers are sometimes found in parts of oak forests and sometimes they might be missing from parts of conifer forests. You would expect them to be always found near the conifers that they feed from. Why is this not always the case? The explanation is that the self-world of a bird is very different to our human self-world. A bird's self-world is a 30 mile an hour flight over the tree tops. The senses and capabilities of a bird's self-world make small patches of conifers easy to spot and travel to even if they are quite widely distributed. A central patch of oaks that is surrounded by many conifer patches is a very attractive hub to locate in, but a small conifer patch in the middle of a vast area of oak trees is unattractive. The bird's self-world – how it senses conifers as well as how easily it travels – interferes with the checkerboard of patches of different trees. Together they create an interference pattern that would bring joy to any data scientist. It is a pattern that enables the bird to choose where to look for food and where to locate its base. The bird is not necessarily found near the conifers that they feed from because it uses a different pattern to make its decisions than a human would.

Retailers make similar choices when they choose where to build new stores. Data on shoppers' home addresses and competitor's store locations will not give the best pattern for choosing store locations. To make these decisions a retail analyst also needs data on where and when shoppers shop. Many people shop on the way home from work. It depends on what they are shopping for, but many times the best place to build a new store is near to workplaces or near to the nearest train station from a work place. So, the retail analyst's self-world should include access to data about customer's travel habits and what they might buy on these travels. Sometimes interference effects produce locations where many different organisations with similar business models congregate because of a combination of beneficial characteristics. For example, fast food outlets group together near transport hubs and roads with space for parking cars. Petrol stations do a similar thing at the entrance and exit to cities. A map of convenience stores across a large city would follow patterns of the tastes of the people who live in different patches of the city as well as how they travel across it.

Accommodation is where over time one species turns what another species does from a negative to a positive, or to a neutral effect. It is an unfolding process of adjustment between two species or between a species and its environment. For example, on the west coast of North America, some garter snakes have evolved to become resistant to the extremely poisonous skin of the Taricha species of newt (Yong, 2008). As one species accommodates itself to the actions of another species, or to a regular event, a negative action or event gradually turns into a benefit. The species can even begin to rely on it. Another example of this is a Canadian jack pine, which grows resin-sealed cones that hang on the tree until a fire melts the resin to let the cone pop open and the seeds drop out for distribution (Herring and Simmon, 1999). They rely on fires as part of their reproductive cycle.

In business as well as in nature, accommodation is a process of starting to work together. Relationships between organisations might start off as competitive but there might be useful biproducts. Just the fact that there is a relationship, even if it is competitive, is a basis for some form of development. An example of this would be when competitors decide to form a joint venture to take advantage of different but matching capabilities. 'Coopertition' is a well-known type of relationship between organisations where they compete in some ways but cooperate in others (Brandenburger and Nalebuff, 1996). Even the most direct competitors will join the same industry associations and band together to lobby governments to further their mutual interests. An organisation can learn to accommodate a significant effect on its business model, like strong competition, or some other change force. The main thing is that the organisation must eventually find a way to derive some benefit from the change force, for example, when competition sparks an organisation to improve its operational effectiveness and innovate.

The community viewpoint helps us to understand how the self-worlds of organisations 'mesh'. Sometimes organisations form communities of beneficial relationships and sometimes they do not. But thinking about these relationships in terms of communities and how they start and develop is very useful in a globalised and increasingly digitally linked up world.

The landscape viewpoint

Landscapes are single locations of any size, with their own significant geographical features. The landscape viewpoint helps ecologists to focus on a place and analyse how the features of that place affect the species in it. In nature, these features include mountains, valleys and hills, or cliffs and rivers. These features all have fundamental effects on the species that live there and the relationships between them. They all restrict or loosen the flows of materials on which these species depend. Mountains act as barriers to competition, or they can limit food sources. For example, the side of a hill in the northern hemisphere will get more sun if it faces south. Rivers can be barriers, or they can be migration routes. Landscapes in nature can be as big as a continental rock formation, or as small as a leaf. Organisations and organisms are both directly affected by their landscapes.

With organisations, the physical space that they operate in will influence the success of their business model. There are things that limit or help organisations to distribute physical products (like rivers, canals, or flat dry ground), such as the advantages of being near to customers and partner firms. Large scale landscape features like the footprint of high bandwidth Internet services are also very beneficial to the business models that rely on them, such as on demand video providers like Netflix. What we call a landscape in terms of organisations is the area occupied by a significant geographical feature that affects the business model of the organisations near it. The landscape viewpoint is not defined by its scale, it is the geographical feature that is important.

With organisations this includes not just physical effects, but also cultural and regulatory 'landscape' features. These come from operating in specific national legal systems or national cultures that exist in specific locations. Cultural footprints can be much bigger or much smaller than a country, and they might be based on age rather than ethnicity or citizenship. For example, the settlement of Irish and Chinese immigrants in specific neighbourhoods of New York and San Francisco left cultural footprints, which affected the types of local shops and industries. Other organisational landscapes include technology clusters like in Silicon Valley and Bangalore. The characteristics of the place itself directly affect its inhabitants' ability to grow business models of a certain type. In the cases of Silicon Valley and Bangalore, this includes access to highly educated staff and high quality educational and research institutions. In Bangalore's case, the availability of good Internet services helped organisations there to take advantage of the global outsourcing boom over the last two decades. Another example of a landscape effect is a landscape of customer tastes. Salsa manufacturers in the US change the spiciness of their sauce to fit to local tastes of each landscape: 'Salsas are often labelled mild, medium or hot. But one cannot find national brands that are actually "hot" salsa in the Middle West of the US. Even if the label claims the salsa is hot' (Shaw and Allan, 2017). Another example is free ports. Free ports are areas where a government sets special tax rates for specific things (Partington, 2019). Import taxes are not paid on goods in a free port until the goods move inland, so they can be stored or processed more cheaply. Goods might even be exported without ever moving inland. Other taxes are reduced in a selective way that encourages economic development by attracting companies to that location. The landscape viewpoint helps us to understand how the direct effects of where an organisation operates affect the success of its business model. It also suggests questions about current or potential locations for an organisation to operate in.

The biome viewpoint

Biome viewpoints are similar to landscape viewpoints because they are single locations of any size, with their own significant features. But biomes are only *indirectly* defined by their location and its physical features. A landscape viewpoint is *directly* based on its location, but a biome is only directly affected by its climate. What constitutes a natural biome is heavily influenced by the organisms that live in the biome. The organisms affect the biome's climate, and the climate also affects the organisms. For example, forests keep their local climate relatively cool by providing shade and by discharging water from their leaves. Another example is grazing animals that nibble back trees that would try and colonise a grassland. In a biome viewpoint, the focus is on how organisms affect the climate as well as on how the climate affects the organisms.

Organisations' biomes are affected by the cultural, regulatory and tax 'climates' that they operate in. Some communities of business models profit from the climates produced by the physical, cultural or legal situations of a geographical area. For example, special economic zones have different legal climates to the rest of a country, like Shenzhen and some other Chinese cities. China has opened many special economic zones. For example, in Shenzhen in the 1980s the purpose was to experiment with market-oriented reforms to what was a planned economy, and later in Zhangzhou and other cites the purpose was to stimulate economic growth by opening coastal cities to overseas investment. In all cases, special economic zones are areas where laws have been changed from those in the rest of the country, and where their laws might be adjusted more depending on how the zones develop.

On a smaller scale, city planning laws change the climate for firms in different parts of a city. When small suppliers locate themselves near to a large car plant, they benefit from the biome that the larger firm creates just by being in that location. These benefits include quicker delivery, easier communication, and the exchange of experienced staff. In a similar way to how animals and plants change the climate of a biome, organisations shape their climates as well. Climate shaping by organisations includes lobbying regulators and seeking to change public sentiment with public relations campaigns. Other recent and continuing examples of changes to public opinion that lead to changes in legal systems and cultural values are the feminism movement and the Black Lives Matter movement. These two movements are widespread social movements that include the actions of commercial and social organisations as well as individuals. Public attitudes to new technology are a major force in causing change in regulatory and cultural climates. The law and the cultural attitudes of every nation lag behind technological changes like the ability to record and link our individual identity to every single website that we visit, every key that we type and every mouse click that we make online. But they eventually catch up in different ways and at different speeds. Organisations, especially when they come together in communities, are a strong influence on these changes.

The biome viewpoint helps us to analyse how organisations can work together to influence their regulatory and cultural climates, and how these changes in turn affect business models. This two-way relationship between organisations that change their climate and a climate that affects business models is a prime illustration of why the forces of change depend on the 'personal' situation that each organisation is in. It is also an illustration of how change is a process of linked stages that can feed back on themselves. The biome viewpoint links together ideas about many organisations working together in communities with ideas about how each organisation's business model is affected by its personal situation. It helps us to ask questions about how an organisation's community might change and how the community can influence that change. Figure 2.9 summarises all five viewpoints from a natural perspective and an organisational perspective.

Viewpoint	Natural viewpoint	Organisational viewpoint
Self-world	Organisms with similar genomes have similar senses and capabilities. So, they live in a similar self-world and behave in similar ways in similar situations. Example: all breeds of dog	Organisations with similar business models can get access to similar data, analyse it in similar ways and have similar capabilities to act. They have similar self-worlds. Example: supermarkets
Population	A natural population lives within a single space or shares the same group of ancestors. A population viewpoint gives insights about the maximum possible population and variations in population. Example: the pressures on animals that are close to extinction	A population of copied business models operate within a single space or historically share similar business model ideas and implementation methods. Example: when organisations start with the same business model but then diverge. This viewpoint gives insights about the maximum market capacity and variations in the growth and number of these organisations. Example: comparing the financial performance of burger chains
Community	A community of mixed species is defined by how they accommodate, compete, and mutually benefit each other over time. Individual species join or leave the community. The self-worlds of species mix with each other and their environment to produce interference effects. Example: when mixtures of plants produce patterns of changing colours across a large field	In a community of organisations, organisations work tightly together in their different roles. Example: the linked business models of a supply chain. Organisational interference effects include variations in competitive intensity from pure competition to partnerships like joint ventures

(Continued)

Viewpoint	Natural viewpoint	Organisational viewpoint
Landscape	A landscape is a single physical area. The area's features shape the flows of nutrients and energy, which sustain the species in it. Example: when rivers provide migration pathways and mountains increase or reduce rainfall	The features of a single physical location shape the flows of resources, capabilities and stakeholder values that business models are made from. These features include cultural and legal characteristics that are specific to that area, like a smart city's attitudes, policies and laws
Biome	A biome is directly based on its climate and only indirectly based on its location's features. Organisms in the biome change and are changed by its climate. Example: rainforests help to produce regular rainfall in their microclimates	Organisational biomes are based on the cultural, tax and legal climates of specific locations. These climates help to sustain some communities of business models. Together, organisations can change these climates. For example, with lobbying for changes to city planning or other local government policy

Figure 2.9   Five viewpoints for analysing how organisations' personal situations influence their responses to change. Adapted from Shaw and Allen (2017) and Allen and Hoekstra (2015), and conversations with Professor Judith Bronstein.

The next chapter introduces a method called the 'Open Systems Change (OSC) model', which uses the ideas in this chapter to sense change forces and plan how to respond to them.

Chapter summary

Many aspects of society change, and these change forces strongly affect organisations. Changes in technology, markets, competition, legal regulations and the public's concerns about environmental sustainability affect organisations by changing their business models. But each organisation's local situation also affects the impact of change forces. Research into natural ecosystems gives us five viewpoints for analysing the local situation of an organisation. These viewpoints include an organisation's 'self-world', the population of similar business models, its business community, its business landscape and business biome.

Further reading

Atluri, V., Dietz, M. and Henke, N. (2017) 'Competing in a world of sectors without borders', *McKinsey Quarterly*, July 12. https://www.mckinsey.com/business-functions/mckinsey-analytics/our-insights/competing-in-a-world-of-sectors-without-borders (accessed 2 April 2022).

Andreessen, M. (2011) 'Why software is eating the world'. Andreessen Horowitz. https://a16z.com/2011/08/20/why-software-is-eating-the-world (accessed 2 April 2022).

Conde, J. and Pande, V. (2017) 'The century of biology', Andreessen Horowitz. https://a16z.com/2017/06/21/jorge-conde-bio-fund (accessed 2 April 2022).

Dixon, C. (2010) 'The next big thing will start out looking like a toy', Cdixon. https://cdixon.org/2010/01/03/the-next-big-thing-will-start-out-looking-like-a-toy (accessed 2 April 2022).

Gazmararian, L. (2020) 'Time for trust: How blockchain will transform business and the economy', PWC, https://www.pwc.com/timefortrust (accessed 2 April 2022).

Panetta, K. (2019) 'Gartner top strategic technology trends for 2020', Gartner, https://www.gartner.com/smarterwithgartner/gartner-top-10-strategic-technology-trends-for-2020 (accessed 2 April 2022).

Panetta, K. (2020) 'Gartner top strategic technology trends for 2021', Gartner, https://www.gartner.com/smarterwithgartner/gartner-top-strategic-technology-trends-for-2021 (accessed 2 April 2022).

Press, G. (2016) 'A very short history of artificial intelligence (AI)', Forbes, https://www.forbes.com/sites/gilpress/2016/12/30/a-very-short-history-of-artificial-intelligence-ai (accessed 2 April 2022).

ANALYSING HOW CHANGE FORCES AFFECT ORGANISATIONS

KEY IDEAS

- The Open Systems Change (OSC) model is a method for using the ideas in Chapter 2 to respond to change forces.
- Using the OSC model starts with sensing changes to any change forces and analysing how these might affect an organisation's business model.
- The OSC model helps with planning a response to change forces including influencing them.
- The OSC model can be used to monitor how a response is working and if this affects the overall purpose of the organisation.

LEARNING OBJECTIVES

After reading this chapter you will be able to:

- Describe how to sense the build-up of change forces.
- Explain how to find out where a change force will affect an organisation.
- Describe how organisations respond to change forces.
- Describe how organisations influence the strength and effects of change forces.
- Explain how and why a response to change forces can be successful and at the same time damaging to an organisation's fundamental purpose.

Analysing how change forces affect organisations

This chapter introduces the Open Systems Change (OSC) model as a method for using the ideas in Chapter 2. You can use the OSC model to sense changes in the size of the change forces that affect organisations and then analyse how they might affect business models. Then you can plan a response. The OSC model can be used to continuously monitor an organisation's environment to check how a response is working. It also helps to evaluate how changes to a business model might affect the overall purpose of an organisation. This chapter explains how to use the OSC model to see the build-up of change forces, to understand how they affect an organisation and to plan a response.

How change forces affect business models

In the last chapter, I described five different change forces that affect organisations by acting on their business models. A business model describes the balance of the three elements – the supplies of resources, the capabilities to change those resources, and the values of the stakeholders who supply those resources and capabilities. Change forces change the balance of these three elements according to each organisation's specific situation. This is the special situation that each organisation is in, and it can be understood using the five viewpoints from ecology in the last chapter. Together, these viewpoints provide a powerful metaphor for analysing business models. Analysing how change forces affect an organisation requires an understanding of these three things: the change forces, the balance of the organisation's business model, and the situation that the organisation is in (see Figure 3.1).

Next, we will look at how to do this using a systematic method called the OSC model. I will use the phrase 'your' business model or 'your' organisation to mean the business model and organisation that is being analysed. But many analysts do not work for the organisations that they want to analyse. For example, they may be analysing a competitor, or a potential acquisition target or partner, and they might not be able to get direct access. If this is the case, then you will need to think about proxies for the organisation or the data sources. Proxy organisations are similar organisations that you are familiar with or that there is other information available for. For example, you might be a customer of a similar firm, or you might know someone who works for a similar organisation. Remember that an organisation can be a proxy for this analysis even if it is only similar to your target organisation in one of the things that the OSC model directs you to look at. For example, it might have similar customers, similar capabilities, or its business biome might function in a similar way. A proxy organisation does not have to be a complete substitution for your target organisation.

You can use as many proxy organisations as you have time for to build up a more likely picture of each part of your analysis. Likewise, proxies for the sources of the data that you will need to use with an OSC model only depend on their fit with what the OSC model requires. There are many ways to get access to the required data. Sometimes you will need to assemble it from different sources. Sometimes you will need to buy it or spend time gathering it from scratch, as primary data. But if you are clear about what information is required by the OSC model and why, then it is likely that you can find proxy data, such as an academic case study on an industry, a government report or some document on the web. Of course, you must judge the data quality, but that depends on what you want to use it for. In this way, you can build a 'patch work quilt' of proxy organisations and proxy data sources that fit the data needs of your OSC model analysis.

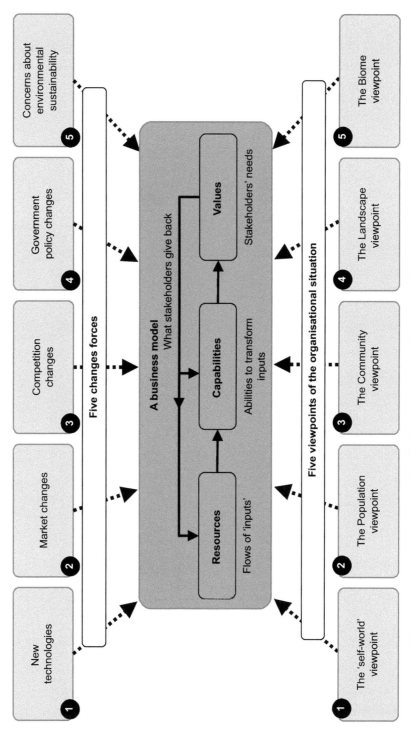

The OSC model

The OSC model can be used to systematically monitor the build-up of change forces, analyse their likely affect on an organisation and then plan a response. The OSC model uses open systems ideas to look for downstream changes to an organisation's business model based on what you can sense happening upstream. Think about this metaphor. Imagine that you are looking upstream on a river. You can see heavy rainfall and a flood moving rapidly downstream. The flood water might get caught and delayed, or it might reach you very soon. Either way, if you first look out for rising water levels and debris, and keep monitoring their progress, then you can take action to limit the damage.

This might seem like a very practical way to look for oncoming changes, and it is. But wouldn't it be better to avoid the effort of regularly monitoring the unfolding process of change and forecast it using some clever model of cause and effect? Yes, it would, if that were possible. But as the renowned philosopher David Hume pointed out, the relationship between a cause and an effect is all in our minds. It is made from logic and analysis rather than our own experience and data. Helen Beebee gave an example of turning a key in a lock and then hearing a sound that we associate with the key unlocking the lock (BeeBee, 2016). We would bet a million dollars that the sound was caused by turning the key, but we cannot know for sure. We cannot see inside the lock; we just use a causal model in our heads based on our experience of using many keys. These types of assumptions work quite well for locks and many aspects of our daily lives. But when it comes to the vast change forces that we are dealing with here, and their complex interactions with the individual situations of organisations, these assumptions are not that reliable. The connections between an apparent cause and an apparent effect that seem clear to us are just assumptions. They might seem highly likely, but they are not necessarily probable, real or true. Change forces are large scale, far off and long-term events that gradually unfold; they are very distant from our human-level senses. They come from far outside the self-world of humans, and even outside the much richer self-world of our organisations.

A common saying in **data science** is 'correlation is not causation'. Just because one event always seems to follow another does not mean that the first causes the second. Yes, some events can have an association if they frequently happen near to each other. But we cannot say if one has caused the other. They may have a common cause, or they may be accidentally near to each other in time or space. For this reason, it is better to use a 'process method' rather than a 'variance method' to analyse how change forces affect organisations. Process methods record the stages of what happens and look at the whole process, like a video. Variance methods are like comparing two photos. They are very useful for noticing the difference between two sets of data because they filter out all the information except for two 'data photos'. There are many strategic analysis tools that use variance methods to understand how the environment of an organisation interacts with its internal workings. These include the ESCO model (Heracleous et al., 2009) and Porter's 5 Forces model (Porter, 2008), strengths, weaknesses, opportunities and threats (SWOT) analysis (Dyson, 2004) and others like the Blue Ocean Strategy and the Balanced Scorecard (Lynch, 2021). But the limited snap shots of variance methods cannot tell us about the unfolding process of events in the way that a video can (Markus and Robey, 1988). Process methods do not actually prove that some event caused another event, but they give us enough information to produce an explanation of why something probably happened and why something is likely to happen (Rescher, 2000). Process methods are useful for understanding changes in organisations because they give us a detailed 'audit trail' of what has happened. This is critical for getting senior managers in organisations to sponsor organisational responses and to sign-off the costs, and even more importantly for persuading other stakeholders to change how they work.

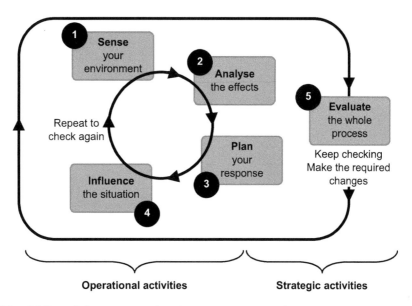

Figure 3.2   The OSC model's operational and strategic activities for sensing and responding to change forces

The four operational activities are: 1. Sensing changes in the size of change forces, 2. Analysing how these changes will affect an organisation's business model, 3. Planning the response, and 4. Influencing the situation to mitigate or guide the change. The operational loop must be repeated by continuously rechecking the organisation's environment to see how the response is working. The single strategic activity (Activity 5) connects to two of the operational activities: 5. Evaluating how the operational cycle is doing by repeatedly comparing the results of the analysis (Activity 2) to the organisation's purpose, then changing the plan (Activity 3) accordingly.

So, the OSC model uses a process method to monitor changes to the system of business models that each organisation is in. Business models are **open systems** rather than **closed systems**. They have input flows and output flows; the inputs are used up, so the system needs a continuous flow of new inputs to sustain itself. This process is the river in our river metaphor. The OSC model is designed to continuously look up river to monitor changes as they head closer and closer downstream, all the time preparing the organisation. Eventually the likelihood of their effect becomes easier to guess and action can be taken. In a world where ideas of cause and effect are trickier than they seem, the OSC model relies on continuous updates and short-term expectations rather than long-term guesses. It only suggests the next stage in the process flow, not some far future stage in time.

The OSC model in Figure 3.2 is made up of five activities, which are arranged in two connected cycles. The operational activity cycle and the strategic activity cycle. The operational activity cycle collects data, decides on a planned response, and then checks that plan. It plans and re-plans according to how upstream change forces develop over time. The strategic cycle keeps checking the operational plan and changes it to satisfy the organisation's purpose. The five activities of these two cycles are common to many models of organisational action such as Haeckel and Nolan's Sense and Respond model (1993) and data feedback loops, which Observe, Orient, Decide and Act (OODA) (Mayhew et al., 2016).

In these models, a loop compares information about an organisation's environment with what needs to happen. This loop is the fundamental basis of cybernetic control systems (Wiener, 1948).

The OSC model has an operational cycle and a strategic cycle because the model links the internal operational activities of an organisation with the external strategic forces that they are responding to. It also integrates these with the local operating situation that the organisation is in. These two cycles reflect two overlapping internal and external perspectives, which work on two different timescales. Internal operational activities tend to be on a timescale of minutes to weeks, whereas strategic evaluation activities happen on the scale of weeks to months and years.

Using the OSC model

ACTIVITY 1

Sensing changes in change forces

Activity 1 starts by looking for upstream causes of change. 'Change' is the difference between how things are before and after a change. It is this difference that seems to 'power' changes like the chemical energy in the fuel that moves cars, or the mechanical energy in a spring that powers a clockwork toy. Or it might be something that motivates people to do something, something that they value. The difference between the before and after states explains why a transition was able to happen. So, you need to look for potential before and after states and check if everything is there to enable a transition between the two. For example, a car with a full petrol tank and a driver, a toy with a wound-up spring and a child to trigger it, or a person with a need for something they value and the money to pay for it. The before state can be recognised from the current situation, how things are right now. The after state needs some imagination to think up and a re-examination of the current situation to check if everything is present to enable the transition.

This activity gathers data on potential differences that might already be powering an ongoing change to an organisation's business model, or which could do so in the future. Things might be changing already, but you might not have noticed yet. For example, changes in customer sentiment towards green and 'eco' products have been building for decades. But for many years, market changes were just limited to a demand for organic products. It is only in the last few years that ecologically sound products like reusable nappies and alternative materials to plastic have started to become mainstream. More recently, this movement in consumers' expectations about what they want to buy has changed again. It now includes consumers' concerns about the ethical position of the company, not just the materials that the product is made from. This means that customers now expect changes in how firms treat their staff: customers are interested in issues like what benefits a firm gives to its gig economy workers and how the workers at a company's suppliers are treated. The spotlight has shifted from covering products, to manufacturers and eventually to whole supply chains.

The change forces that we focus on in this section are causes of change in organisations. But they themselves have causes as well. To understand and look out for the downstream effects of changes to organisations we must look backwards for early warning signs. Many types of differences can potentially power a change force. For example, technological development can be powered by wars and pandemics; what we have and what we need motivates us to change jobs and our skills; and in the case of the original moon landings, it was a vision of

(Continued)

what might be possible. Market changes are driven by many factors such as changing tastes, demographic and economic fluctuations, which form great gaps to be filled. Competition is driven by not enough of something that different parties all want. If there is enough to share, then there is no competition. Regulatory change is driven by organisations not being allowed to do something, for example, when organisations behave unethically, when they harm society or the government itself. In all these examples, changes are caused by other changes that are further upstream, such as society's rising concerns about environmental sustainability, which are driven by a desire to avoid an impending ecological disaster. If you can sense that tension between the situation now and what the situation could be, then that tension might be able to power a change. Sensing such a tension, like the tension in a wound-up spring, gives you a warning. You can look for conditions that might release that pent-up change energy.

But before we can gather data to sense the size of the differences that could power potential changes, we need to ask the right questions. We need to ask questions that will allow us to monitor the types of potential difference, their size right now and the trend in how they are changing. For each type of difference, we must ask, 'Is it growing or reducing, and how fast?'. Designing specific questions helps us to gather the information we need by targeting the right data sources. Also, a single measurement of potential differences is not enough. Regular measurements over time will tell us the trend. They will tell us if the change itself is changing, maybe accelerating or decelerating, which will warn us of powerful downstream effects. An example of this is when dissatisfaction with a government in a major oil producing nation builds to the point where there is a revolution, which disrupts oil supplies. Alternatively, a trend might give us the data to suggest a reduction or an end to a change force. 'Peak coal' in the US is an example of this. Decreasing use of coal led 2009 to be the year when US coal mines finally reached their maximum coal output, and this has fallen ever since (EIA, 2020). The forces that had for many years increased the US' ability to mine coal had started to reduce. Changes in the size of a potential difference help us to assess how soon the change will start to be felt and for how long. A trend for US coal production capacity to keep falling for over a decade suggests that there have been and will continue to be direct downstream changes to employment levels in the industry and in coal producing areas, as well as to coal prices and in other industries that directly depend on the coal industry, like mining equipment. However, this trend will not necessarily lead to a reduction in emissions from burning coal in the US if more coal is imported.

Questions to ask of the data

Sensing change is an information gathering activity, so it needs to start by creating and asking the right questions. This section describes and explains some practical ways to do this for each of the main change forces in this book. When trying to sense any changes to the size of the upstream differences that might power a change force, the questions to ask depend upon the type of change:

- Technology changes.
- Market changes.
- Competition changes.
- Regulatory changes.
- Rising concerns about environmental sustainability.
- Other change forces.

Technology changes need scientists, engineers and other specialists to learn how to do new things, which requires investment. So, ask yourself where is research and development money being spent now to develop technology changes soon? For example, a widespread and deadly disease like AIDS or COVID-19 will trigger huge amounts of research funding over many years. Look further upstream and ask: in which technological areas will research and development funding change in the next few years? Which technologies seem to be getting better at what they do very fast? For example, many AI technologies have been researched for decades but AI using neural network technology only became powerful enough to be really useful from around 2010. Which are the specific capabilities that newly useful technologies enable and where else could they be used? For example, neural network technology AIs are very good at being trained to recognise images, sounds and other things that are recorded as digital data.

Market changes are about changes to customers. So, ask yourself: how are customers or customers' tastes changing? The number of customers involved will shrink or grow as a result of their changing tastes. But also think about the types of products and services that they need, e.g., what do your products and services enable customers to do in their lives? What is the outcome that you help them to get to? Umbrellas keep people dry, food will entertain as well as feed a person, cars move people, and videos educate and amuse viewers. Is there a change in how customers are using your products and services? Look further upstream and ask: is the purpose that customers buy your products and services for changing?

Competition changes are about your current competitors and organisations who might compete with you in the future. Who are your current competitors and exactly how do they compete with you? Do you each target the same resources, capabilities, or stakeholders? In the near future, which organisations might target those same stakeholders with products and services that satisfy the same values as you do? Start by looking at organisations who already sell to the same stakeholders or use the same resources or capabilities. Is their demand for resources, capabilities or stakeholders changing? Are they likely to grow, so that their resource and capability needs will also grow?

Regulatory changes are changes to government regulations, which take effort as they use up limited government time and governments always have too much to do. As a result, regulations only change when large-scale events happen upstream, such as when a political party with very different ideologies is elected, or when some disaster produces a national public call for change. For example, a fire in the Grenfell tower block in London in 2017 killed many residents and led to major reviews of building regulations concerning the materials that towers could be covered with. Another example is when the murder of a young girl in the US led to the creation of Megan's law, which gave parents access to information about paedophiles living in their area. Even after powerful events like these, where the public demand that governments act, every government will have a legislative process that can provide valuable information and alerts about timescales, and likely changes to regulations. The legislative process will also have opportunities for public feedback on the details of potential regulation changes, which can provide information in what those changes might eventually be. Some exceptionally catastrophic and emotionally charged events will stimulate emergency actions, which provide much less of a warning and may not follow the normal process. For example, at the start of the COVID-19 pandemic, there were emergency orders for tens of millions of pounds worth of gowns, masks and gloves for UK NHS workers, which bypassed normal government procurement processes (NAO, 2020). Another example is the legal changes in Japan after the catastrophic earthquake and tsunami in March 2011 (LOC, 2013). With regulatory change forces, you should ask what the normal legislative process is for the governing body or ministry in charge of your sector. Monitor their legislative workload to understand the pipeline of future regulatory changes and their timetables.

Rising concerns about environmental sustainability are held by all the stakeholders in your business model. So, ask yourself: who are they and what do they each think about the resources and capabilities that your business uses? What do they think about the values that you satisfy? All stakeholders are integral to balancing your business model by contributing something to it in return for something it provides them with. This includes all the organisations in your supply chain. For example, microbeads are very small pieces of plastic that are used for abrasive cleaning in face washes, toothpastes and body scrubs. Rising concerns about microbeads spreading plastic throughout the natural environment has led to them being banned in the US, Canada and the UK. Other countries are also considering bans. The public's concerns about environmental issues like plastic pollution drive technology changes, market changes and regulatory changes. They force companies to develop new technologies when capabilities like cleaning teeth with microbeads become disapproved of by customers, or illegal.

In this book, we focus on five major ways of looking at change forces. There are many other change forces and many ways to look at them. However, what really counts is the outcome: the effect on the balance of resources, capabilities and values in your business model. Try to work backwards from your business model's three elements to look for changes that might affect them, whatever they are called. These changes might be in the amount and type of resources and capabilities that your organisation can acquire, or it might be in the amount or type of stakeholders' values that it can satisfy. All these things should be closely monitored to see if they are increasing or decreasing. Do not just look for a change that has already started. Also, look for a build-up of potential change energy that has no medium for releasing it yet. For example, industries where there are high levels of customer dissatisfaction, but no alternative products are ripe for new start-up firms to destabilise them, like when the telephone and videoconferencing industries were disrupted by Skype.

Sources of information

Sources of information include:

1   Technology forecasting sources: specialist research firms like Gartner (www.gartner.com) and Forrester (https://go.forrester.com), specialist news publications like New Scientist (www.newscientist.com) and Scientific American (www.scientificamerican.com), and technology-oriented venture capital businesses like Andreessen Horowitz (www.a16z.com). The technology practices of major consultancy firms like McKinsey Quarterly (https://www.mckinsey.com/quarterly/overview), Deloitte (www2.deloitte.com/uk/en/insights.html) or PwC (www.strategy-business.com) are worth signing up to for their newsletters. Also, look at the technology sections of mainstream news agencies like the BBC (www.bbc.co.uk), the websites of top newspapers, and online news sources like BuzzFeed (www.buzzfeed.com), Reuters (www.reuters.com) and HuffPost (www.huffpost.com).
2   Market analysis firms like Euromonitor International (www.euromonitor.com), Frost and Sullivan (www.frost.com), Hoovers Research (www.hooversresearch.com) and Mintel (www.mintel.com) provide very detailed information on specific markets.
3   Other market analysis firms look more closely at customer behaviour, for example Nielsen (www.nielsen.com), Ipsos (www.ipsos.com) and Kantar (www.kantar.com).
4   Some firms specialise in consumer credit information, for example Experian (www.experian.co.uk) and Equifax (www.equifax.co.uk).

(Continued)

5   Political think tanks are a good source for forecasting regulatory changes and there is a large number of them in every country with different specialities and different biases. Examples include The Brookings Institution in the US (www.brookings.edu) and The Adam Smith Institute in the UK (www.adamsmith. org). Also, see the political news sections of mainstream news agencies and online news sources, especially if a regulatory change force affects or is affected by the public in some way.

6   World institutions and international organisations are also good sources for monitoring global level change forces, for example the World Health Organisation (www.who.int), the World Bank and the World Economic Forum (https://www.weforum.org/reports). Governments also publish useful reports but like any data source there will be an inherent bias.

7   The online sources and databases that are accessible through university libraries.

ACTIVITY 2

Analysing how this will affect your organisation's business model

The OSC model analyses how change forces affect the balance of the elements in an organisation's business model. Stakeholders supply resources and capabilities because they get something that they value in return, which can be anything: products, services, information, permissions, suggestions. It depends on who they are. Balancing all this can be complicated and sensitive. Change forces affect organisations by *unbalancing* these elements. They work by changing the amounts of specific resources and capabilities that are available, and by altering what stakeholders value. This activity uses the data from Activity 1 to look for changes that might unbalance a business model. If a business model is unbalanced, then it must be changed to rebalance it. But any changes produce follow-on changes. Change is an ongoing process, not a single event. All changes have repercussions, implications and further consequences, and all of these can further unbalance a business model.

Activity 1 looks for upstream changes that could potentially power downstream changes. Activity 2 analyses that information to see how these changes might affect your business model in the near and medium future. Near future changes like shortages of certain resources are worth looking for because they will affect you soon. Medium term changes are worth looking for because they are roughly predictable. There is little point in looking far into the future because there are too many possible permutations of what might happen to accurately predict it. The uncertainty and the probability of errors get too high. The OSC model is a monitoring tool not a crystal ball.

The forces that change business models and business models themselves are both part of the same open systems. If they were not part of the same system, then there would be no connection and they would not affect each other. A business model is like an engine. Resources are the fuel, which get used up at a certain rate to produce value, by capabilities. The capabilities a business model uses to burn fuel limit its capacity, which is the maximum rate at which it can use up resources to create value. This is the difference between the quantitative idea of capacity, i.e., 'how much?', and the qualitative idea of capability, i.e., 'capable of what?'. One car engine can burn fuel to give a maximum speed of 100 miles per hour. A more efficient car engine design might have the capability to burn the same amount of fuel in the same car and give a higher maximum speed.

(Continued)

Resources may become more available or less available, or more expensive or less expensive. They might become unavailable, or illegal. Capabilities may become more – or less – efficient at converting resources into useful outputs, or they might be swapped out for other capabilities that do it in a different way. How much customers value something, or what they value might change. Continuing to produce exactly the same products, or to use the same capabilities, in the face of these changes might cause a business to fail. An example of this is Kodak. Kodak was a hugely successful manufacturer of analogue film cameras and film, but its management failed to act fast enough when digital technologies replaced chemical capabilities for recording images. It entered the digital camera industry but was too slow to respond when this industry was flooded by low cost but high-quality competitors like Canon and Nikon. The camera market was then further pressurised by the new competition from mobile phones as many people started to use them to take pictures and record videos, instead of using dedicated cameras. Eventually Kodak filed for bankruptcy protection in 2012. This is a good illustration not just of how the flows of resources, capabilities and what customers value change, but also how change forces merge together.

Resources, capabilities and what customers value are 'input flows' to business models. They all have maximum limits and they can run out. Oil resources were originally found bubbling up from the ground or very near to the surface. As these deposits were used up, oil firms had to drill deeper and deeper (Tainter and Patzak, 2012). Now oil firms must drill deep under the sea or develop new capabilities like fracking. Fracking can extract petrochemicals from shale deposits. But what customers value also has its limits. Most people only own a maximum of one car each at any one time – that is their car owning limit. It is the same for many other products. Even products that we collect lots of, like books, shoes or ties have limits to what we can afford or fit in our cupboards. Disposable products that we use up quickly like milk also are limited by the amount that we can buy. This is because our ability to use them and our ability to pay for them are limited.

There are many limits on the three business model elements. All of them have limited availability. Customer numbers depend on the size of the market and suppliers for specialist goods or in new markets are frequently very limited. Every stakeholder will also have a limit on their capacity to contribute whatever it is that they contribute to a business model. For example, they will have a maximum rate of delivery or a maximum rate of dealing with whatever it is they do. They will also have strict limitations on the types of roles they have in the business model. Suppliers specialise in particular niches, like car dealers that supply only certain brands or shops that only sell shoes. Customers also specialise, in the sense that they have specific needs.

The capabilities that any stakeholder contributes will not be able to do everything, they will have a limit. It is these limitations that set the balance of a business model. Simple physical systems are only limited by constraints. Simple machines or organisations run at their maximum rate unless a person limits that rate. Fire will burn at a maximum rate, which is set by the available fuel and oxygen – fires are not like dimmer lights that can be varied between high and low settings. Dimmer lights are not simple physical systems, they contain variable switches in addition to their lighting circuit. But business models are simple physical systems – they are either on or off. Full speed or stopped, they do not have a dimmer switch. Managers only reduce the speed that an organisation operates at if they have to. The only thing that regulates the operation of a business model is not enough of a resource, a capability or something customers value. That is what the regulator in an engine does, it starves it of fuel to slow it down, or increases the flow of fuel to speed it up.

Questions to ask of the data

Sensing changes is an information gathering activity, so it needs to start by creating and asking the right questions. This section describes and explains some practical ways to do this for each of the main change forces in this book. Analysing how the changes you sensed in Activity 1 will affect your organisation's business model means studying how they will affect the following:

- The resources that your business model consumes.
- The capabilities that these resources feed.
- The stakeholders' values that your business model satisfies.

Here are some practical questions to ask about these three elements for each of the main change forces in this book.

Don't forget to consider the specific situation of the organisation that you are analysing using the five viewpoints from Chapter 2:

- The 'self-world' viewpoint: how does the business model affect the organisation's ability to sense, analyse and respond to change?
- The population viewpoint: how are organisations with similar business models doing and is there a cycle of variation in their prosperity? Can the market support them all?
- The community viewpoint: which other organisations are part of the same organisational community, how do they affect each other and what does this imply for your organisation?
- The landscape viewpoint: are there any physical, legal, or cultural features of the organisation's location that should be considered?
- The biome viewpoint: are the organisation's cultural, regulatory or tax climates affected and can the wider communities in this biome help with a response?

For resources, first ask yourself, what are the resources that your business model feeds on? Make a list. Do you have a manufacturing process that depends on certain raw materials? What information is a prerequisite for your services? What are the inputs that your business model needs to consume for it to operate? From the information that you gathered in Activity 1, which of these resources are becoming – or will become – harder or easier to acquire? An example of this is if an increase in biofuel crops and solar farms caused the space for food crops to start to decrease. How is the supply of these resources likely to change? Think of it like a bucket with a hole in it being filed by a water tap. If the flow of water from the tap increases *or* the leak decreases, then the water level in the bucket will rise. If the flow of water from the tap decreases or the leak increases, then the water level in the bucket will fall. A change in the water level of the bucket shows a change in the balance of supply and demand for a resource. The water level changes because of the inflow of water as well as the outflow of the leak. Change forces affect these inflows and outflows to the whole economic system.

You can look for changes to inflows and outflows of resources by focusing further upstream to monitor indirect changes. Is a new technology causing firms to use more of one of the resources on your list? For example, improvements in battery technology are increasing the distance that an electric vehicle can travel on a single charge, and the demand for lithium and other materials is greatly increasing as more people decide to buy electric vehicles. Or is a new technology enabling firms to use less of one of these resources, or to use an alternative resource? An example of this is power stations using wood pellets rather than coal. Are market changes causing an increase in demand for some of the resources that you use? For example, China's dietary transition to consuming more meat per person resulted in an increased demand for meat (Shimokawa, 2015). Or do you expect your competitors to change how they consume resources? Maybe they will start to compete for the resources you use as well as for your customers.

Regulatory changes also affect the inflows and outflows to your markets by limiting the inflows of some resources. For example, trade tariffs and regulatory checks at customs all increase barriers to trade. Changes in laws are frequently designed to reduce demand. An example of this would be a law requiring manufacturers to add pictures showing the effects of cancers and other smoking related diseases to cigarette packets. Rising concerns about environmental sustainability will reduce demand for some resources and increase demand for others. For example, many shops in Europe have stopped supplying free disposable plastic bags, but the demand from consumers for alternatives to plastics, like bamboo or steel lunch boxes, is rising.

For capabilities, first ask yourself, what are the capabilities that your business model uses to function? Make a list. For example, do you depend on people with critical skills or specific machines, which means things grind to a halt when they are not available? Are there bottlenecks in your organisation, some function that would increase your overall capacity if it was more productive? Any bottleneck will do much worse than limiting your maximum capacity if it is reduced in some way. According to the information you gathered in Activity 1, which of these capabilities are becoming – or will become – harder or easier to acquire? For example, for a long time, the race to use big data and AI technologies in organisations has been limited by the availability of experienced data scientists. But universities and other education providers have greatly increased the flow of people with sophisticated data analytics capabilities. New AI services from IBM Watson, Google, Microsoft and other providers have also helped by automating large parts of the analytical process. The leaky bucket metaphor applies to the varying power of a capability as much as it does to the amount of a resource.

Which of the capabilities in your list are currently based on technologies that are improving fast? For example, cheaper sensors and Wi-Fi have enabled even low-cost appliances like toasters and electric toothbrushes to become connected together as Internet of Things devices. Which technologies might be replaced by another technology? For example, mobile phones replaced the use of many landline phones and brought many new capabilities with them, like mobile Internet access and continuous location monitoring, as well as easy video and audio recording. Fewer people buy separate cameras, watches and calculators anymore. Which of the capabilities on your list are based on human capabilities that will soon be augmented by technology? In the past, separate software applications could only be joined together and automated using special internal connections in the code, called application programming interfaces (APIs), or with additional scripting code. But improvements in image recognition, text recognition and AI technologies have enabled Robot Process Automation (RPA) technologies to learn how to do this by watching how people use the software's user interface. The 'robot' in RPA software is the software pretending to be the person using the software, for simple decisions and repetitive tasks.

Market changes also cause changes in the demand for capabilities, like when the COVID-19 pandemic increased the forecasted demand for hospital beds and China built several hospitals, each with hundreds of beds and each in about ten days. Also, your competitors might change the capabilities that they use. For example, in late 2020, several UK ports like Felixstowe and Southampton became blocked. This was due to the COVID-19 pandemic disrupting global shipping timetables, several extremely large shipments of protective masks and gowns to the NHS, Brexit preparations and the usual Christmas supply chain pressures. Felixstowe and Southampton are giant ports and critical for the operation of shipping companies, and two of the biggest shipping companies, Maersk and MSC, said they would reroute their cargos to Liverpool port instead (Nunis, 2020).

As when analysing resource flow changes, you can also check to see if market changes are leading to an increase in the demand for some of the capabilities that you use. But do not forget to check if your competitors are changing the capabilities that they use as well. Regulatory changes will affect your capabilities in two ways. First, they will limit the supplies of capabilities that you can access by potentially changing how these capabilities are produced, like when training specialists. This is particularly relevant where educational accreditations and quality assurance is required, like in medicine, law, engineering or accountancy. Second, regulatory changes will affect your capabilities by limiting or relaxing how you use these capabilities, i.e., what you can do with them. For example, in Ontario, Canada it is illegal for a truck driver to drive more than 13 hours in a day (MTO, 2017). They are capable of driving for longer, but the laws limit them, which means they can only be used as drivers at certain times of the day. Finally, rising concerns about environmental sustainability will change the supply of some capabilities. For example, concerns that burying household rubbish creating greenhouse gases mean that municipal waste collectors have been forced to gradually use more incinerators instead of landfill sites (Harrabin, 2018). Also, certain rubbish items like batteries cannot be disposed of in landfill sites in some countries. Alternatively, there has been a vast increase in the availability of electricity generated from solar and wind energy sources, as the technologies have improved and more generation capacity has been built to take advantage of this.

What your stakeholders value are also affected by change forces. But their values are subjective, so you need to start by asking who the *stakeholders* are whose values your business model satisfies. Make a list. Then add to it what each stakeholder contributes to your business model, and what they get in return. A Value Flow Analysis diagram (VFA) is a practical way to list all your stakeholders, how they contribute to your business model and what they gain from it (see Chapter 2 for an explanation of a VFA). For each stakeholder, you should ask what their values are. Are they suppliers that supply raw materials for money? Are they customers that pay money in return for your products and services? Are they partners who get something else out of the relationship? Are they a government department, a not for profit or some other organisation or group of people? Make a VFA diagram and put all this information into it as well (see Figure 3.3). This will help you ask targeted questions to analyse your original business model and decide how to change it. Are any of these stakeholders becoming harder or easier to sell to? Are their values changing? Is the population of stakeholders with these values and these contributions becoming smaller or larger? If the population of one type of stakeholder is changing or what they value is changing then it will potentially unbalance your business model, unless you see it coming.

Stakeholders' values are particularly sensitive to rising concerns about environmental sustainability. But what they value and what they will contribute in return is also affected by market changes and what your competitors do. Another thing about stakeholder values to look for is which of these values are becoming harder or easier to satisfy? For example, car buyers are starting to expect their cars to be less polluting, which is forcing engine manufacturers to change. You can prepare for a potential threat to the balance of your business model by paying attention to changes in the tastes and expectations of stakeholders, and what they consider important.

Figure 3.3, Figure 3.4 and Figure 3.5 illustrate how to use VFA diagrams to analyse your 'original' business model in response to problems, redesign it into a 'new' business model and build it up by recruiting new stakeholders from an 'outer VFA' of potential and temporary stakeholders. These illustrations

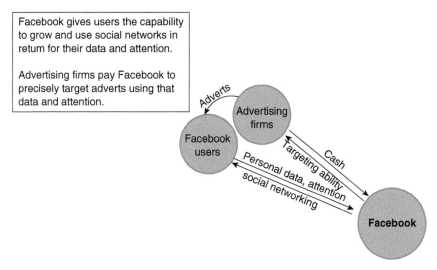

Facebook gives users the capability to grow and use social networks in return for their data and attention.

Advertising firms pay Facebook to precisely target adverts using that data and attention.

Figure 3.3   Example of original VFA diagram illustrating an original business model and where it was reportedly affected by change forces

are based on activities by Facebook taken from news sources (Cellan-Jones, 2018; Grothaus, 2018; Nix et al., 2018; Courea, 2020; Frenkel and Barnes, 2020). These news sources only give a general view, with little detail, and things changed as the situation developed over several years. But they are a useful illustration of how an organisation responds to developments in new technological capabilities, how people use these technologies in unforeseen ways, and how this forces further changes to a business model. In this case, the changes involved recruiting new types of stakeholders from outside the pool of stakeholders in the 'original VFA'. The examples in this illustration concern the problem of 'fake news' that our society is dealing with as I write this book. So, they could apply to almost any social media organisation at this time. In the next few years, social media organisations will rebalance their business models to accommodate and deal with issues like this.

ACTIVITY 3

Planning your response

Activity 1 looks for build-ups and reductions in the change forces that could affect your organisation. Activity 2 analyses these to see how they might affect your organisation, by changing the balance of elements that your current business model relies on. Activity 3 plans how to deal with increases or decreases in the supply of these resources, capabilities, or stakeholder contributions. This can be done either by planning how to deal with changes to their supply, or by changing other parts of your business model. I will explain how to change business models in Chapter 5.

(Continued)

Planning how to deal with changes to your supplies of resources and capabilities means looking for alternative suppliers for them, or redesigning your products, services and business processes so you do not need them. Alternatively, it might mean looking for alternative stakeholders who can contribute to your business model. When resources and capabilities become much harder or much easier to get, or when what customers and other stakeholders want changes, your business model will become unbalanced. The collective product of what your stakeholders do will not satisfy what they require in return. Some stakeholders, maybe customers, maybe suppliers or others, will stop contributing. They will stop or reduce whatever they do as their role in the business model. So, either you need to find something else that will persuade them to play their part, or you will need to replace them. That is how Activity 3 plans to rebalance a business model. A business model maintains itself by functioning. If it stops then it begins to fall apart. This is why companies that are still operating as a business can be sold as a 'going concern' for much more than companies that have closed down. Closed down companies have turned the lights off, switched off the power, and their staff and customers have gone elsewhere. They are then sold just for their separate assets. Working companies are worth much more than the sum of their assets because value is calculated by what they do, not by what they could potentially do.

Rebalancing your business model

The analysis in Activity 2 might detect a potential destabilisation in the flows that balance the business model elements in your VFA diagram (Figure 3.3). You can plan a response to this either by:

1   Increasing the supply of whichever resources, capabilities or stakeholder values are reducing.
2   Finding alternative sources from elsewhere.
3   Changing the mix of your business model to use different resources, capabilities, or to satisfy stakeholders' values in a different way.

This will mean redesigning your products and services and your business processes to use alternative resources and capabilities. It may also mean educating your customers to expect a very different product or service. For example, when Netflix started to stream films over the Internet using a subscription service, most customers were used to physically renting or buying individual DVDs.

Start by going back to the VFA diagram that you made in Activity 2 (see Figure 3.3). You will need to draw out several new versions based on your ideas for rebalancing it. These VFAs can be used to test your ideas with internal and external stakeholders, to strengthen them and eventually reach a consensus. This will provide you with a much better response as well as the support to make the changes to your organisation.

Figure 3.4 shows two simplified VFA diagrams. Panel (a) shows how problems with inappropriate content and fake news reportedly caused some voters to complain to government legislators and politicians. They apparently wanted tighter regulation of companies like Facebook. Panel (b) illustrates how Facebook apparently worked to rebalance their business model by reducing the causes of these complaints. The company reportedly developed new AI filtering and Oversight Board capabilities to deflect potential new legal responsibilities. These capabilities included resources and capabilities to construct its Oversight Board, which came from the new stakeholders in Facebook's outer VFA, in Figure 3.5.

(a)

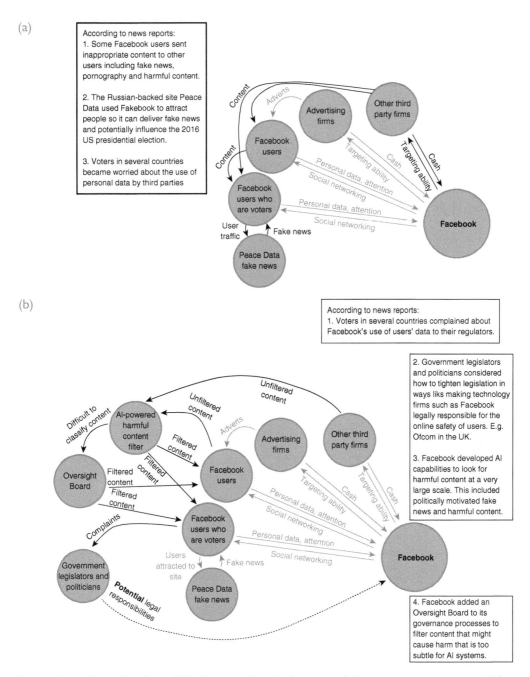

According to news reports:
1. Some Facebook users sent inappropriate content to other users including fake news, pornography and harmful content.

2. The Russian-backed site Peace Data used Fakebook to attract people so it can deliver fake news and potentially influence the 2016 US presidential election.

3. Voters in several countries became worried about the use of personal data by third parties

(b)

According to news reports:
1. Voters in several countries complained about Facebook's use of users' data to their regulators.

2. Government legislators and politicians considered how to tighten legislation in ways liks making technology firms such as Facebook legally responsible for the online safety of users. E.g. Ofcom in the UK.

3. Facebook developed AI capabilities to look for harmful content at a very large scale. This included politically motivated fake news and harmful content.

4. Facebook added an Oversight Board to its governance processes to filter content that might cause harm that is too subtle for AI systems.

Figure 3.4   Example of new VFA diagram showing how to rebalance your business model (try out several versions)

These are simplified VFAs. Panel (a): Problems with inappropriate content and fake news apparently made voters complain. Panel (b): A rebalanced business model with new AI and Oversight Board filtering capabilities to deflect potential new legal responsibilities

Table 3.1 Example priority list of changing supplies of the three business model elements with planned responses

Examples of supply increases			Examples of supply decreases		
Business model elements	What increases in supply	Planned response	Business model elements	What decreases in supply	Planned response
Resources E.g., solar cells for products			**Resources** E.g., energy used to generate electricity		
New types:	More efficient solar power cells are developed	Change product design to use fewer cells, to reduce product cost	New types:	Fossil fuels become unacceptable to customers due to pollution	Investigate use of wood pellets for sustainable forests
New sources of same type of resource:	More manufacturers start production	Check for better quality/ price for other sources	New sources of same type of resource:	Bio fuels production reduced because it uses food cropland	Look for foreign suppliers or suppliers using bio reactors not cropland
New cost:	Solar cells become cheaper as supply increases	Check product design for increased power or higher quality cells	New cost:	Oil costs increase	Consider alternative energy sources like wind
Capabilities E.g.: automatically finding patterns in customer data			**Capabilities** E.g.: data science skills		
New types:	Real-time voice recognition	Add a hands-free voice interface to products	New types:	The supply of data science skills is much lower than organisations need	Cloud service tools are automating many data science tasks, so less data scientists are needed
New sources of same type of resource:	New AI cloud services open for rental	Add AI functionality to Internet of Things products	New sources of same type of resource:	The supply of data science skills is much lower than organisations need	Train more data scientists, recruit internationally
New cost:	Cost of AI image recognition reduces	Add function to many phone apps	New cost:	Data scientist salaries are rising	Retrain business analysts to do part of the job, so less data scientists are needed

(Continued)

Examples of supply increases

Business model elements		What increases in supply	Planned response
Stakeholder values E.g.: customers value their health	New types:	Retail customers want to monitor their exercise in detail	Add sensors, Internet connections, analytics, and social features to exercise products
	New sources of same type of stakeholders:	Both healthcare and data privacy are increasingly monitored by regulators in different countries	Makers of digital health apps, equipment manufacturers and insurance firms must understand the likely implications
	New cost:	Alcohol taxes increased to change citizen's behaviour	Develop low or zero alcohol versions of products

Examples of supply decreases

Business model elements		What decreases in supply	Planned response
Stakeholder values E.g.: customers' health	New types:	Health insurance used to be standardised, based on averaged sample data	New fintech health insurers are personalising premiums using rich personal data
	New sources of same type of stakeholders:	Legislation and customer concerns have reduced cigarette consumption in some markets	Expand other markets with easier legislation and lower concerns about the dangers
	New cost:	Healthcare markets like the US have become too expensive for many people	New start-ups are testing low-cost, no-frills business models

In this activity, start with your original VFA (in Figure 3.3). First, make a list of the resources, capabilities and stakeholder values that are changing. You should think about the effect of increases in supply as well as decreases in supply because both will change the balance of your business model. For example, an increase in the available supply of a resource might attract new competitors who suddenly find that resource very attractive at its new low price. Remember that stakeholders' values change when the number of stakeholders change as well as when what they value changes. For example, an increase in a resource or capability would be great if it reduced the price you paid for it. But an increase in supply might still change your business model if you take it as an opportunity to use this resource in new areas. An example of this occurred in 2020 when a group of firms started the Green Hydrogen Catapult project. This project aimed to produce a 50 times increase in the production of hydrogen made from renewable electricity in just six years. Clean hydrogen like this works very well for trucks, buses and other heavy vehicles that currently use diesel. But diesel engines do not burn hydrogen and diesel transport and storage systems are very different to the high pressure and low temperature systems used for hydrogen (Harrabin, 2020). So the mix of resources, capabilities and stakeholders had to change.

Second, put your list in order of priority. At the top of the list, place things that are going to affect your business model the most strongly, and the soonest. Which resources and capabilities have been reducing for some time but are only starting to be in short supply now? Which stakeholders' values are changing the most radically? For example, when a high proportion of regular customers of a burger restaurant turn vegan? Next, start at the top of the prioritised list and think about how you can deal with each item. The forces that drive the change in each list item will suggest questions for you to ask. In Table 3.1 you can see an example of this type of list, including examples of increases and decreases in the supply of each of the three business model elements. These are split into new types of elements, new sources of the same type of element, and new costs for the element. There are also examples of planned responses. This format of list can be used to prioritise responses to as many changes in the suppliers of business model elements as you have time to analyse.

Finally, use this list to make a new VFA diagram (see Figure 3.4) to try out ways of rebalancing your business model. Test your ideas out, first by asking colleagues and then by checking carefully chosen parts of the VFA with external stakeholders. Of course, these VFAs are highly confidential documents because they describe the detail of how your business model might change. Competitors would love to know what is in them. But it is possible to check the logic and accuracy of individual parts of a VFA without giving away the full picture.

ACTIVITY 4

Influencing the situation to lessen or guide the change

Activity 1 looks for changes in what is driving change forces. Activity 2 analyses these changes to see how they might affect your business model, and Activity 3 rebalances the business model by changing how an organisation accesses or uses its resources, capabilities or stakeholder contributions. In Activity 4, organisations

(Continued)

try to 'reach upstream' and influence the fundamental drivers of the change force. Organisations must plan how to deal with changes to their business model in Activity 3, but change is a process. It takes time; it is not instantaneous. If an organisation can sense the early stages of the build-up of the fundamental causes of a change, then it can be ready for the likely downstream effects. But it can also try and shape how these effects turn out. Activity 3 plans how to deal with the change. Activity 4 is where organisations try to lessen the causes of the change itself, or they try to guide it to their advantage, which means to the advantage of the organisation's stakeholders.

For example, many organisations fund lobbyists to persuade key decisions-makers in governments to do or not do certain things, or to change the details of incoming laws and regulations. Strong lobbying was used for years to delay anti-smoking legislation in some countries, or to support the use of fracking against the wishes of environmental protestors. Another way to influence a situation is if a whole supply chain is being held back by a lack of key skills, then larger companies sometimes invest upstream in educating and upskilling their supplier's staff. This is common in industries that are pushing the limits of what can be done, such as nuclear energy, pharmaceuticals or renewable energy sources. Maybe it is because their products are new as well as highly complex, or because there are tough safety requirements. A customer company relies on the quality of what its suppliers give it, so if a company is already at the upper limit of what it can buy in terms of amount and quality then the only way to increase these is by helping suppliers to do more and do better. Supplier development programmes are a common way of helping to create new capabilities in suppliers (Webb, 2017).

Organisations plan for changes that are heading their way, but they also try to head them off, or divert them. The ability to do this depends on three things: what the change is that the organisation senses coming, which resources and capabilities it will affect, and which stakeholders will be involved. Every change force has the potential to make changes, but how this unfolds is limited and constrained by the resources and capabilities in business models, as well as the decision-makers and other stakeholders that are involved in the change. Every change will affect different resources and different capabilities and influencing that process of change will mean influencing different people: people in government, groups of customers, staff, or parts of the public.

Some ways to influence change forces

Influencing is an indirect action; it means affecting something's behaviour without directly controlling it, like getting car drivers to slow down rather than driving their cars yourself. In this case, influencing change forces means causing actions that are far upstream in the change process. Usually this is done through people who are far outside the organisation and probably not listed as stakeholders on your VFA diagram. People who are far outside your organisation can still be called stakeholders because if there were no connection then they would not be able to help you. If they were not stakeholders, you would have no connection at all, they would be outside your self-world so they might as well not exist. When you think of how a person, or an organisation could influence things in a way that helps you then they could become a stakeholder – a connection becomes possible. But they might not want or need to help you, or they might not even be aware that they have a potential role to play that could help your business model. They are like potential new suppliers who you want to invite to join your business model and play a role. You have to figure out what they would ethically and legally accept in return. Ask yourself, 'what do they value?'.

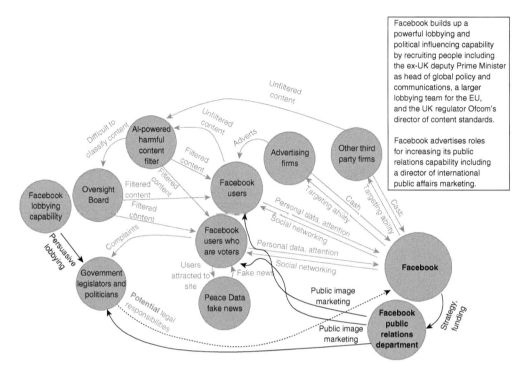

Figure 3.5   Example of a reported 'outer VFA' made of non-core stakeholders

For example, lobbyists need to be recruited and then paid to persuade government decision-makers. Such a persuasion project might contain many new stakeholders all by itself and would make a nice offshoot for your VFA diagram. Another example of recruiting temporary stakeholders to a business model is using consultants to acquire new expertise or an external viewpoint. Similarly, employing an external public relations firm helps organisations to deal with crises. This is similar to the ecosystem building process that we will cover in Chapter 7, except that these new stakeholders are part of an 'outer VFA', rather than the core of the business model. It means that they might be more temporary in the sense that they are useful for shaping changes to the business model as they arise rather than being central to what your business does. New stakeholders might start off in the outer VFA and later become part of the core VFA. But all parts of the VFA, the outer VFA and the core, must change over time. All of the parts of any business model are temporary.

In Figure 3.5 you can see how Facebook has apparently tried to influence government regulators as well as the voters that influence them. The company reportedly increased its capability to lobby and influence law-makers by recruiting people who understood that process and who knew and understood the people who worked in that process. These new recruits included the ex-UK deputy Prime Minister Nick Clegg as the head of global policy and communications, a larger lobbying team for the EU, and the UK regulator Ofcom's ex-director of content standards. Facebook also advertised roles for increasing its public relations capability, including for the role of director of international public affairs marketing. This was apparently targeted at influencing voters. Figure 3.5 shows how you can expand a VFA diagram to include an 'outer VFA', which includes all the stakeholders that are not directly involved in the business model but could be. These new stakeholders are particularly useful for developing new and innovative capabilities, and for accessing new resources. They might be temporary in the sense that they are useful for dealing with influences on a business model, which do not last. For example, a single event or crisis.

In this activity, start with the new VFA diagrams that you made in Activity 3 (see Figure 3.4). First, make another list of the resources, capabilities and stakeholder values that are changing, the change forces are driving them and what is powering these change forces. Influencing and shaping the change forces here in Activity 4 might help you to decide which new version of your VFA to choose.

Second, put your list in order of priority based on the business model elements that will be affected the most strongly and soonest. Use the same order as the last list because the priority is still the same. But keep in mind that one change force might cause changes to several business model elements, like when cloud computing technology made it much easier to outsource many different capabilities that until then had to be in-house. To decide how to influence specific change forces look at the outer edges of your new VFA (Figure 3.4). Most VFA diagrams cannot fit all the organisational stakeholders on them, no piece of paper is big enough. I have seen managers draw VFAs on multiple flip chart sheets and still run out of room. The reason is that in economies and supply chains every organisation is ultimately connected to every other, and you have to stop somewhere. That is why these activities use prioritised lists (see Table 3.1 and Table 3.2).

Third, study the lists and VFAs that you have created as your tools. Look at how your business model's elements are being affected. Think about which stakeholders have the capability to influence these change drivers. Do your current stakeholders possess these capabilities, or do you need to recruit new stakeholders for your Outer VFA? Which capabilities would shape the change drivers that you are dealing with? Table 3.2 breaks these questions down and sets them out in a process, with examples. The secret, as with many process methods, is to start at the outcome and work backwards. Prioritise which business model elements to focus on, then think about the changes that affect them and the drivers of these changes. Then think about who has the capability to influence how those drivers work. Focusing on an element tells you the change force, which then leads you to its driver, which in turn tells you the capabilities that are needed to shape the driver. This finally points you to the owner of that capability. The owner might be a stakeholder who is already in your VFA diagrams, or you might need to recruit new stakeholders to form an outer VFA (Figure 3.5). For example, in Figure 3.5 Facebook recruited people who really understood how government and regulators functioned to help them try and influence the direction of potential new legislation.

Change forces can be influenced by delaying them, as well as reducing or reversing them. For example, lobbying for longer deadlines for new regulations or reversing public opinion by providing education to help people make informed decisions. I do not personally agree with delays to well-designed environmental legislation or legislation that is designed to reduce unethical employment practices. But progressive past environmental legislation can be reversed by subsequent governments, as Donald Trump did during his administration. Also, the influencing techniques here can be used to accelerate change as well as to slow it down. Another option is to divert a change force so that it changes something else. For example, if your organisation depends on a huge customer who is thinking about moving a manufacturing site away from your business to consolidate their operations, then try and persuade them to centralise near you rather than move away. Think about who is making the decision and what options they might have thought of. Try and influence the options that they hold as well as which option they eventually choose. Also, your influencing process does not need to act fast if you can spot the build-up of a change force early before it starts to hurt you. For example, if a business customer starts to investigate alternatives to your products because their customers do not agree with your business practices or the materials that you use, then you could offer to work closely with them to change the situation and actually strengthen your relationship. Give them some good news to tell their customers. Influencing the dismantling of a change process is a process in itself.

Change forces take time to build, and so does an influencing process. For example, large-scale changes like shifting public opinion or removing unethical practices from your whole supply chain demand large-scale networks of influencers. Sometimes dealing with a change means moving with it rather than against it. Whatever the change is though, it always comes down to finding the stakeholders with the right capabilities to help you respond to the change. Then you must find out what they value enough to give their help. In other words, your response to a change needs a business model of its own. This is what the outer VFA is and why it is closely linked to the core VFA.

Moving between the operational activity cycle and the strategic activity cycle

After Activity 4, keep repeating the operational activity cycle to monitor the response to your planning and influencing activities, and to look for new changes. Repeating the operational cycle rechecks 'upstream', to see if the causes of a change force are increasing or decreasing. It also allows you to see

Table 3.2   Example priority list linking changes to business model elements and their influencers

Change in business model element	Change force(s) that caused it	Drivers of change force(s)	Stakeholders with a capability to influence change drivers
Resources			
According to the UN, fresh water is becoming scarcer around the world (Ruz, 2011)	Freshwater is only 2.5% the world's total water, and most of that is locked up permanently in ice and snow	Climate change Increased use of fresh water by households and businesses	High-use organisations that could be more efficient, e.g., some water companies have very old and leaky pipes Governments could regulate for higher efficiency in water use by businesses and households Researchers could develop more efficient technologies for high volume users
Capabilities			
Automatically finding patterns in customer data is rapidly changing what products and organisations can do	The increasing digitisation of society. Recent improvements in machine learning and AI systems	Increased use of ecommerce shopping, phone apps and cloud software. Businesses digitising activities and joining up their digital operations	Partner with providers of AI services (Alexa, Google Assistant) to get access to AI capabilities Recruit more data scientists and train more business leaders about understanding and using AI capabilities
Stakeholder values			
Customers and government regulators are becoming worried about personal data privacy leading to tighter data privacy laws	Personal data is rapidly becoming much easier to gather and use	Increased public understanding of the uses of personal data and business-to-business data sharing	The public, customers and governments: • use marketing campaigns to increase trust in the organisation's brand • publicise the organisation's data security strengths and internal data privacy training

if the downstream effects are changing. This is partly to check on the effect of your influencing work in Activity 4, but also to check if the plan in Activity 3 needs to be updated, because maybe the change itself might be accelerating or decelerating. The frequency of the operational cycle needs to be appropriate for monitoring the things in it, the rate that change forces build and the rate that they affect the elements of your business model. In parallel to the operational activity cycle, but one which happens less regularly, is the work of the strategic activity cycle.

ACTIVITY 5

Evaluating the operational cycle against the organisation's purpose

The operational activity cycle plans and re-plans according to how upstream change forces develop. The strategic activity cycle keeps checking this plan and changes it to satisfy the organisation's purpose. This is the start of the strategic activity cycle in Figure 3.2, and it compares how Activities 1 to 5, in the operational activity cycle, are either supporting or opposing the overall purpose of the organisation. Activity 2 and Activity 3 both work with the three elements of a business model: the resources, the capabilities, and stakeholders' values. Activity 5 works with the organisation's purpose, which is an expression of the values of its stakeholders.

The purpose of an organisation is the reason that it was created, not just the direct effects of its products and services. The main purpose of for-profit organisations is to create profits for the owners. But the purpose of for-profit and not-for-profit organisations can also be to produce a change itself, as a by-product of its normal organisational activities. Ford's original stated purpose was to bring affordable cars to the masses, a bit like IBM and later Dell did with Personal Computers. The purpose of an organisation can be much more than making money. The purpose of an organisation can motivate staff and help it to attract customers and other stakeholders, who can provide it with useful capabilities. A purpose helps to coordinate the firm and its ecosystem of partners by providing a common goal. A purpose can be designed into a business model as a useful capability to help it operate, and as an end in itself. For one company that I worked with, its purpose meant using new technology to help make a real difference to society. It was a for-profit software firm, but the firm and its staff were committed to protecting and supporting young people with their software. The purpose of the firm closely aligned with being commercially successful and helping society. Organisations can be vehicles for change, and organisations with a clear purpose can drive change across their whole ecosystem of stakeholders.

The way to evaluate the progress of the operations activity cycle (Activity 5) is to check the changes to your business model from your analysis (Activity 2) and your planned responses (Activity 3) against your organisation's fundamental purpose. The purpose of an organisation should be reflected in the values of its stakeholders; it is the values that come from the purpose not the other way around. The purpose of the organisation is the fundamental reason for building and operating it. Stakeholders and their values might get swapped out and changed, although the purpose would need to be derived from the values of a group of stakeholders if it were to help that group. It is important to regularly check the fit between an organisation's purpose and adaptations to its business model because rebalancing the business model might reduce that fit. There may be a gradual but fundamental change in what the organisation does and how it behaves, and this might move it away from its original purpose. Activity 5 is there to check for this. For example, the goal of the Swedish bank Handelsbanken is to support customers, the goal of India's Tata Group is to support the

(Continued)

communities it is in, and the goal of HCL Technologies is to support its employees (Birkinshaw et al., 2014). These goals have helped these firms' business models to run because they help to balance the values of all the stakeholders in each business model. Staff change, the leaders of an organisation move on, events and emergencies cause changes to plans, and elements of a business model gradually shift. Over time, it can be very easy for what a business model's stakeholders value to become misaligned. So, Activity 5 regularly compares the values that the business model is set up to satisfy with the stated purpose of the organisation. The frequency of this cycle needs to be appropriate for monitoring the things in it, so it needs to be at least as frequent as the rate at which stakeholders and their values change.

How to evaluate the operational cycle

Every organisation has values, overriding things that stakeholders value and that give the organisation goals and a purpose. You can evaluate the effects of your activities in the operational cycle in Figure 3.2 by comparing a list of values that your organisational purpose sets out to satisfy with a list of the values that your current business model is designed to satisfy. For each of these two lists you must start with the stakeholders whose values are currently being satisfied. Keep in mind that values are subjective, just like customer experiences. Different outcomes mean different things to different people. The important thing to check is what an outcome of your business model means to specific stakeholders. It is the personal experience of outcomes that count, not general outcomes. For example, does a service help customers to get to the end point of what they need, or does it just get them half way and then stop? Does working for an organisation help staff to develop and fulfil more needs than purely financial ones?

Each row in Table 3.3 shows an example of a type of stakeholder and something that this stakeholder values, something which the original business model was designed to satisfy. Then, an event

Table 3.3   Example priority list comparing stakeholder values in new business models with an organisation's original purpose

A. Type of stakeholder B. One purpose of the organisation	Original stakeholder value (original business model)	Event that caused a value change	New stakeholder value reflected in changes to new business model	Comparison of how the changed value affects the organisation's purpose	What to do about it (i.e., changes to the planned response in Activity 3)
A. Retail customer B. Produce low-cost meals	Retail customers want cheap packaging that protects food	Micro-plastic contamination starts to seriously worry many customers	Start to use biodegradable packaging that protects food	A move from plastic to biodegradable packaging may increase the price of the meals	Look for new partners to supply low-cost biodegradable packaging (cardboard, bioplastic), so costs will start to reduce

A. Type of stakeholder B. One purpose of the organisation	Original stakeholder value (original business model)	Event that caused a value change	New stakeholder value reflected in changes to new business model	Comparison of how the changed value affects the organisation's purpose	What to do about it (i.e., changes to the planned response in Activity 3)
A. Staff B. Trust staff rather than micro-manage	Staff want freedom and autonomy to use their brains and training	New legislation threatens huge fines for staff errors (e.g., EU privacy legislation, some banking laws)	Add monitoring software and restrict key decisions to senior managers	Senior staff are overloaded with decisions and feel scared of consequences where they can Other staff feel untrustworthy and micro-managed	Explain the threats, provide better training, support and safety nets to reduce risks to all
A. Government B. Fairness to users of products and services	Voters expect fair treatment of customers that fulfils the 'spirit of the law' not just the 'letter'	There are very high commercial pressures on social media firms to monetise the data they collect	Social media firms start to share users' data with third party firms in ways that do not necessarily benefit users	Worries increase about social media firms misusing personal data Legislators may tighten laws	Strengthen governance processes, increase transparency, strengthen public relations and lobbying

causes a change to this value, so the business model must change or lose this stakeholder. Next, the old and new values are compared to see how this could change the organisation's purpose. These steps help to check for a potential misalignment between a rebalanced business model and the original organisational purpose. Finally, having done this for specific stakeholder values it is much easier to think what to do about it. What changes (if any) must you make to the planned response? In the examples in Table 3.3, notice how the values of individual types of stakeholders need to be balanced with other possibly conflicting values in the business model. If this is not possible then the stakeholder type needs to be swapped out. This is difficult but not impossible for some types, like government stakeholders.

Chapter summary

The OSC model uses the ideas in Chapter 2 to plan a response to organisational change forces. It starts by sensing changes in any change forces and analysing how they might affect an organisation's business model. Then it plans a response, which includes changing the business model and influencing the change forces themselves. Finally, the OSC model shows the way to monitor how a response is working and any effect on the overall purpose of the organisation.

Further reading

Atluri, V., Dietz, M. and Henke, N. (2017) 'Competing in a world of sectors without borders', *McKinsey Quarterly*, June. https://www.mckinsey.com/business-functions/mckinsey-analytics/our-insights/competing-in-a-world-of-sectors-without-borders (accessed 7 April 2022).

Andreessen, M. (2011) 'Why software is eating the world', *The Wall Street Journal*, August. https://www.wsj.com/articles/SB10001424053111903480904576512250915629460 (accessed 7 April 2022).

Conde, J. and Pande, V. (2017) 'The century of biology', Andreessen Horowitz. https://a16z.com/2017/06/21/jorge-conde-bio-fund (accessed 7 April 2022).

Dixon, C. (2010) 'The next big thing will start out looking like a toy', Cdixon. https://cdixon.org/2010/01/03/the-next-big-thing-will-start-out-looking-like-a-toy (accessed 7 April 2022).

Gazmararian, L. (2020) 'Time for trust: how blockchain will transform business and the economy', PwC. https://www.pwc.com/timefortrust (accessed 7 April 2022).

Panetta, K. (2019) 'Gartner top strategic technology trends for 2020', Gartner. https://www.gartner.com/smarterwithgartner/gartner-top-10-strategic-technology-trends-for-2020 (accessed 7 April 2022).

Panetta, K. (2020) 'Gartner top strategic technology trends for 2021', Gartner. https://www.gartner.com/smarterwithgartner/gartner-top-strategic-technology-trends-for-2021 (accessed 7 April 2022).

SECTION 2
HOW ORGANISATIONS ARE RESPONDING

4

HOW TO BUILD NEW TYPES OF RELATIONSHIPS WITH CUSTOMERS

KEY IDEAS

- What customers value is subjective: everyone values different things. Customers all have different aims, objectives, tastes and interests.
- Each customer travels along their own individual journey to reach their personal aims and objectives. These are work journeys, shopping journeys, education journeys, recreation journeys as well as journeys where they physically move.
- Organisations help customers to progress through the stages of their individual journeys by providing products and services, including information, advice and guidance.
- Journey-based Thinking is a way of analysing the stages that customers need to go through to help make their journeys easier, more useful and a better experience. It is a way to think about how data can be gathered, analysed and used to improve the journeys of large numbers of customers and other stakeholders.

LEARNING OBJECTIVES

After reading this chapter you will be able to:

- Explain what people's values are and why this is important in business. Explain why it is also very complex.
- Describe what customer journeys are and how they can be used to find out what each customer wants, even when they all might want different things, and when they might not even know what they want or need themselves.
- Describe some ways of helping each customer to get what they want, to reach their objectives and satisfy their personal needs.
- Explain Journey-based Thinking. Describe how customer journey models help to improve customer experience and customer journeys, and how they help with the strategy of using customer data.
- Describe how customer data can be used to strengthen and change relationships between an organisation and its customers.

Sometimes my students ask me why I talk about customer journeys so much. My answer is that customers will only continue their relationships with an organisation if they get what they need from it. If a customer's experience of dealing with an organisation is amazingly useful, easy and pleasurable then they will always come back and buy again, and they will tell everyone about this experience. They do it not because they are loyal – customer loyalty does not exist – they do it because the organisation is indispensable to them. Understanding, analysing, and improving customer journeys is the start and end of what everyone does in an organisation. There is nothing else. If anyone says that their job is nothing to do with customer journeys, then they do not understand the full picture. Every staff member of an organisation is there to give customers a great experience, and every stakeholder is a type of customer. So, in this chapter we will learn how to find out what customers really need to make successful journeys.

This chapter explains how each customer travels along their own individual journey to reach their personal aims and objectives. These are work journeys, shopping journeys, education journeys, recreation journeys as well as journeys where they physically move. Organisations must help their customers to progress through the stages of their individual journeys by providing products and services, including information, advice and guidance. Here we introduce Journey-based Thinking, a way of analysing the stages that customers need to go through to help make their journeys easier, more useful and a better experience. It is also a way to think about how data can be gathered, analysed and used to improve the journeys of large numbers of customers and other stakeholders. This chapter explains how organisations are creating completely new types of customer relationships using Journey-based Thinking ideas to understand their customers better and help them progress along their individual life journeys.

What are customer values and what are customers?

What do you value the most?

Have a think for a moment about what you value the most. Is it money, or is it family and friends? Or is it your health? I have asked my students this question many times over the years. The answers have included children, parents, chocolate, cars, football, a degree certificate and many other different things. Some answers are very common (especially chocolate). But then I ask my students to be more specific. If they say football, I ask them 'which team?'. If they say chocolate, I ask them 'what type of chocolate? Dark, light, chocolate with nuts, chocolate with dried fruit or chilli in it?'. Then it starts to get interesting. The more specific their answers are then the less likely it is that they value similar things. In a group of people that love chocolate there is always a big split in terms of types of chocolate and what is in the chocolate. I even have a lot of students who do not like chocolate at all – the chocolate lovers in the room find that particularly hard to understand.

With football and other sports, it is the same. When I ask a football fan which team they love then they will name a variety of different teams, and it is very important to be specific. They all love football, but it is usually one team that they love, not all teams. Football fans also find it hard to understand that I have no interest in football, except for the business side.

It turns out that what people value is highly subjective (Lepak et al., 2007; Priem, 2007). Everybody values different things, they have different tastes, different priorities and different needs. You could say that 'value is in the eye of the beholder'. It is different for every person, and it is based on what each individual need, or thinks they need. In addition to this, people want to get what they value in different ways. Whether you are talking about cars, toothpaste, sandwiches, or books to read, people want products with different variations – different colours, prices, quality levels and delivery times. To make matters even more complicated, what a customer values changes minute by minute, second by second and transaction by transaction. One second, I want a drink of coffee, then I drink it and I do not want another coffee straight away. If I have a sandwich, then I do not want a meal straight afterwards. The things that a customer values are dynamic, they keep changing.

All stakeholders are customers.

Why are customer values subjective and dynamic? The reason is that everyone is on a different life journey, and we are all at a different stage in our life journey. I say 'everyone' because all stakeholders are a type of customer (see Chapter 2). A stakeholder is anyone with a 'stake' in the business. Customers, staff, investors, suppliers and partners, government regulators, even competitors. If someone has something 'to do' with the business, then they are a stakeholder, and their 'stake' is whatever this connection is. In Chapter 2 we use the idea of stakeholders and their connections to draw Value Flow Analysis (VFA) diagrams for analysing the system of stakeholders that make up an organisation's business model. Stakeholders support a business model with their resources and capabilities because they get something in return. That is why all stakeholders are like customers, they all contribute to the business model in return for what they get back:

- Customers contribute cash and information such as their needs, feedback and new ideas.
- Staff contribute time, knowledge, ideas and their activities.
- Investors contribute capital, advice and introductions to their connections.
- Suppliers and partners contribute their resources, capabilities and connections.
- Government regulators contribute limitations that focus an organisation's business model.
- Competitors contribute pressure to improve and lobbying for common causes.

Do you notice how a stakeholder always contributes several different things and that without them the business would not be able to continue? The secret to business model innovation is to think of new things that stakeholders can contribute and new things that they will value in return. Stakeholders always give as well as take. This is called **co-creation** (Ramirez, 1999; Vargo and Lusch, 2004). Customers give businesses information about their needs as well as cash payments, they do not just take a product or service. At the very least customers provide information on what product they want, how and when they want it and some payment information, like their bank account details.

To keep stakeholders happy, it is worth treating them a bit like customers. For example, take the staff that every organisation relies on. All the effort that organisations put into designing super smooth services, amazing experiences and easy-to-use products for customers should also be applied to their staff. Think about it. The success and happiness of an organisation's staff is directly related to the success of the organisation, just like it is directly related to its customers' success. Every stakeholder is a customer. After all, isn't your business model just a description of what all your stakeholders need to do in order to get what they value?

Customer journey models

The most sophisticated organisations carefully plan out their relationships with their customers using models of customer journeys, which are sometimes called journey 'maps' (Richardson, 2010; Lemon and Verhoef, 2016; Rosenbaum et al., 2017; Tueanrat et al., 2021). These are detailed descriptions of the stages and routes that different types of customers go through. Every journey can be broken down into a series of stages, and every type of customer goes through a slightly different collection of stages. Most journey models focus on the early part of the relationship from when a customer first starts looking for something they need up to them buying it. But the stages in a customer's journey after they buy a product or service are even more important. If the experience of receiving a product and starting to use it does not go smoothly then they will be unlikely to buy anything else from that organisation.

In Figure 4.1 the **Customer Buying Process (CBP) model** shows the main stages of finding and choosing a purchase, purchasing it and then what comes afterwards (Kotler, 1991). The CBP starts with the problem recognition stage, where customers become aware that they need something, maybe without knowing what it might be. Then in the information search stage they look for ideas and assemble a 'long list' of potential purchases. Then in the evaluation of alternatives stage customers find out more information about the product. For example, from product reviews or from the manufacturer's website. They use this information to filter their 'long list' into a 'short list' of choices. Then in the purchase decision stage they actually choose which product to buy, and then buy it in the purchase stage. The stages after the product have been purchased are even more critical than the pre-purchase stages because they contain all the events that happen when the customer uses the purchase. This includes their experience of using the product or service, their subsequent feelings of satisfaction or dissatisfaction, and their whole relationship

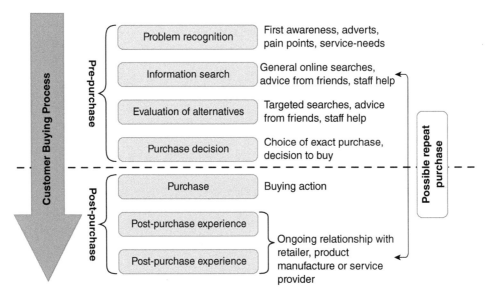

Figure 4.1   The high-level stages of the Customer Buying Process (CBP) model
Adapted from Kotler (1991)

with the retailer, including repeat purchases or going to another retailer next time. The pre-purchase stages are critical because they contain many sub-stages where customers experience buying, receiving, preparing to use and then using their products and services. Any small barriers or problems can stop a customer from going back to a retailer for another purchase. The pre-purchase stages are where whatever is purchased joins with the customer's life journey, which this chapter is all about.

A second model, which is similar to the CBP model, is Mckinsey's **Customer Decision Journey model** (CDJ) (Court et al., 2009). The CDJ starts with the initial list of brands and products that a customer has in mind as buying options that will satisfy their specific need. This is called the initial **consideration set**. Then the customer searches for more information to help them improve these buying options or to check how closely they fit what is needed. Eventually the customer chooses one option to buy and then buys it. After purchasing, there are the usual stages of using and experiencing the product, and if these are positive then the customer might loyally buy the same product again when something in their life causes a new need for this type of product (Figure 4.2).

The AIDA model is a third way of looking at the process of converting potential customers into actual customers over several stages. There are many other models that do this. The stages in the AIDA model are first getting customers' attention with advertisements, then generating interest with marketing communications, then turning this into desire for the product or service by explaining how it satisfies their needs. Then finally, the action stage is where customers make the purchase (Lemon and Verhoef, 2016). Notice how these three models can be used from the perspective of customers looking to buy things as well as from the

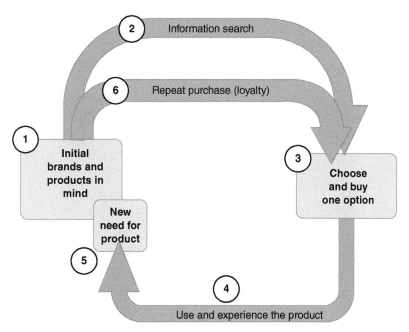

Figure 4.2 Mckinsey's CDJ model.
Adapted from Court et al. (2009)

perspective of retailers looking to sell things. All three models look at customer journeys from slightly different perspectives. The CDJ model is different from the other two models in two ways. First, it helps us to think much more about the decisions that separate one stage from another. Each stage ends with a decision about which stage to do next. This is the same on a shopping journey and any other life journey that people make, like which drink do we purchase from a Starbucks service counter? Or before that, which place do we go to buy a drink? Or before that, deciding if we are hungry or thirsty or both? Second, the CDJ model highlights how real customer journeys are actually loops. Customers move along the same journeys many times as they repeatedly purchase the same things or go to the same stores and websites. The CDJ model also helps us to think about how customers move backwards as well as forwards on a journey. Customers frequently change their minds: they might go into a Starbucks looking for a coffee but change their mind and buy orange juice, or decide that they are hungry, or that they want another coffee shop instead.

The most important stages in a customer journey model are after the purchase stage. You might think that all an organisation's efforts should be directed at getting customers to choose its products and then buy them. But what will happen if customers are disappointed? What if the coffee in the above example is unpleasant or hard to drink? What if the cups leak and scald customers? What if customers worry about the environmental effects of throwing away plastic cups? This is very important. The after-purchase experience must be frictionless, enjoyable and useful. The after-purchase experience must be these three things to the customer because you want customers to keep coming back. You also want them to tell other potential customers who are on an earlier stage of their own customer journeys and have not decided what to buy yet.

> **The after-purchase experience must be easy, enjoyable and useful.**

When you make a customer journey model, it is very important to include all the before-purchase stages and all the after-purchase stages. It is also very important to break the journey down into very small

Table 4.1   Some of the many stages in a car buying journey

1. Old car makes a strange noise	16. Visit car dealer to look at cars
2. Ask wife to listen to it	17. Choose car (a blue Kia Niro Hybrid)
3. She laughs, says 'talk to mechanic'	18. Phone dealer to tell them
4. Mechanic looks at car	19. Check bank account for cash to pay
5. Mechanic laughs, says 'this is dead'	20. Transfer money to dealer
6. I Google 'new car'	21. Change insurance to new car
7. Look at car websites	22. Change breakdown cover to new car
8. Look at review websites	23. Check dealer received the money
9. Go to car showroom to test drive	24. Collect car keys from the dealer
10. Pick short list of options	25. Drive car home
11. Discuss with wife	26. Use car to get to work for the first time
12. Look what people say online	27. Use the car to go shopping for the first time
13. Discuss with wife	28. Use the car to go on holiday for the first time
14. Discuss with kids	29. … more stages that connect to the rest of my life
15. Daughter says 'your car is 100 years old'	

stages that you can then examine closely, like putting them under the microscope. For example, in a car buying journey many events, large and small, need to happen before you even decide to look for a new car (Table 4.1). Every high-level stage in the above three models includes a series of small events, or sub-stages, that need to happen in order to progress to the next stage. Breaking the journey down into very small sub-stages lets you discuss each sub-stage with people in the organisation and with customers, which helps you look for problems, like anything that stops customers' journeys from being a super smooth experience. Examining small sub-stages also enables you to link the journey of a customer choosing and experiencing your organisation's products and services to their wider life journeys. This is important because it helps you to check whether your organisation is actually helping customers to get to the end point of whatever they value in their lives, the thing that your organisation is there to help them with.

There are many models that help us to think about customer journeys. What is important is how they help us to focus and ask questions. When you pick a model or use a mixture of several models you need to:

- Pick the model that covers the part of the customer journey that your analysis is about, plus a few extra stages before and afterward. If you include a few extra 'before-purchase stages', you will better understand the context for the customer. This is how the customer got to the situation that you are analysing. If you include a few extra 'after-purchase stages', you will be better able to pass the customer on to your colleagues or partner organisations who support the customer in the stages that come next. After all, what counts is the ultimate success of that customer's journey, not just your part in it.
- Use the model to divide the whole journey into stages, and bigger stages into smaller sub-stages. Think about what needs to happen for each stage to go smoothly for the customer. Each stage ends with a decision by the customer making that journey. Decisions like, which product to choose from on a short list. Before that, which products to add to a short list. Before that, which information sources to use to look for information about potential products. Just before purchasing, customers need to make choices about delivery times, locations and methods, as well as pricing and payment choices. After purchasing, customers need to decide how to open the box or assemble the product. They will certainly need to figure out how to use it successfully if it is their first time. Divide each stage into very small stages so you can accurately specify what resources and capabilities are needed for each stage to work smoothly.

For a more in-depth description of how to use models like this, see Chapter 10.

Journey-based Thinking

Journey-based Thinking is a way of thinking about a customer's life as a metaphorical journey that is made up of stages. The stages of a journey can be the second-by-second clicks of a mouse, as the customer moves through the pages of a website. Or the stages can be the day-by-day progress of each week, or the weeks of a semester, or the years of a degree course. In Chapters 9 and 10 we will apply Journey-based Thinking ideas to other stakeholders but in this chapter, we start by focusing on customers' journeys.

A journey can be any timescale – seconds, minutes, hours, weeks, years, or a whole lifetime. Journey-based Thinking is a way of analysing part of the life of a customer to help them to move along their journey in a better way and to get where they want to go. A customer journey might be a physical journey, or a **learning journey**, or the duration of a single project. The idea of a journey is used as a metaphor (although some journeys are physical) to focus on the different goals and destinations of each customer and their individual routes to get there. Goals and destinations are always based on what customers value, which are highly subjective. So, customer journeys are different for every customer. They each have different goals and destinations, and they each take different routes to get there.

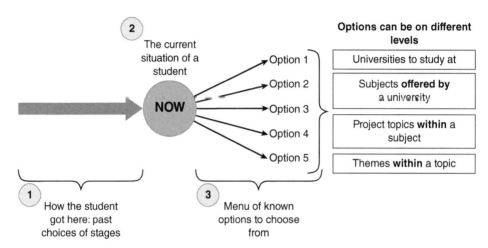

Figure 4.3   Decisions break stages into the smallest components of a customer journey

Every stage in a customer journey is the result of a decision and every stage ends with another decision. Decisions join stages together, and each is a choice between several options. Figure 4.3 shows an example of the journey of a student. The current situation of a student is a result of all the past stages they chose to take (Figure 4.4). The qualifications that they chose to study, the amount of work that they did and many other large and small choices. When the student is at the stage of choosing a university to go to, they have lots of different options. There are high level options like which university to go to, or even which country to study in, and there are low level options like which topics are included in which subjects and which themes in which topics. But they can only choose from the options that they are aware of. Before every decision is the previous route of past choices, which got the individual to this stage (Court et al., 2009; Iyengar and Agrawal, 2010).

The best way to support customers in reaching their stated goal is to give them better quality options than they had before. The options to choose from can range from high level strategic decisions down to very small choices at any level of fine detail. High level stages are themselves divided into sub-stages by the micro decisions. If completing a stage requires one or more decisions, then it can be divided into smaller sub-stages at these decision points. Decisions separate stages and sub-stages in a customer's route. For example, deciding you are thirsty not hungry; deciding you want a hot drink rather than a cold drink. Journeys are made up of many stages and you can see this in the research into areas like digital innovation and retail customer journeys (Hall et al., 2017; Henfridsson et al., 2018). Customers move forwards towards their goals by choosing between options. For example, choosing between drinks, food or both. Or choosing between hot or cold drinks, and their flavours.

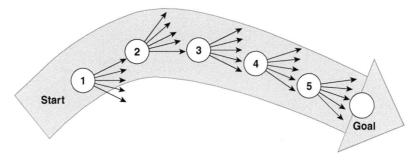

Figure 4.4   Decisions between stages add up to the route of a customer journey. Stages are separated from each other by decisions, which are choices between several options. Options are like branches on a path. Small decisions separate sub-stages, large decisions separate higher level stages

The options that customers choose from can be improved by giving them higher quality options. Giving customers higher quality options does not mean giving more options. It means swapping current options that they know about with better options. Better options help them reach their individual goals in a quicker, easier, cheaper or more enjoyable way than the options that they already know of (Lemon and Verhoef, 2016).

Each customer makes different choices to other customers, one after the other, so they each move along a different route (Figure 4.5). Each route includes different problems, opportunities and barriers. For example, two customers might choose to buy a coffee, but they might start off in different locations and buy it from a different Starbucks outlet. Or one customer may start off with less money or less time than the other so they may end up making a coffee at home. Each route can lead to a different goal, or a single goal can be reached by more than one route. For example, two customers might end up at the same

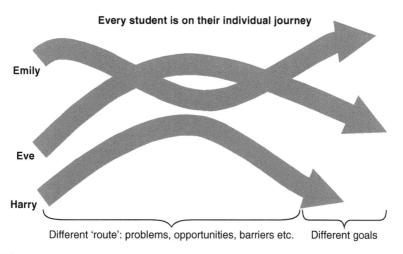

Figure 4.5   The individual journey routes of three students

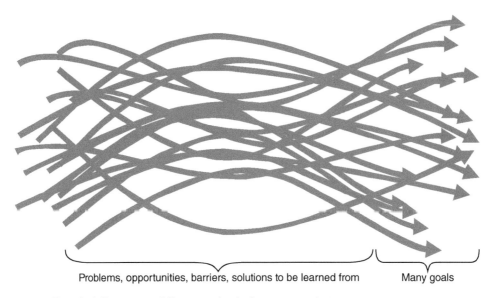

Problems, opportunities, barriers, solutions to be learned from   Many goals

Figure 4.6   People follow many different individual routes on their journeys

Starbucks outlet in the same train station even though they arrived on different trains, and one never usually goes to Starbucks. Journeys are a series of decisions and choices that can be repeated. When customers use a route to successfully get to their goal then that route can be thought of as a record of the problems that they encountered on the journey and how they solved them. Every customer is on their own individual journey, and each customer travels along a different route, which is made up of different stages and different goals.

Guiding customers along their many different individual routes is a complex task. Customers have different start points, different decisions to make and different goals to get to (Figure 4.6). They will meet different problems and opportunities and they will overcome different barriers with different solutions. But large numbers of these customer journeys can be recorded in datasets, and useful patterns can be found. At the lowest level of detail, every person follows a different route, but organisations have become very skilled in finding high level regularities to the patterns of problems, opportunities, barriers and their solutions that are in the journey routes that customers take. For example, Amazon can spot people that are similar to you and use this similarity to make predictions and recommendations for products that you might like, based on what those people did. This is done by finding patterns in a dataset that describes what people buy as well as their profile data. There is nothing magical about it: similar people do similar things in similar situations – not all of the time but enough to make useful predictions.

Example of a customer's journey

Think about the last time that you bought some washing-up liquid. It seems a bit trivial, but we all do it at some time or another and there are a bewildering number of choices of washing-up liquid available.

Next, I'll use the Customer Buying Process model to divide the journey of buying this product into stages and for each stage I'll illustrate how to think about the journey that each customer is on.

1   The problem recognition stage

Picture Dave standing at his kitchen sink. There is a pile of dirty dishes in front of him and a frustrated look on his face. It is his turn to wash up but there is no washing-up liquid.

This is the first stage of his dish washing journey and like every stage it is the context for the next stage. Thinking about Dave helps you to understand who he is, where he is and what he is thinking and feeling, as you start to consider his next stage. This helps you to understand his current situation. The problem recognition stage is how this small dish washing journey branches off from Dave's main life journey. It will take just a small number of stages to get a product that he needs so he can progress along his evening meal journey.

2   The information search stage

Dave has noticed that he has a problem and thinks, 'What do I need to solve this problem and where can I get it?' (I'll leave out what he says about whoever was supposed to buy washing-up liquid last week.) From the last stage, you know he's standing in the kitchen, probably looking in a cupboard and scratching his head. Imagine that he's just moved into the house and doesn't know the area. So, you can guess that he will probably pull out his phone and look for a solution on a search engine, maybe from nearby shops, or an online supermarket delivery service. Or he might ask someone in the house, or message someone else for suggestions. Looking closely at this stage helps you to guess where Dave will look for solutions so you can make sure that your solutions (your products) are there and highly visible. This might mean that your products need to come up as high-ranking search engine results for the sort of search terms Dave would use, or they need to be easily remembered products and brand names that will come to mind when he asks for suggestions. Thinking through this stage helps you to see what sort of information Dave needs before he can start the next stage. This includes where and how to get the product, not just which product to get. If he needs to get the washing-up done quickly then he also needs the locations of nearby shops, or the next available delivery slots for online grocery shopping. Notice that Dave or his information sources must have heard of your brand and know that your dish washing products exist. If they have never heard of your brand, then you will not make it past this stage. This is why organisations spend so much money on brand advertising, so that people will be aware of them at the start of the journey.

We pretend that customer journeys are one-way and linear, but Dave may rewind or fast-forward. He may skip stages and repeat stages, as will anyone who is analysing his journey. The key is to work backwards: use the description of the next stage to think through all the sorts of information that Dave will need to find out in the stage before, and then make sure that he's got easy access to your organisation's version of that information. Your brand name, your advertising messages, your product details, where to buy your product, your top advice tips and even your current deals.

3   The evaluation of alternatives stage

After his information search, Dave has got a rough idea of the sort of washing-up liquids that are available and where to get them. He's got most of the information he needs, and he's certainly removed a few candidates from his consideration set. A consideration set is a short-list of potential options to choose from. In the last stage he made a long list of product options with the information he had found. He used the characteristics of each option to decide whether to keep it in his consideration set or to filter it out. Characteristics can be anything about a product: its price, colour, design or the material of its packaging. Its smell, size, shape, the effect on his skin, or even the feelings that he associates with it from adverts and other experiences. It depends what characteristics are important to Dave.

It is important to make it very easy for Dave to get information that influences him to keep your products in his consideration set. In this case, understanding the problem that Dave needs to solve – the situation he is in with dishes to be washed and no washing-up liquid – tells us what information he needs and how to get it to him. Organisations make sure that their potential customers have the information they need with advertisements, product pages on their websites and lots of other sources. Some very important product characteristics are the small differences between product or service options, like different colours or quality levels. Organisations usually produce a range of variations on their core products to fit the diverse needs of a wide range of customers. This is why customers must choose which specific product variant to buy before they make a purchase decision. For example, laptops have different chip speeds and storage capacities, phones have different camera types and memory sizes, and cars have different engine sizes and added extras.

4   The purchase decision stage

Now Dave has got enough information to make his decision on exactly which washing-up liquid to buy, where to buy it from, how to get it and how to pay for it. He has finalised the details of all the stages that will end up with him holding a new bottle of washing-up liquid (or a refill sack, or a huge wholesale carton) as he stands in front of his kitchen sink. Standing there is how he will start the first post-purchase experience stage. It is important to think carefully about everything that needs to happen before he gets to that stage because he can only buy the product when he has completed all the previous stages and decided exactly what to buy. Think of all the questions that a retailer's website asks before a customer clicks on the buy-now button. All the different choices and variations about the product, its payment and its delivery options. It is the same when buying in-store. Before you purchase, you need to specify exactly what to purchase.

5   The purchase stage

This is simple, Dave just acts on his decision. He clicks the buy-now button on a website or phone screen, after adding all the transaction details. Or he gives cash or card details in the checkout lane of a store. But then it starts to get tricky…

6   The post-purchase experience stage

The previous stages are important, and organisations that do not make them smooth and easy do not get many sales. But the post-purchase experience stage is much bigger than all the previous stages and much riskier for the organisation and its reputation. This is because owning a product or being provided with a service is just the start of a series of sub-stages that are absolutely critical. From this stage onwards, Dave has to be the most successful user of washing-up liquid in the history of the world... ever. It sounds silly but think about the alternative. Do you want your customers to be unsuccessful at using your products and services? Do you want it to be hard, annoying or difficult? The most important thing about the post-purchase experience stage is making your customers successful with a combination of your product and the services that your organisation provides. This includes delivering the product, product manuals, and your customer service and support activities. Even getting a product out of the box must be easy and smooth. For example, a well-designed device like a phone or a game will include a quick start guide as well as a more in-depth manual. Owning a product is just the start. Every physical product must be surrounded by information and support services that enable it to be used easily and successfully. Quick start guides help customers to quickly use products for the first time; cooking appliances come with recipe ideas. Product users need more than just the product itself to be successful and they need to be successful over several journey stages after the purchase.

When you make a customer journey model you should spend at least as much time and effort thinking about and analysing all of the stages that come after the purchase as you do for the stages before purchase. These need to be frictionless, easy and as enjoyable as possible (see Chapter 9). Modelling the post-purchase stages of Dave's washing-up liquid journey is the only way to find things that could go wrong. Like with the pre-purchase stages, you have to break the main stages down into smaller and smaller journey sub-stages to make a detailed customer journey model (see the car buying example in Table 4.1).

> **Dave has to be the most successful user of washing-up liquid in the history of the world ... ever.**

Let's have a think about the stages of Dave's post-purchase experience. After purchasing his washing-up liquid, Dave will either get it delivered or he will take it home. It depends on the route of his washing-up liquid journey. He will do both at different times in his life. If the retailer delivers it then Dave's experience needs to be smooth, easy and free from problems. This means that booking an online shopping delivery needs to be easy as well as the delivery itself arriving on time with the right items. Using a product for the first time also needs to be easy. The washing-up liquid's top must come off easily and there must be no mess, either when using it in the sink or when filling the washing-up liquid bottle from a refill container. Any information that Dave needs to use the washing-up liquid should be easy to understand and quick to find. For example, relevant details are usually printed on the side of the bottle or on a small piece of paper that comes with the product. This part of a customer journey model is a chance to think about how a product is used and to foresee what questions a customer might have and what could go wrong. For washing-up liquid, the post-purchase stages start with the purchase stage and only end after the washing-up liquid has been used up and its container has been recycled. For repeat purchase products like washing-up liquid, you can see that the post-purchase stages eventually lead to the pre-purchase stages in a new loop. For one-off products, like an undergraduate degree, or products that are bought occasionally, like cars, the customer journey model will finish with a final stage. But even this will start off a new set of stages in that customer's life journey.

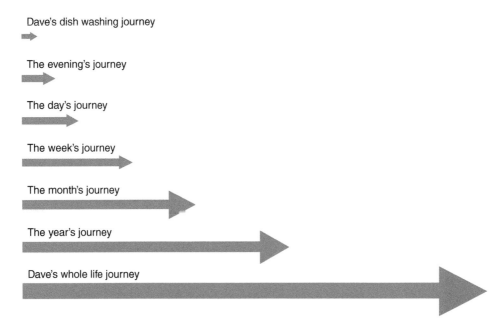

Dave's dish washing journey

The evening's journey

The day's journey

The week's journey

The month's journey

The year's journey

Dave's whole life journey

Figure 4.7   Journeys are nested – smaller journeys become stages in larger journeys

This example of Dave's washing-up liquid journey is itself just a small stage of his larger evening journey, which is part of that day's journey, which is part of his week, his month and so on up to his whole life journey (see Figure 4.7). But there are two more things that we need to add to Dave's customer journey model to make it useful. First, this customer journey model is just for one person, Dave. Every customer is different. They value different things, so they have different objectives. They also have different starting situations and different capabilities and resources to work with. All customers have different journey routes, but you can find patterns of similar routes with common stages, like Frequently Asked Questions, common problems, reusable ideas and clever solutions. A customer journey model for Dave is just for Dave. A single standardised customer journey model is like a single shoe size – the shoes don't fit many people and they won't get you very far. Dave started from the situation of a surprising lack of washing-up liquid, and he needed some immediately. But other customers will start with more time before they need to wash the dishes, and just add washing-up liquid to their list for their weekly shop.

Dave's customer journey model only fits customers like Dave. These are people with Dave's profile characteristics, objectives and needs. Organisations usually target several main types of customers, which they call 'customer segments' and try to understand them by describing their 'customer personas' (see Chapter 10). So, a useful customer journey model needs to include the routes that all the main customer segments take. The more customer segments you add to your customer journey model then the more useful it will be. Similarly, adding more and more detail with smaller and smaller sub-stages will also make it more useful. The more detail you add then the more you see the gaps where even more detail can be added. Like anything, the closer you look then the more you will see. But where should you stop? When is 'enough' enough? There are two very practical answers to these questions. One is 'when your time runs out'; the other answer comes from thinking about what a minimum viable customer journey model can do for you. As with any analysis you should start by defining the answers you need from it and working backwards. So, it depends on what you are using the customer journey model for. Start with a customer's desired goal and work backwards; model the stages that they need to go through to get to that goal. You can do this by thinking of the decisions that mark the end of each stage and the start of the next. It is best to begin with the main stages first, then each main stage can be broken up into smaller sub-stages (see Chapter 8 for how to make a customer journey model).

You can add more and more stages and more and more customer segments. But try and use the purpose of your customer journey analysis to tighten your focus. Are you interested in specific customer segments, and the rest are not relevant for this analysis? Is your job only concerned with particular stages in one part of the customer journey? Think of your analysis project as a journey in itself – what insights, decisions and actions are you trying to get to? If you can tightly define those by discussing the project with your boss and other stakeholders, then you can work backwards from that to fully define it.

Second, a really useful customer journey model is based on high quality data. If you know your job and your customers, then you can start by roughly drawing a first draft version by hand. The purpose here is to set out a rough description of the high-level stages of the main journey routes that the main customer segments use. What are the high-level stages, the main customer segments and the main journey routes? If you are new to a job, then you have a small advantage in doing this. When you start a new job people will expect you to be famous for asking questions about the job, the products and services, and the customers. Whether you are new or have been doing the job for ages, this first rough draft is just a basic framework to add more data to. The first data comes from inside your organisation, from interviews with people who deal with customers every day, from reports and other documentation, and later on from digital datasets. The aim is to divide the high-level stages of the main journey routes into lower and lower-level sub stages. This is qualitative analysis – before you count something you first have to figure out what to count. When you have a qualitative description of the stages of the main journey routes of the main customer segments, then you can get some quantitative data to check how important those routes are to your organisation (see Chapter 10). This will let you quantitatively check to see if these are the right routes, stages and segments to focus on. Be careful about definitions – some people in your organisation might use different words and definitions for the same things; this will cause problems when you start the quantitative stage of your analysis, when you start to count the numbers and amounts of these things. Part of a qualitative analysis is to search for useful definitions and to mould them together into a useful qualitative model of ideas.

You can use your qualitative journey model to specify the datasets that you need and where to get them. A qualitative model for a customer journey just means a clear description in words of the customers' routes, stages and segments. You will need all that information to get your quantitative data. The first qualitative model comes from interviewing people inside your organisation. After that, you can refine it by interviewing customers and other external stakeholders, like suppliers and a customer's customers. Quantitative and qualitative analyses are part of a cycle. A qualitative analysis forms the questions, and sometimes guesses the answers, and a quantitative analysis will look to see how much of this is true. Then another qualitative analysis will form deeper questions and another quantitative analysis will look to see how many times different answers come up. These quantitative and qualitative cycles are used with questionnaires and all types of data analytics to search datasets, to look for data patterns within them (see Chapter 10).

Customer life journeys are chains of linked services and 'service-needs'

The end of each stage of a journey model always has a mixture of outputs, like cars at the end of a factory assembly line or a new haircut at the end of a process of cutting and combing. But another way to look at it is that every stage needs inputs, and the inputs of one stage are the outputs of the stage before it. Inputs are like the parts to be assembled into a car or the cutting and combing actions in a haircut.

You can think of a customer journey as a process for producing needs for inputs, not just for producing outputs. We call these needs '**service-needs**': they are the things that every stage requires before it can be completed. 'Service-needs' are the things that a service satisfies (Shaw, 2007). If the output of a process is a service, like the process of cleaning a car, then each stage of that process requires inputs. And these inputs satisfy the service-needs that the process produces as it runs.

The start of every journey stage is always joined to the end of the last stage. The products and services that are the outputs from the last stage must satisfy the service-needs, which are the inputs to the next stage. A customer journey is a chain of stages that are linked by services (products) and service-needs. Thinking about customers and their life journeys in terms of a chain of service-needs makes it much easier to see how to help them because if you understand exactly what a customer needs at every stage of their journey, then you know what to do to help them. If you do not know then helping them is impossible.

Customer life journeys: helping customers to choose the right products and services for themselves

If you have a detailed customer journey model then you will have a good idea of the chain of service-needs and services (products) that most of your customers will require to get to their goals, to get the things that they value. You can never include every microscopic stage for every single type of customer, but you can get a good idea of the main customer journey routes that most customers take (see Chapter 9).

Each stage – at any level – is separated from the one after by choices between options and it is your job to guide customers to help them choose the best options for themselves. This is what customer journey models are for. Ultimately, customers must decide themselves what they want to choose but the best way to help them is to recommend options so that they are more likely to end up with what fits their values and their lives the best. You can do this by giving them better quality options than they already know about.

> **Better quality options replace options that customers already have.**
>
> **They do not make options multiply like rabbits.**

Giving customers too many options is confusing, and it will scare them away. A well-meaning intention can end up looking like a dog's dinner of too many confusing options. Better quality options means giving each customer new options based on a deep understanding of customers like them.

Personalising a customer's journey means helping them to meet their goals more quickly, more easily and in a less costly way. Personalisation also gives customers better quality destinations as well as better quality routes. You can learn from the options and choices that past customers made by studying the journeys that they went on. The click journeys of customers using a website and the questions and problems that customer service staff deal with are all valuable customer journey data. Other sources of customer journey data include what people say they are interested in on social media and what they search for and look at online (see Chapter 9). Customer journey data can be used to record the journeys of past customers so you can learn from them, learning that includes which options to suggest to which type of customer and when to do so. Recording of past customer journeys helps organisations to recommend better quality options to current customers. For example, Spotify uses listening and profile data to recommend music tracks to millions of users, Stitch Fix recommends clothing to buy, Amazon recommends all sorts of products and services, and LinkedIn and Google even recommend what words to type in messages and searches (Kinni, 2020). Recommendations include better ways for customers to get to their end goals, like different payment and delivery options. Or for earlier stages, they include different advice and information to help customers decide what to buy. However, you can also give customers better quality end goals – end goals that they never even thought of, but you have learnt of them from analysing the journeys of other customers.

The idea of 'better quality options' comes from my research into careers guidance networks, as well as from retail marketing (Hall et al., 2017; Court et al., 2009; Iyengar and Agrawal, 2010). When I interviewed careers advisers, they told me how a good adviser gives three levels of help. The first and quickest is information, the next is deeper advice and the third level is in-depth guidance.

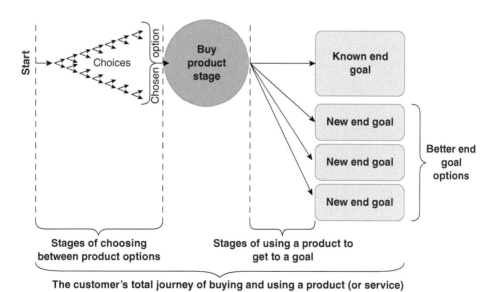

Figure 4.8   Customer journey models can guide customers in three different ways:

1. Choosing a product based on an end goal 2. Choosing a specific version of a product 3. Suggesting completely new end goals

Each level of help depends on the information that they have from the person looking for a new job. Quick information is quite ad-hoc, the adviser might be helping somebody on a computer with their CV and gives them information. Advice is usually given in a proper interview. Here, the careers adviser does more of an assessment, which involves exploring and asking questions about what job they are looking for to help a job seeker with their main issues. But with careers guidance, a careers adviser also tries to get below the surface to understand the things that a job seeker does not say straight away. An adviser tries to understand the motivation of the job seeker and what is driving their ideas about potential jobs. When giving information, a careers adviser will help a job seeker with small pieces of information, like access to job websites. When giving advice, a careers adviser will give suggestions of how to progress along the job seeker's journey to get the job they have chosen, like advice on formatting a CV to best fit that job. When giving guidance, a careers adviser will try to give better quality options, not just how to get a job but suggestions of jobs that a job seeker may never have thought of themselves.

Journey-based Thinking can be used to make a customer journey model that will help to guide customers in three different but related ways (Figure 4.8). First, it can be used to help customers to choose a product that they want based upon what they need it for, their end goal. Remember, umbrellas keep you dry, cars move you from A to B: customers buy things for a reason. Second, a customer journey model can be used to plan out all the questions that customers need to answer and the choices that they need to take as they choose between different versions of a product, or as they choose different service options. Third, a customer journey model can be used to suggest completely new end goals and products to a customer. End goals that other customers have thought of in the past and which are part of the information recorded in the customer journey model. As long as suggestions for new end goals for a customer are consistent with the wider life journey of that customer then they will fit. If they fit better than the end goals that the customer is currently aware of then they are better quality options (Rosenbaum et al., 2017; Richardson, 2010).

Journey-based Thinking and customer journey models can be used to design products, services, business processes, machines, software and the organisations themselves. Whenever people use something, need help from something or take part in something they are a type of customer. They get some benefit, advantage or assistance, which helps them along the journey they are on, their job journey or their life journey. Every customer's progress along their journey depends on successfully using a lot of products and services. These products and services do things for a customer and give them information that they use to decide which stage to choose next. A model of a customer journey helps organisations to design their products and services, to design how they work together with other products and services, and even to design how customers can find and choose them in the first place.

Examples of using Journey-based Thinking and customer journey models

Here are a few examples of how organisations help customers using Journey-based Thinking and customer journey models. Notice how the help customers receive comes from a combination of products and services. Every organisation produces products and services even if they think of themselves mainly as a product manufacturing organisation, or mainly as a service provider. There is always a mix of products and services, even if the services just provide customer information (see Chapter 5).

- Helping customers to find and choose *your* product or service: helping customers with information and suggestions is an ideal opportunity to persuade them to buy your products and services. For example, washing-up liquid customers want different smells and prices, and some need the product to be 'green'. So Ecover provide lots of information about their washing-up liquid's biodegradable ingredients and their zero waste certified factory (Ecover, 2021). This information is on the Ecover website and on the product pages of retailers' sites to attract customers, as well as to help them decide what to buy. Other customers will value products for sensitive skin. The key customer data here is knowing which customers value 'eco' products, certain smells, low prices or other product characteristics.
- Designing a product: designing a product is itself a journey for the designers who must design products that help customers get where they want to go to in their life journeys (see Chapter 9). The key customer data here is knowing exactly what customers need a product for. What are their aims and objectives? Designers use that information as an end point to work backwards from, to design the whole customer journey. From receiving the new product and opening the box, then using it successfully for the first time and so on. For example, when you buy an iconic Billy bookcase from IKEA (IKEA, 2021), the objective is to store and display books and other possessions off the floor using the vertical space of the room. But the journey to get there requires successful assembly, timely and undamaged transportation to where you live, and choosing the type of Billy bookcase required. The key journey stages here are designing the product so that the bookcase is easy to assemble and making sure the package is secure and light enough to transport. Also, the designer must choose a mix of bookcase variants that fit the maximum spread of customer requirements, whilst not being too confusing for them, or too expensive to manufacture.
- Designing information services to go with a product: in the Billy bookcase example, the information service part of the design includes the assembly instructions, which need to be very clear and easily available – on paper for the first assembly and online for disassembly and reassembly in the future. Services that complement products can be designed by carefully modelling all the stages that a product and its user go through, to understand when and why they are required, as well as who needs them and how best to provide them. Sources include delivery advice pages, Frequently Asked Questions, user groups and community support, or other website information.
- Designing phone apps: phone apps and other software development apps can also profit from thinking of each project as a journey. All project Gantt charts are like storyboards for a movie. A Gantt chart lists the activities in a project using horizontal bars to show the activities' starts and ends. But to understand individual peoples' needs, we must also describe the journey of writing the software from the perspective of the developers, and the journey of users using the software. Gantt charts do not do this because they are objective not subjective. For the developers a journey model's stages describe who does what work and when. For the app user the journey model's stages describe what it is like to use the app, how clear and easy it is, how intuitive the screens are and where a user might run into problems. Together, these two detailed descriptions of staged events can be used to organise workflows and coordinate staff. They can also be used to manage data flows by seeing where information needs to be collected and where it is needed. For example, key stages in the software project journey will collect information about progress and user feedback. Modelling these two journeys at once helps them to be coordinated. For example,

there will be key stages on the journey of using the app where user feedback can be asked for and collected to feed into the software project journey. The processes of designing other information systems like websites and web pages can also profit from Journey-based Thinking.

- Designing and analysing business models: whenever multiple stakeholders interact in an ongoing basis there needs to be a way of analysing how their life journeys intertwine. This applies as much to staff interacting in the same organisations as it does to staff and customers or organisations and their business partners. All business models rely on the smooth coordination of multiple stakeholders over time (see Chapter 2). Stakeholder journey models help to design this coordination, to 'choreograph' it or 'orchestrate' it. This is because they show the stages all stakeholders must progress through to get to their goals, and many of these stages are enabled by contributions from other stakeholders, which is what a business model is.

The future: super apps and concierge services

Customer journey models are particularly useful for helping organisations to see what additional products and services their customers need. Crucially, organisations already have a working relationship with customers and should have their attention and their trust. Journey models help organisations to expand what they sell to these same customers to cover more and more parts of their lives. Even if organisations do not currently offer certain products, then they can always get a new partner to supply them. What counts is understanding what customers need in their lives and having a strong enough customer relationship to suggest it to them and be listened to.

For many years, the huge supermarket chain Tesco has built on its early relationship with customers selling groceries, by adding banking, insurance, holidays and other services. Tesco gained a deep knowledge of its customers' lives by recording many of their buying activities with loyalty cards. What they bought week to week gave Tesco a detailed understanding of the events in their lives and the opportunities for helping them by offering new products and services. When shoppers had a baby, moved house, started a degree course, or moved to a different phase in their lives, they changed their shopping habits. These changes were reflected in the loyalty card data that Tesco recorded. More importantly, every loyalty card holder was familiar with receiving frequent letters or emails from Tesco with the loyalty points they had earned and suggestions on what to spend them on. Tesco knew about the current events in customers' lives, and it had a frequent, strong and trusted way to communicate with individual customers. It could guess the new products that customers needed and was able to offer them to customers. Information always flows in two directions. The more products that an organisation sells to a customer then the more it knows about that customer's life journey and their unmet needs.

Tesco uses a highly sophisticated customer loyalty programme to understand customers' lives, but this two-way flow of information works to some extent for all transactions. The two-way information that flows between organisations and their customers applies to the rich data streams from customer loyalty programmes. But it also works with much simpler high frequency services, super apps (Chan, 2020; KPMG, 2020).

Super apps are simple high frequency services, like a food delivery service or a taxi app. They act as a gateway to lots of other products and services. Each simple transaction gives a very limited picture of a customer's life but over time the data from many frequent transactions adds up to a more detailed picture. Better still, the high frequency of the interactions provides many opportunities for an organisation to suggest additional products and services. Every transaction with a customer has a data exhaust.

This is the customer data that is needed to let the transaction happen plus the data that is created during that transaction. For example, when a customer uses a taxi service like Uber or Lyft, their pick-up and drop-off locations at certain times are recorded. Even if this data is anonymised, information about picking-up and dropping-off thousands of customers gives the taxi app firm a very detailed picture of commuter flows in a city. Super apps use the data exhaust to understand which other products and services a customer might need and give them the high frequency relationship to offer them. An example of this for taxi apps is when the app suggests useful information about the shops and restaurants at a drop-off location. The app knows when and where the app user is – if the time is near to breakfast, lunch, dinner or an evening snack and there are food outlets nearby, then the app user might find that useful. If the location is well known for other activities – maybe it is near a football stadium or a tourist area – then the app can use that information to guess what the user might need. If the user accepts the suggestion, then the app will have even better data to base its next suggestions on.

Alipay and WeChat are super apps. Amazon Prime is also a super app, because it uses rich data from Amazon plus a high frequency and trusted relationship with customers to suggest more and more services to its users. Super apps are interested in increasing their sales per customer rather than just the number of customers. The more services they sell to a customer, then the more they will know about that customer's life journey, and the more extra services they can recommend. This is an example of a powerful positive feedback loop, a flywheel business model (see Chapter 5).

In every high-end hotel, there is a desk near the reception with a person on it 24 hours a day. That person is the concierge, and the concierge is very different to the reception desk staff. The reception staff are specialised, they mainly check people in and out and deal with payments and questions about the room. The hotel concierge is a general point of contact for a much wider set of services and lots of information about local services. For example, you can use a concierge to get transport, a table at a restaurant, tickets for shows, advice about food and entertainment, ideas for what to do during your stay and many other services that are external to the hotel. Digital services, like super apps, are starting to expand what they offer along the customer journey models of peoples' lives and they are starting to become more like concierge services than the very focused apps that they started as.

Chapter summary

The purpose of everyone in an organisation is to give customers a great experience. If a customer's experience of dealing with an organisation is amazingly useful, easy and pleasurable then they will always come back and buy again. Customer loyalty does not exist, they do it because the organisation is indispensable. Understanding, analysing and improving customer journeys are the responsibilities of everyone in an organisation. Each customer travels along their own individual journey to reach their personal aims and objectives. Journey-based Thinking is a way of analysing the stages that customers need to go through to help make their journeys more successful. It is also a way to think about how data can be gathered, analysed and used to improve the journeys of large numbers of customers.

Further reading

For more about super apps and lifelong concierge services see: https://www.linkedin.com/pulse/super-apps-recycle-your-data-exhaust-power-whole-ecosystem-shaw and https://a16z.com/2020/01/23/four-trends-in-consumer-tech (accessed 7 April 2022).

McKinsey & Company (2021) 'Journey analytics', McKinsey & Company. https://www.mckinsey.com/solutions/journey-analytics (accessed 7 April 2022).

Schrage, M. (2020) *Recommendation Engines*. Cambridge, MA: MIT Press.

Vargo, S.L. and Lusch, R.F. (2004) 'Evolving to a new dominant logic for marketing', *Journal of Marketing* (68): 1–17.

5

HOW TO DEVELOP NEW WAYS OF CREATING VALUE AND NEW BUSINESS MODELS

KEY IDEAS

- A business model is like an 'equation' with four variables – its stakeholders, their values, their capabilities and their resources.
- Reengineering a business model is a response to the change forces that disrupt it (Chapter 2).
- Business models can be reengineered to create entirely new business models.
- Emerging data technologies are disrupting business models by changing all four business model variables.
- Products are turning into services, and services are being turned into software and generated in the cloud. This alters business model variables by generating new capabilities and resources to use, and new services to offer.

LEARNING OBJECTIVES

After reading this chapter you will be able to:

- Explain why a business model is like an equation, with variables that need to balance.
- Describe the difference between rebalancing a business model and reengineering it, and why this is sometimes required.
- Describe what business model disruption is and how emerging data technologies can cause it.
- Explain the differences between a product and a service.
- Explain how some products have been turned into services and how this disrupts business models and creates new ones.

This chapter explains how the elements of a business model can vary and change, but they must balance for the business model to work. The stakeholders that contribute capabilities and resources to a business model must get what they value in return, or the business model will fail. These are the variables in a sort of business model equation, and every business model equation must balance. Business models can be reengineered and rebalanced to respond to the change forces described in Chapter 2. They can also be created from nothing as long as they balance. This chapter systematically examines the many changes that can be made to a business model's variables to reengineer and rebalance it. This includes all combinations of changes to stakeholders, their values and the capabilities and resources that they contribute. The final part of the chapter introduces the idea of business model disruption and explains how new data technologies are disrupting many business models by turning products into services, and creating new types of business models such as Software as a Service (SaaS) business models and subscription business models.

Reengineering and rebalancing a business model equation

In Chapter 2 we looked at the three elements of an organisation's business model: the values of its stakeholders, the capabilities, and resources that they contribute to the business model. In this chapter we separate the stakeholders' values element into two parts, stakeholders and values, to give a total of four parts. A business model is a bit like an equation with these parts being its variables. All four variables are changed by the forces that affect organisations and the business model's 'equation' needs to be rebalanced to adjust to this or it will fail. In a balanced business model, the stakeholders mutually satisfy each other's values using their combined capabilities and resources (Figure 5.1a). If they do this well enough then stakeholders will keep contributing. The 'balance' of a business model is a metaphor for its sustainability, its ability to keep on going and persist. Whatever a stakeholder gets out of their stake in a business model needs to be at least equal to what they put in, in their opinion. If they do not get a good enough return, then they will leave the business model. So, business models are actually inequalities not equations (Figure 5.1b). The return must be greater than or equal to some perceived minimum. Customers need to get something that they think is worth what they pay. Staff need to be compensated for their time and effort, so do suppliers and partners. Here I will use the word 'balanced' in the sense that stakeholders get enough of a return, rather than exactly what they think is fair.

Business models are also multi-sided equations, and each side is represented by the needs of a different stakeholder. Business models have lots of stakeholders and so lots of sides (Figure 5.1c). Every single stakeholder is a side of the equation, not just every stakeholder group but every individual stakeholder person or stakeholder organisation has to feel that they get at least as much as they give because as we know valuation is subjective (see Chapter 4). Each business model is a multi-sided equation with as many sides as it has stakeholders.

You can see examples of these multi-sided relationships all around. Free email services like Hotmail are paid for by advertisers who want to put their brands in front of email users. It is the same for many other free online services like social media. The difficulty of trying to balance sometimes conflicting stakeholder values explains why some social media firms are accused of not putting their users' interests first (Wells et al., 2021). In their business model the user is not the cash paying customer. Like the well-known saying goes: 'If you do not pay for the product then you are the product'.

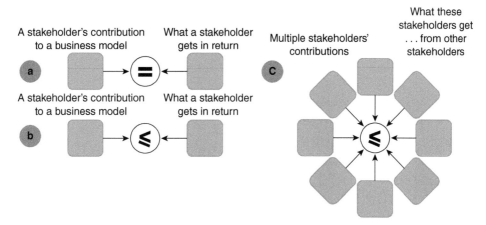

Figure 5.1   Business models are like equations with many sides and many variables

Realistically, we cannot give every single person exactly what they value ... yet. But modern customer relationships are aiming to get there, as we saw in the last chapter. Right now, it is good enough to divide stakeholders into smaller and small groups and give them things that fit their individual needs enough to keep them. It's important to note that no business model is perfectly balanced. Some customers always feel like they get a great deal. Also, dissatisfied stakeholders are always leaving, or they just join for one transaction. That is normal customer **churn** or staff churn. But as long as enough stakeholders get enough of what they value in return for what they contribute then the business model will continue to function. Customers will keep returning or new ones will replace them, staff will turn up for work or be recruited, and suppliers will supply or be replaced. The business model will continue to turn resources and capabilities into what its stakeholders value.

Business models also have a sort of 'momentum', like flywheels that store kinetic energy in their rotation. The idea of a **flywheel business model** emphasises the idea of creating and storing value as well as strong positive feedback loops in a business model. The more stakeholders that get enough of what they value then the faster the business model will 'turn'. The more they feel that they do not get this then the more it will slow down. A flywheel is a good metaphor for a business model because flywheels gather and store energy from energy sources and then share it out to energy users. Business models are a way to gather and share the products of resources and capabilities between stakeholders, with outputs that stakeholders value. Business models can also 'spin' faster or slow down; small changes to the design of a business model will change its balance to create more value or less value. Another aspect of the flywheel metaphor is the positive feedback loops that business models contain. Every contribution from a stakeholder provides resources to create value for another stakeholder and so on. A positive feedback loop is a circular process that keeps amplifying an input. Uber's business model was designed so that more geographical coverage of the service led to faster customer pickups, which led to more demand, which attracted more drivers, which led to more geographical coverage and so on. Amazon's business model was designed with another positive feedback loop; better **customer experience** led to more web traffic, which attracted more sellers, which led to a greater selection of products, which produced a better customer experience (Subramanian and Rao, 2019).

Rebalancing a business model

The idea of a balanced business model equation suggests that business models could be rebalanced, to deal with the change forces we saw in Chapter 2. We can reengineer a business model's equation to a new but still balanced equation. We can even set up completely new business model equations, as long as they balance. One way to look at a business model is to list all its variables and then systematically look at the effects of changing them in every combination. Truth tables are a useful tool for doing this systematically. A **truth table** is a method used in Boolean algebra to set out all the possible combinations of several binary variables. In this case the four variables are based on changes to a business model's three elements: its stakeholders and their values, resources, and capabilities. In Table 5.1 I have divided the stakeholder values element into two columns of 'stakeholders' and 'values' because either half of this element might change without the other changing. For example, a stakeholder like a customer could leave the business model, but another customer with the same values might be recruited to replace the first. Or a customer might remain but change what they value. So, there are four columns of variables in Table 5.1.

Table 5.1   All combinations of four variables staying the same (0) or changing (1)

Stakeholders	Values	Resources	Capabilities
0	0	0	0
0	0	0	1
0	0	1	0
0	0	1	1
0	1	0	0
0	1	0	1
0	1	1	0
0	1	1	1
1	0	0	0
1	0	0	1
1	0	1	0
1	0	1	1
1	1	0	0
1	1	0	1
1	1	1	0
1	1	1	1

Table 5.1 contains every combination of 1 and 0 that is possible for the digits in the four columns. It does this by counting in binary from 0 at the top to 15 at the bottom. As we move down the rows of the table the 0s stand for business model variables that stay the same and the 1s stand for variables that change. Table 5.2 shows all the combinations of staying the same or changing for these business model variables, like the 1s and 0s in Table 5.1.

Table 5.2   All combinations of changes for stakeholders, values, resources, and capabilities

Stakeholders	Values	Resources	Capabilities	Key differences between rows
Same	Same	Same	Same	1. No change to all the business model variables
Same	Same	Same	**CHANGE**	2. Capabilities change but other variables stay the same
Same	Same	**CHANGE**	Same	3. Resources change but other variables stay the same
Same	Same	**CHANGE**	**CHANGE**	4. Resources change, and capabilities change to balance that
Same	**CHANGE**	Same	Same	5. Stakeholders remain the same but what they value changes
Same	**CHANGE**	Same	**CHANGE**	6. Stakeholders remain the same but what they value changes; capabilities change to adjust
Same	**CHANGE**	**CHANGE**	Same	7. Stakeholders remain the same but what they value changes; resources change to adjust
Same	**CHANGE**	**CHANGE**	**CHANGE**	8. All business model variables change except the stakeholders
CHANGE	Same	Same	Same	9. Stakeholders change but all other variables remain the same
CHANGE	Same	Same	**CHANGE**	10. Stakeholders change and capabilities change; all other variables remain the same
CHANGE	Same	**CHANGE**	Same	11. Stakeholders change, and resources change, all other variables remain the same
CHANGE	Same	**CHANGE**	**CHANGE**	12. All business model variables change except the stakeholders' values
CHANGE	**CHANGE**	Same	Same	13. Stakeholders change, and their values change
CHANGE	**CHANGE**	Same	**CHANGE**	14. All business model variables change except resources
CHANGE	**CHANGE**	**CHANGE**	Same	15. All business model variables change except capabilities
CHANGE	**CHANGE**	**CHANGE**	**CHANGE**	16. All business model variables change to make a radically new business model

Next, I will describe each of the 16 rows in Table 5.2.

Row 1: No change to all the business model variables

No change to the stakeholders, values, resources, and capabilities of the business model.

Row 2: Capabilities change but other variables stay the same

In this row the organisation gets the capability to do some of the same things differently, e.g., it might use new technology to become better at doing the same thing or be limited by new regulations and become worse. The same stakeholders' values can be better satisfied, e.g., by using customer data to recommend products or by using product platforms to cheaply produce many product variations. The organisation can become better at doing the same thing if new capabilities make it more efficient. Or it might be worse at doing the same thing if regulatory changes limit how it operates. In that case, the change to the capability is a legal limitation not a technological improvement. For example, in many countries there are legal limits on using highly effective pesticides – like neonicotinoids – because they also kill bees.

A change in capabilities might mean the same stakeholder values can be better satisfied, e.g., by using customer data to recommend products that better fit customers' needs. Or by using product platforms to cheaply produce many variations of a product to give a more customised experience for customers. For example, car manufacturers use a basic design platform for each model of their cars, which is easy to add customisation options to, like different engine types and sizes.

Row 3: Resources change but other variables stay the same

In this row the resources that a business model uses change, but other variables stay the same. So, the organisation uses different raw materials to produce the same products and services. The organisation's capabilities remain the same so the current capabilities must still be able to work with these new resources. For example, many organisations are changing from using electricity to using renewable energy sources like wind turbines and solar power, or to using bamboo packaging instead of plastic wrapping. In these examples the organisation still receives electricity and still buys in packaging materials for its products. Here, the buying organisation does not need to change its capabilities to be able to deal with a radically new resource that might not fit its current machines or ways of working. Instead, the change to the resource variable must be dealt with by the supplier of the electricity or the packaging. Those suppliers may have to change their capabilities.

Notice how you can change the definition of the variables slightly so that one minute you are thinking about the business model variables of a single organisation and next you are thinking about the business model variables of different stakeholders, e.g., suppliers' capabilities or customer values. This can be confusing but it is actually a great way to get ideas. If you look at the variables of a business model in different ways and they do not seem to fit together then do not worry. Just use the ideas like you would in a brainstorming process: do not judge them at this stage, store them up for later. You can check if they all work together when you put the complete system of business models into a Value Flow Analysis (VFA) diagram, which we will discuss later.

Row 4: Resources change, and capabilities change to balance that

In this row resources change and internal capabilities change to balance that. This is like a combination of rows 2 and 3, e.g., when new machines must be bought to make packaging from bamboo rather than plastic. Another example is when someone replaces their car with an electric car. The business model of the car user changes, and an electric vehicle requires recharging with electricity rather than by adding petrol.

This second example shows how a business model can be used to think about all its stakeholders, not just the manufacturer of the car at the centre of its business model. Business model ideas apply to all stakeholders: in this example the car users are at the centre of their own business models as much as the car maker is at the centre of its own. All stakeholders are a part of as many different business models as they have relationships with other stakeholders. Business models are systems of value flows between stakeholders, so, in every business model analysis it is very important to clearly pick whose business model you are analysing – we call this 'Asking the right Analysis Question' (see Chapter 10). Also, stakeholders continuously change the collection of business models that they are part of as they change their relationships and move between different communities of other stakeholders. A car user will join another manufacturer's business model when buying a car from another brand. From the perspective of one organisation and its business model, that movement is customer churn, staff churn, supplier churn or the churn of some other type of stakeholder. From the perspective of the stakeholder who buys a different brand or moves jobs, it is the organisation that changes, even if it was the stakeholder's decision to change.

Row 5: Stakeholders remain the same but what they value changes

In this row the business model has the same stakeholders but some of what they value changes. These can be changes in customers' tastes and requirements, or the prices that suppliers charge, or the non-financial reasons why partner organisations work together, like when brands strengthen and raise customer awareness to other brands, or when organisations share data. Satisfying a stakeholder's values is the only reason why they play their role in a business model and these values can easily change faster and to a greater degree than variables like resources or capabilities. The reason for this is that values are subjective and can be emotionally driven, especially with retail customers.

The problem in this row is not stakeholders changing what they want, it is that other business model variables remain the same. How can the business model satisfy new requirements from its stakeholders whilst keeping everything else the same? The answer is that it must be flexible. The business model must either be flexible enough to change what it produces for some stakeholders, or it will fail. Usually, a radical change to what stakeholders require will force a change to other business model variables, like a change in stakeholders when an organisation looks for new markets or new suppliers that it can more easily satisfy. For example, customers in countries that still smoke cigarettes when demand reduces elsewhere. If it cannot be flexible when an organisation wants to keep the stakeholders whose values have changed then it will have to change its capabilities (row 2), or the resources that it uses (row 3).

Row 6: Stakeholders remain the same but what they value changes; capabilities change to adjust

In this row the business model has the same stakeholders but some of what they value changes, like in rows 5 and 7. Any adjustments are made by changing the capabilities that the business model uses, like in row 4, where capabilities also change to balance things.

Row 7: Stakeholders remain the same but what they value changes; resources change to adjust

In this row the business model has the same stakeholders but some of what they value changes, like in rows 5 and 6. Any adjustments required are made by changing the resources that the business model uses, like in row 4 where resources also change to balance things.

Row 8: All business model variables change except the stakeholders

In this row all the business model variables change except the stakeholders. The values of all stakeholders do not necessarily change, nor all the capabilities, nor all the resources. But some of each change. The important point is that if the values of some stakeholders change then an adjustment in how the business model uses resources and capabilities is required to rebalance it. This is like rows 6 and 7 but both capabilities and resources change.

Row 9: Stakeholders change but all other variables remain the same

What the new stakeholders value is the same as what the old stakeholders valued, so no major changes are required to rebalance the business model. New stakeholders will have some differences so there is a need for 'business model flexibility'. This is like in rows 2 and 3, which also contain a single variable change that has to be adjusted for without any other variables changing.

In this row some of the business model's stakeholders change, and even if their overall values remain the same then the situations that each of these stakeholders is in changes. The new stakeholders want the same as the old stakeholders. Here, 'new stakeholders' means more of the same types of stakeholders as the old ones; a different type would have different values (which is why they would be considered a different type). What the new stakeholders value has not obviously changed from what the old ones valued. But new stakeholders can never be exactly the same as the old stakeholders. For example, the new stakeholders might be new customers that buy a product when old customers do not repeat their purchase, like for products that you only buy once (coffins) or that last a long time (houses). Companies that sell these types of products always have to look for new customers. Another example is that organisations with a high staff turnover are always looking for new staff to do the same old jobs. But even so, the subtle differences in the new staff and their advice and information needs will demand some flexibility from the business model. New stakeholders cannot be the same as the old ones, new customers have questions, and new staff need training. In this row the capabilities and resources variables are the same because the business model is able to absorb the slight differences between new and old stakeholders without changing any more. For example, customer service departments might cope with the added new customers' requests for help and human resources departments might have the capacity to recruit and train more new staff. But it does raise a question about business model flexibility: how much can some business model variables change without having to change others to rebalance the model?

Another example of new stakeholders being added to a business model and where no other variables change is when a product is early in its life cycle. New customers will come from the same targeted stakeholder group because there is likely to be many more of the same type of customers left in the market to be sold to. Having said that, adding more and more customers would also require a firm to increase its manufacturing capacity, which will eventually lead to a change in its production capabilities as it builds more factories or outsources production to new partners.

Row 10: Stakeholders change and capabilities change; all other variables remain the same

This row is like row 9 in that stakeholders change to others with the same values, which makes no material change. But in this row capabilities also change. So, this row is also similar to row 2 where capabilities are the only material change. It is in effect a single variable change and single variable changes need the business model to be flexible enough to adjust to the change. In this case the business model might become better at satisfying stakeholders.

Row 11: Stakeholders change, and resources change, all other variables remain the same

This row is like row 10 in that stakeholders change to others with the same values, which makes no material difference. But there is also another variable change, in this case the resources variable. So, this row is also similar to row 3 where resources are the only material change, and row 11 is another variable change. For example, when the change just makes satisfying stakeholders cheaper or more expensive because of resource changes.

Row 12: All business model variables change except the stakeholders' values

In this row all the business model variables change except the stakeholders' values. Not necessarily all stakeholders, all capabilities, and all resources, but some of each change, like in rows 9, 10 and 11, new stakeholders are never exactly the same as the old stakeholders. The situations that these stakeholders are in will change even if their overall values remain the same. In this row some capabilities and some resource variables will change to balance the changes to some of the stakeholders. This is a much greater adjustment than the business model flexing in row 9. Row 12 includes a rebalancing that changes how the business model uses some capabilities and some resources. For example, new stakeholders with the same values as the old stakeholders might live in different legal and cultural situations, or different geographical situations. They might be at different stages in their lives, if they are retail customers, or they might be at different company growth stages, if they are organisations.

Changing some capabilities and some resources is a much greater change than adjusting by using the inherent business model flexibility that comes from the natural 'give' and tolerances for change in any human activity or operating machinery. For example, if an organisation focuses on different markets with similar tastes, it might still have to change its transport, legal, linguistic and other capabilities to do business in other countries. Governments and regulators are also stakeholders so different delivery locations, laws and languages count as a change in the values of stakeholders, i.e., they are not part of row 12. But it depends on how you use and interpret these business model ideas; you are in charge of your own Analysis Question (see Chapter 10). The objective is to use business model ideas to think of useful insights that help organisations, not to use the model 'perfectly', like a robot. You should feel comfortable in playing around with definitions and their interpretations when you analyse business models because each new way to interpret something provides a new way of looking at your analysis.

Row 13: Stakeholders change, and their values change

In this row the business model has some different stakeholders with some different values. But the capabilities and resources remain the same, like in row 5, this means changes in customers and their tastes, or different suppliers with different price requirements. But even though the stakeholders change, what the new stakeholders value must be quite similar to what the old stakeholders valued, or new capabilities and resources will be required. The ways that the organisation uses capabilities and resources must be flexible enough to keep the balance.

Row 14: All business model variables change except resources

In this row all the business model variables change except some of the business model's resources. This does not necessarily mean all stakeholders, all stakeholders' values and all resources, but some of each change. This row does not describe a common occurrence. The logic that causes an organisation to choose any particular business model is based around the 'tools' that it has available, i.e., the capabilities, resources and stakeholders that it can attract to join in acting out a business model. It is rarely worth changing everything about a business model's variables but still replicating the same resources it had before; new suppliers can usually be found to provide similar resources to those in the old business model. There must be some powerful reason to go to the trouble of changing every variable but one. One reason for doing this might be a change in the purpose of the organisation. An organisation might have a long-term purpose of providing some service or bringing about some large-scale change to society that overrides any evolution in what it consumes to do this. Examples for this are government services like education and health. The stakeholders change, their values change and so do the resources and capabilities of the organisation, but the service still continues. Although the question must again be asked: if you change most of the variables of a system, is it still the same system?

So, this row represents a radically different business model with the same resources, rather than a rebalancing of a single business model. This row is similar to row 15.

Row 15: All business model variables change except capabilities

This row is similar to row 14, but capabilities are the only variable that remains the same, not resources. Again, this row represents a radically different business model with the same capabilities, rather than a rebalancing of a single business model.

Row 16: All business model variables change to make a radically new business model

In this row all the business model variables change to make a radically new business model. A change to all four variables is complex and significant. If all stakeholders, all stakeholders' values, all capabilities, and all resources change then this is a completely new business model rather than an adjustment to an existing business model. A completely new business model is usually executed by a new organisation. Sometimes an existing organisation contributes resources or capabilities to a new subsidiary company, much like a major supplier stakeholder, or for example, when an organisation starts a joint venture with a partner or contributes capital, intellectual property, and transfers staff to start an off-shoot. This row is different to rows 14 and 15 in that everything changes. This is not an example of business model rebalancing, which is a more graduated change.

The granularity of business model variables

In real life, the divisions between the examples in Table 5.1 and Table 5.2 are not as clearly separated as the 16 rows. When business model variables change as a response to the change forces in Chapter 2, they do not change in just 15 discrete ways like in the tables. In real organisations the changes to each variable in rows 2 to 16 are much more granular and parallel. Not all stakeholders, stakeholders' values, resources, and capabilities change, only some of them: some customers, some suppliers and some staff always stay with a firm over long periods, some do not. The characteristics of resources and capabilities always slowly change. Packaging, processes, functionality, designs and even colours and shapes will change as time goes by. These changes also work in parallel; the four variables will change at the same time, such as when staff join as well as leave at the same time. This is a natural situation and an opportunity to promote flexibility and a readiness for future changes, as long as it does not overwhelm the organisation. The main thing is to keep the mix right to balance the business model.

Also, the rate of these changes varies as well. Some business models, like university education, have not changed much in decades. Over the years more people have gone to universities and got a degree, there has been an expansion in the number of master's level degrees, and more people have studied away from their home countries. But recent changes to business model variables like technological capabilities and the type and use of teaching and learning resources have led to radically new versions of the university education business model. Online learning platforms like Teachable, Khan Academy, edX and Coursera have recruited many new types of stakeholders with different values to the old types of university stakeholder groups, like students and academics. These new business models use modern online technologies to give a much cheaper educational experience to a much larger set of customers by using teaching resources and capabilities in new ways.

The flexibility and balance of business models

Large changes to a single business model variable are always difficult to accommodate because every business model needs to balance. Change one part and another needs to change to compensate. But no business model is completely balanced. There is always a churn of stakeholders as staff join and leave, as customers find a new brand and then migrate to it, or as business partnerships are created and ended. The more customers, staff and other stakeholders there are in each group then the more granular this churn will be. One customer leaving a firm that only has three big customers is a huge shock; one customer changing from Walmart to another retailer is hardly noticeable. But the number of stakeholders that join plus what they contribute must be at least as much as what is lost from those that leave. If the contribution of the leavers is more than the contribution of the joiners then the capability of the business model to mutually satisfy its stakeholders will gradually reduce, stakeholders will become less satisfied, more will leave and eventually the business model will fail. Think of it as a bucket with a hole in it being filled by a water tap: the leak from the bucket must be less than or equal to the flow of water from the tap, or the bucket will empty.

However, there will be a certain amount of 'give' or stretch in any business model. Most will be flexible enough to be able to deal with small changes to a single variable without immediately failing. A single variable change could happen without any need for adjustment on the level of the whole business model. Single variable changes happen when a change to one business model variable is cancelled out by parallel changes in the same variable, in a 'swap', for example, when one customer or staff member leaves and is replaced by another. This sort of swap is a change to a business model variable that does not change the overall mix of variables at the level of the whole business model. Business models are not rigid 'ice crystals' that immediately shatter when you try to bend them. They have flexible qualities.

The first flexible quality of business models is like the leaky bucket example above. Business models are always growing and failing at the same time. Stakeholders are always churning. The larger the organisation, the more who are joining and leaving every day. Organisations keep monitoring the flows of joiners and leavers to work out how the balance of contributions will increase or reduce an organisation's ability to satisfy its stakeholders. Here, the flexibility of the business model is in its stock of stakeholders and the resources and capabilities that they contribute. As long as the organisation's stocks of stakeholders, resources and capabilities do not run out then the business model will not fail – there is time to replace them. Obviously, some are more critical than others. There are always top performing staff, key suppliers and most profitable customers, and there needs to be a minimum of each, although this minimum is based on what they can contribute rather than how many there are. Stocks and flows are valuable ideas that help us to look at business models in two complimentary ways. Measurements of flows are completely different to measurements of stocks. Like data that describe production rates versus stock levels in manufacturing, or the difference between income statements and balance sheets in accounting. Flows like production rates, income and cash flows are rate dependent characteristics; stock levels and asset balance sheets are rate independent characteristics (Allen and Starr, 2017). Flows are concerned with questions of how much over time; questions about stocks just ask, 'how much?'. The rate of the flow from a tap is utterly different to the level of the water in the bucket.

The second flexible quality of business models is to do with the granularity of changes to business model variables. I introduced granularity in the last section, and the flows and stocks of stakeholders and their contributions in a business model can be made up of large pieces or very small pieces. A small business might have very few customers and losing one is a big impact. Firms with many suppliers or many customers can more flexibly accommodate a reduction of one because the reduction is a smaller part of the total. Here the flexibility of a business model is in the size of changes to a business model variable relative to the size of the whole variable. Losing or gaining one customer when a retailer has a million customers in a year is highly granular: the 'grains' are small. This is not the same as the rate of flow of leavers or joiners, which is the size of the change over time. The granularity is just the minimum size that the change can be. The smaller the minimum change size then the more flexible a business model is; changes will not necessarily cause a severe unbalancing.

Tools for rebalancing and reengineering business models

The VFA diagrams in Chapter 2 are very useful tools for analysing a business model's stakeholders, what they contribute and what they value in return. They are helpful for getting the ideas and experience of many people out of their heads and onto a medium where they can be easily shared and commented on. This helps to get more brains and experience involved in an analysis, and to build consensus. I have found that online whiteboards like Miro, or physical whiteboards and flip charts, work well with this.

The Journey-based Thinking ideas and the journey models in Chapter 4 are very useful tools for analysing how the flows between each of the stakeholders in a VFA unfold or progress. These might be the transportation of materials or information, or the learning journey of a student. They are particularly good for finding and removing barriers and problems that impede these flows. They enable the qualitative analysis that will specify where data should be gathered and used in preparation for a systematic quantitative analysis (see Chapters 8, 9 and 10), which can be automated and very large scale.

Business models that use data technologies

Disruptive business models and business model disruption

Interest in business models really took off in the late 1990s when organisations started to use Internet technology to add to and rebalance their business models' variables (Osterwalder et al., 2005). For example, Amazon started to connect with retail customers online, and then made its warehousing and IT infrastructure capabilities available as a service to business customers, and Ebay built an online platform to connect many different retail buyers to many different small sellers. The Internet and the World Wide Web (WWW), which it was built on, disrupted the business models of incumbent firms because they enabled individuals and organisations to do things differently – they enabled people to connect up in radically different ways. Business models depend on capabilities and if you add to or change any of these capabilities then what is possible as a business model can also change. For example, Netflix disrupted video rental store businesses like Blockbuster by renting films on DVDs and then by delivering them by mail, so no store was needed. Later, Netflix disrupted the industry again by streaming films over the Web, and then again by actually producing video content itself (Hicks et al., 2021).

Another good example of business model disruption is when Amazon's capability to sell books online disrupted the business models of off-line bookstores in several ways including how they interacted with customers. Amazon could display a much wider range of books and other products than a store with limited shelf space. Its web pages were a much easier and more convenient way for a customer to search for the right book, to get a taste of the content and to even learn what other readers thought about it. All this could be done in a physical book store but not very fast and only after leaving home to go out. Furthermore, Amazon's website was also a marvellous way for the firm to learn about customers, what they were looking for, what they eventually chose and how they behaved afterwards. One of the first data analytics tools that Amazon used was product recommendations: customers would be told what customers like them went on to buy after looking at the book they were currently looking at. Amazon's website held data on what customers looked at, what they eventually bought and most importantly, customers' profile data from when they joined, plus other data like geographical location. This allowed Amazon to give really useful product recommendations.

As we saw in Chapter 4, helping a customer or any other stakeholders to progress along their journey will persuade them to take part in your business model because it is obviously in their interests to do so; it helps them get what they value. Amazon and any other online shop can record what customers buy and compare it to these customers' profiles to look for a pattern. A pattern that connects the books that are eventually bought with the profiles of the types of customers that bought them. Then they can use that pattern to recommend books to other customers because the pattern links specific books with specific groups of customers. The website gathers data on which web page they are looking at, so it knows the book, and the website knows who the customer is from a log in. The pattern shows what other books people like them bought and recording which books that customer bought in the past makes the pattern even more accurate. Offline book stores never had access to this data, so they did not have this capability. This also enabled Amazon to give more personalised and more accurate recommendations than even the most experienced shop staff could give.

This is an example of an organisation using a new technology to change the capability variable in a common industry business model in order to satisfy the stakeholder values variable in a new way. But originally the idea of disruptive business models, which came from researchers like Clayton Christensen, was much more precise. Nowadays, most organisations think of disruptive business models and business model disruption as any revolutionary change to normal ways of creating value in an organisation or an industry. Revolutionary changes are changes in one organisation's business model that harm the business models of other firms in the same industries, or related industries. For example, when Skype's free video calls disrupted the telecommunications industry, just as mobile phone technology did before, or when free to use online news sites, like BuzzFeed and HuffPost helped to disrupt the newspaper industry, or when streaming firms like Spotify and SoundCloud disrupted the business model of the music industry.

But Clayton Christensen's classic ideas about disruptive innovation are much more precise than this and they do not apply to all types of disruptive change that we see today from AI or other new technologies. Christensen's classic ideas are about how incumbents, the main players in an industry, fail to fight off new entrants, firms that are new to the industry and usually much smaller (Christensen et al., 2015). Incumbents try to sustain their capabilities to satisfy their main customers by making their products better in ways that fit the values of their main customers. This is called a **sustaining innovation strategy**. But new entrants focus on satisfying the customers that are left over rather than the most profitable customers. Christensen originally researched how this unfolded in several industries like the disk drive industry and the mainframe computer industry. And his ideas have been tested in many other industries like motorcycles, computers, photocopying, car tyres, management consulting and cameras (Bower and Christensen, 1995; Christensen, 2000; Christensen et al., 2015). Christensen saw how new entrants could gradually expand their market share from a very small start. His key insight was that in many industries the incumbent firms were so focused on satisfying their main customers that they ignored the needs of other customers. By doing this they gave new firms a chance to enter the market.

New data technologies have accelerated business model disruptions in three ways (Geller, 2017). The first way is by improving connectivity. Smartphones and the Internet make it much easier to link businesses and other stakeholders together in new ways. **Cloud computing** provides rentable infrastructure for any firm that wants to produce and deliver digital services to customers, including customers' phones. This works for business-to-business customers (B2B) as well as for business-to-consumer customers (B2C). The second way is about an organisation's focus. New entrants focus on growth and change but incumbents tend to focus on the return on their existing assets – the assets that they have invested in, not new ones that they could invest in. Incumbents will have recruited stakeholders to their business model who have contributed resources and capabilities, like loans from banks or payments for shares in a firm. These stakeholders will want to see the return that they were promised, and it is very difficult to change these relationships quickly. For example, a firm cannot demolish a factory that it has built before the investment has been paid back. The same goes for new machines and the research and development investments that go into improving current products. It is much easier for new entrants who have a blank business model that they are just starting to build up. They are much more flexible because they have no pre-existing investments or agreements with stakeholders. The third way that new technologies have accelerated business model disruption is with barriers to market entry, which benefits incumbents. In some industries, like drugs, past knowledge assets increase in value. Incumbent firms can build on past know-how to race ahead of new competitors. For example, old drug firms are building on their knowledge of drug chemistry by adding new techniques from biology. These techniques use computer simulations and AI systems to look for potential new drugs without slow and expensive experiments in the lab.

In this book I use 'business model disruption' in a much wider sense than Christensen to include more immediate, radical and broader changes to the business model equation of how business capabilities create value for stakeholders. The link between business model disruption and the change forces in Section 1 is in how the change forces affect the four business model variables: stakeholders, what they value, and the capabilities, and resources that they contribute. For many organisations, business model disruption is a surprise. But the four business model variables are constantly changing because change forces themselves change all the time, especially technological change forces. You can use the Opens Systems Change (OSC) model in Chapter 3 to monitor and prepare for business model disruption.

Product business models are turning into service business models

One area of business model disruption is in the relationship between products and services. At first sight, a product and a service are very different. Products tend to be tangible, something that you can touch. Services tend to be more flexible, less visible, less longer lasting. But think about an Apple iPad and an Amazon Kindle. An iPad and a Kindle are both tablets, but one is more like a service, and one is more like a product. Try and guess which is more like a service, and which is more like a product.

The answer is that an iPad is more like a product and a Kindle is more like a service. You can touch them both, but a Kindle is cheaper than an iPad, it does less things and it is made to a lower technical specification. Its memory and storage capabilities are smaller, and it is less sophisticated. I guess you get what you pay for. For Amazon, a Kindle is mainly a way to help customers to buy more Amazon digital services, like eBooks, as well as to buy more tangible products. Like a website, a Kindle is also a valuable way for Amazon to learn about customers and potential customers. On the other hand, an iPad is a major earner for Apple and the focus of much effort and company resources. Both these tablets are used to buy and consume digital services and tangible products. Both of them are physical artefacts in themselves. But a Kindle is more like a service because it is a means to an end rather than the end in itself. It is not a service, but it is service-like.

Another example is the Amazon Dash, a small wand with a bar code reader, a microphone and a Wi-Fi connection. They also used to sell a Wi-Fi enabled Dash button (Figure 5.2). Both were used to make it easier for customers to order products from Amazon. Recently, Amazon seems to have discontinued Dash in favour of Echo smart speakers, which use the Alexa AI to help people to order products and do many other things. Amazon also has a food delivery service called Amazon Fresh, which gets the groceries that are ordered from Amazon to people's doors. Notice how Amazon Dash serviced a customer's needs for ordering products, and Amazon Fresh services a customer's needs for delivering products. It looks like Amazon mapped out the customer journey of grocery shopping from the stage of customers realising what they need to the stage of them getting it, and it noticed two gaps. The first gap was that making an order on Amazon's website could be made easier, especially if someone has their hands full or was in a rush. The second gap was that even after ordering, groceries need to be transported to a customer. Online grocery shopping is normal for many people now, especially after the COVID-19 pandemic. But Amazon brought the Dash wand out in 2014, Dash buttons in 2015 and reportedly it launched Amazon Fresh in 2007 (Ha, 2014; Gartenberg, 2019; Day One Team, 2021).

Figure 5.2   Amazon Dash button

Image: Alexander Klink, https://commons.wikimedia.org/wiki/User:AlexanderKlink

Servitisation is the idea that the differences between products and services are part of a gradual spectrum of differences, rather than a binary contrast. At one end are 100% products and at the other are 100% services. Whole collections of products and services are required for customers to progress along their journeys.

> Servitization involves the innovation of an organisation's capabilities and processes so that it can better create mutual value through a shift from selling products to selling Product–Service Systems (Neely, 2008).

Neely's definition of servitisation fits closely with how we talked about business model disruption in Chapters 1 to 3. Stakeholders get what they value from a combination of things that we call 'products' and things that we call 'services'. Products and services are part of a single Product–Service System. What counts is the outcome as experienced by each stakeholder, like the example of the customer who buys an umbrella to stay dry, not to collect umbrellas. When you focus on the outcome for a customer, rather than how it was achieved, you start to see better ways of achieving these outcomes. For example, in 1962 Rolls-Royce engines started to sell the use of their jet engines to companies like airlines and other aircraft users (Rolls-Royce, 2012). Rolls-Royce's customers now had the option of buying what the engine did rather than buying and owning the engine itself. This held many advantages for customers, including the removal of maintenance and replacement costs. In this way servitisation is a little like moving from selling a product to renting it out. Rental relationships have the potential to last longer than a single sales transaction, so they provide many more opportunities to learn about the needs of customers.

Software-as-a-service (SaaS) business models

Services used to be just one person doing something for another. For example, a shop assistant answers questions, brings out clothes and takes your money; a dentist checks and fixes teeth; a tailor measures your size and makes a suit. These days, parts of many services have been automated. For example, when a spreadsheet automatically adds up numbers, or produces a chart from those numbers. An accountant is still needed to make decisions and feed data into the spreadsheet but lots of the simple and repetitive work is done by the spreadsheet software's service to the accountant, or anyone else who uses that software. All software provides a service to its users. But the cloud is increasingly being used by new start-up firms to provide **software-as-a-service** (SaaS). SaaS is when software runs mostly in the cloud, i.e., in a distant data centre, rather than on your laptop. If you load spreadsheet software and run it on your laptop then the laptop does all the computing and data storage work. But if you use SaaS software through a web browser then most of the computing and data storage work is done in the cloud. There are actually two uses of the word 'service' here. The first service is the cloud running the spreadsheet software in data centres and displaying the results in your browser, as a service to your laptop. The second service is the spreadsheet software providing a spreadsheet service to the laptop user. The 'as-a-service' part of software-as-a-service is the first one.

There are many SaaS firms, from giant old style software companies like Microsoft to thousands of new start-up firms. Many large software companies have been moving to providing SaaS software for years and they sell large and sophisticated software products. For example, Microsoft produces the Office 365 SaaS and many others, and Google services like Gmail, Google Sites, Google Search and lots more are all examples of SaaS software. New start-up firms are being founded all the time and they create much more focused SaaS software applications. For example, Xero just provides accounting software and Slack provides collaboration software, but some firms like Zoho keep adding to and expanding the software that they offer, and they end up providing a large range of different SaaS software services (Zoho, 2021; see Chapter 9 for some examples). There are many other start-up firms that produce innovative SaaS software, which provide services that have never existed before.

All SaaS firms are naturally data driven because their whole businesses are based on software and software automatically produces data. See Chapter 6 for a full description of data driven organisations.

Subscription business models

Four of the ideas that we have covered in this Chapter – servitisation, Product–Service Systems, automating services in software and using cloud computing capabilities to run that software – help companies to operate subscription business models. Subscription business models are turning many things that people think of as products into services. For example, most people would think of clothes as very personal products that you own; they would not want to share them with anyone else. But Rent the Runway provides an online rental service for designer clothing and accessories. If you need very high-end clothes but you cannot afford to buy them just for one party or one meeting, then services like this are what you need. Subscription business models are ongoing in services like Netflix and other video streaming services where you make a regular weekly or monthly payment in return for access to a range of shared goods and services. Another example are wine clubs like Naked Wines. Wine clubs regularly choose and deliver a selection of wines to customers, together with useful information about the wines and their producers. This adds to the customer's experience to make it one of learning about and appreciating wine, rather than just drinking it. Subscription business models all provide customers with a regular mixture of products and services, and they give the provider a regular income. But more importantly, the regularity and growing length of these customer relationships lets service providers learn more and more about their customers. A one-off payment to own rather than rent a physical product, or to buy a single instance of a service, would not preserve the relationship. Subscriptions avoid the need for selling to customers again and again: they make the relationship 'stickier', so they generate more customer data (see super apps in Chapter 7).

In the past, many people thought of services as just an addition to products, which were the main thing organisations provided to their customers. This is probably because products are easy to see and touch, and they stay around, whereas services have a fleeting existence because they are produced and used at the same time. Services are also invisible and sometimes so are their outcomes. Also, many of the digital services that we use today were impossible without modern computers, phones, the Internet and cloud computing. But the idea of a Product–Service System captures a spectrum of different outcomes for customers that are generated by a mixture of product-like things and service-like things. The idea of a Product–Service System explains the outcomes experienced by a customer in terms of what the system of stakeholders does that produces whatever a customer buys. But most organisations do not overthink this, they just welcome the freedom to innovate in how they provide customer experiences and support customers on their journeys. Modern digital services are designed as journeys that their users – customers – travel on and experience stage by stage. You can see this with customers clicking through the separate pages of a website, or the step-by-step instructions (an information service) for assembling furniture (products). Customers are people – product users, customers in a physical shop or a website, or even colleagues at work. Customer journeys are a great way to design the process of how customers look for, find, choose and experience the Product–Service Systems they need to progress along their journeys (see Chapter 4).

Chapter summary

Business models are like 'equations' with four variables: their stakeholders, their stakeholders' values, the capabilities, and resources that these stakeholders contribute. The change forces described in Chapter 2 alter the variables of a business model and potentially unbalance it. In an unbalanced business model, stakeholders are not able to fully satisfy each other, and they will begin to leave the business model. But the business model can be reengineered by changing the four variables to compensate and rebalance the business model. Business model reengineering can also be used to create entirely new business models. The business models of competitors can be disrupted by reengineering business models or by creating new ones that outperform them. A common reason for this disruption is emerging data technologies, which can change all four business model variables to make them function better than in competitors' business models, improvements like a better understanding and satisfaction of stakeholders' values or a better use of capabilities and resources.

A central aspect of business model reengineering and business model disruption is the way that some products are turning into services and some services are turning into software in the cloud. These all alter business model variables by generating new capabilities and resources to use, and new services to offer.

Further reading

Christensen, C.M. (2000) *The Innovator's Dilemma: When New Technologies Cause Great Firms to Fail*. Brighton, MA: Harvard Business Review Press.

Christensen, C.M., Raynor, M.E. and McDonald, R. (2015) 'What is disruptive innovation?', *Harvard Business Review*, December, https://hbr.org/2015/12/what-is-disruptive-innovation (accessed 7 April 2022).

For further reading on servitisation, see Neely's blog: http://andyneely.blogspot.com/2013/11/what-is-servitization.html (accessed 7 April 2022).

6

HOW DATA-DRIVEN ORGANISATIONS ORGANISE THEIR PEOPLE

KEY IDEAS

- Business process models describe the activities that people do at work in products and services.
- The way that people and resources are organised in business processes is based on how decisions are made in each organisation and who makes them – this is the structure of the organisation.
- Decision-making power is being shared out across organisations. It is changing from being top-down and centralised to being more distributed, which involves lower levels of staff and even external people.
- More people have access to the information needed to make the best decisions, and that information is being used in different ways.
- Data-driven organisations use new data sources and new decision-supporting technologies to make decisions in much more systematic, informed and detailed ways than in the past.
- Data-driven organisations use agile management techniques and digital collaboration technologies to be more flexible in how people inside and outside the organisation work together, and act on their decisions.
- Data-driven organisations automate decision-making processes using patterns that they find in data.

LEARNING OBJECTIVES

After reading this chapter you will be able to:

- Describe what business process models are and how they support people's activities at work.
- Explain who the best person to make a decision is, and why who it is depends on each particular decision.
- Describe the different ways that organisations use data to make decisions.
- Explain why the decisions that data-driven organisations make are better than other organisations.
- Explain why data-driven organisations are more agile and collaborative than other organisations.
- Describe how data-driven organisations automate some of their decision-making.

This chapter explains how organisations are starting to organise their staff and their resources differently by making decisions in different ways; decisions about business processes – the activities of its people and machines. When it is not just the top management of an organisation who have all the information, then organisations can let any of their staff make decisions. Changing who makes the decisions and how they do it radically alters organisational structures and business processes. Sometimes the best decision-makers are outside of an organisation, like customers using a **self-service** approach.

This chapter describes how many organisations are starting to use new data sources and new decision-support technologies. These 'data-driven organisations' are much more systematic in how they make decisions about their products and services, about how they use resources, and about how they change their business models. They can also make much more detailed decisions, and the ways that people work together in their teams and departments to enact decisions is different as well. Data-driven organisations use agile management techniques and digital collaboration technologies to redefine who their stakeholders work with and how – both inside and outside the organisation. Lastly, data-driven organisations automate more decisions using patterns that they find in their data.

Decisions and business processes

In this book, the word 'organisation' is used to mean a firm, a company, a department, a government agency, a team, or any group of people working together. This includes any group of people who work together for any purpose, including for-profit or not-for-profit, such as voluntary organisations, public sector organisations and commercial firms. They are 'organisations' because being organised means that the people, their resources and their capabilities are arranged in a way that supports their purpose.

In a business model, being organised means picking the right people, resources, and capabilities as well as specifying how they should work together. The people, resources and capabilities that are best suited to one purpose may not be so useful for another. Also, the same people, resources and capabilities can be arranged in different ways for different purposes. For example, if the purpose is to build houses for families, then you will need construction capabilities and resources like building materials. But construction workers need to follow plans for homes not for offices. Altering the variables of a business model includes picking and recruiting stakeholders in the first place (see Chapter 5). But it also includes deciding how they will work together, which means deciding which activities each of them will do and how they will do them. Before any action there must be a decision to take that action, or there will be disorganisation. How people are organised includes deciding what decisions need to be made, who makes these decisions and how they do it. Many organisations use business process models to plan this out.

Business process models describe what people in organisations do in their jobs. They describe the things that organisations make and the services that they produce. Business processes are stage by stage descriptions of activities that people do; they describe activities like assembling products, having meetings or dealing with customer queries. They also describe what actions other stakeholders and even machines and software need to do for the organisation to accomplish its purpose (Curtis et al., 1992; Hammer and Champy, 1993). A recipe for making a meal and step-by-step instructions for assembling IKEA furniture are both business process models. Business process instructions can also be added to the lines of code in software so that phone apps and other software will do their part to support the activities of a business process.

In a Value Flow Analysis (VFA) diagram the arrowed flow lines that join the stakeholders are business processes, which transform resources and move them from one stakeholder to another (see Chapter 5). Business processes produce what each stakeholder requires and the transport to deliver it to them. A VFA diagram does not describe the business processes that transform stakeholders' contributions into other stakeholders' requirements. It only describes the stakeholders, their contributions and their requirements.

Business processes are made up of stages. Each stage has inputs that are required for that stage to be completed and outputs that the stage produces. In between the inputs and the outputs there are smaller sub stages, which transform the inputs into outputs (see Figure 6.1a). Each sub stage also has inputs and outputs and even smaller stages within it, which also can be broken down into yet smaller stages. Inputs are resources that a stage needs for it to be completed. Each stage has capabilities that transform the inputs into outputs, and then these outputs become the inputs for the next stage. Consumables will be used up or changed and fuel, information or materials will be transformed in some way, e.g., refined, assembled, moved or packaged. The next stage can be described in a business process model as being like the next instruction in a recipe. But it could also be a decision for the person who is following the instructions to make, a choice between several next stages (see Figure 6.1b). The series of three stages in Figure 6.1a has already been chosen so it looks like a line rather than the branching junction in Figure 6.1b. A business process model clearly explains which stage to do next. For example, a recipe for making a truly excellent curry will contain many precise instructions about the amounts of spices and other ingredients to use and how to use them. These instructions are decisions that have already been taken by the author of the recipe. But there may be some decisions that cannot be pre-defined, like when something unforeseen occurs. Then the person who is following the business process must make a decision. Or if a machine is following instructions in its software, it will call for human assistance.

Business process modelling is related to Journey-based Thinking, but there are some differences between the two (Table 6.1). A business process is a description of how people and machines should work together, so it includes many individual stakeholders' journeys. Also, a stakeholder's journey is subjective and unfolds moment by moment, whereas a business process is standard, fixed and generic. Journeys can be recorded, like when customer journeys are recorded to learn how to improve customers' experiences. But a stakeholder's journey is only pre-planned to the extent that a staff member follows their job's business process, or a customer is guided by an app. Furthermore, a stakeholder's journey holds all the detail of every second of a stakeholder's life, however a business process only has as much detail as the model requires.

The route of a stakeholder's journey is a series of stages separated by their conscious and unconscious decisions. Each decision is a choice between potential next stages. Business process stages have outputs that can branch between several decisions, these are choices for the next stages. But a business process model only holds the possible branches that an organisation has decided to provide. However, the life journey of a stakeholder could start by following a business process model, then the stakeholder could choose next stages that are not on the model and those stages may not even include that organisation. A customer could buy from another retailer, a staff member could get another job. Stakeholder's journeys have the infinite detail of real life; business process models are just models of a part of life.

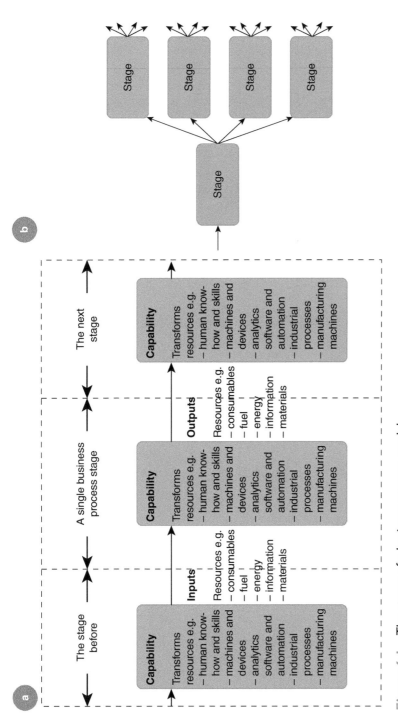

Figure 6.1   The stages of a business process model

Panel (a) shows how each business process stage takes inputs and uses capabilities to transform them into outputs for the next process stage to use as inputs. Panel (b) shows how each business process stage is separated from the next by a decision about which stage to do next. Business process models mostly describe which activities to do next but there are always decisions to make about details or surprises.

Based on Hammer and Champy, 1993

Table 6.1   Comparison between a business process model and a personal journey from Journey-based Thinking

Point of comparison	A business process model	A journey in Journey-based Thinking
Description	A pre-planned description of how people and machines should work together. Stakeholder's journeys can be guided by a business process model	A description of a single person's actual journey that really happens, from their perspective, or a general record of what usually happens on such journeys to many stakeholders
Top-down generalisation or bottom-up detail	A high-level and top-down guide	The bottom-up and precise detail of what happens in real life to the person or people whose journey it is
Separations between stages	A series of stages separated by outputs from one stage, which become inputs for the next. The model advises how to choose between branches	A series of stages separated by decisions. Decisions range from big choices about the future route and final objectives, to small events and choices
Decisions about next stages to take – how top-down business process models meet bottom-up personal journeys	High-level decisions about which next stages to take are chosen from pre-planned options in the business process model. Exceptions and details must be dealt with by humans	People make all the decisions about next stages to take. But they can be guided by personal routines, habits, their training and business process models
The potential inputs that can be used for each stage	Only the inputs for the products and services that an organisation has decided to provide	Any stage inputs including those from different organisations' business models, e.g., buying from a competitor

A business process model describes the activities that an organisation has decided to do, not all that it could do. Shops only stock the goods that they choose to, manufacturers only make the range of products that they want to produce, and even governments cannot provide every service that citizens ask for. Business processes are like railway tracks, they have planned junctions where trains can change direction, but only along predetermined routes. Designing and changing where those tracks are laid out, where they branch and where they go to involves decisions about how the organisation should function. This is **Business Process Reengineering (BPR)**, which involves redesigning the work activities of the people and machines involved in business processes (Hammer and Champy, 1993). But even when the process has been agreed and the track has been laid, choosing which individual trains should take which routes and in which circumstances involves detailed decisions by the people that work in those business processes. For example, a customer service advisor will have clear instructions for which solutions fit different customer problems. But when dealing with any specific customer, a customer service advisor needs to recognise what the problem is and then decide which advice to give. Whenever we tap on an option whilst using a mobile app, we are choosing from the options that have been designed into software that follows pre-defined business processes, like pre-laid railway tracks – we can only choose from a fixed set of options. The choice of options that an organisation makes when it decides on its business processes determine things like the training of the customer service advisors and the design of the software.

Fundamentally, an organisation is not a building, a brand or a legal entity. It is how people, resources and capabilities are organised. Organisation is created by decisions at different levels and at different frequencies, from very low-level detailed decisions to higher and higher-level strategic decisions, from decisions that are taken minute-by-minute and even second-by-second on factory floors, to high-level decisions in board rooms that are taken quarterly, or annually, or at even lower frequencies. Many of these decisions can be foreseen and people can follow the pre-planned tracks of a business process, but a business process only provides guidance up to a certain point. What happens in organisations cannot be completely foreseen and pre-planned. In Journey-based Thinking terms, every decision that we make is a choice between two or more options for the next stage in our lives. In this case, our work lives. Most work is a chain of decisions – a journey of stages that are linked together by decisions between choices for the next stage. Sometimes these choices are suggested and guided by business processes, like choosing between options on a screen. Sometimes they are not, and we first must decide on a short list of options to choose from before we even make a final choice. **Data-driven organisations** use digital data to help people to do this.

What are data-driven organisations?

Data-driven organisations use data to make their decision-making much more systematic and much more detailed (Anderson, 2015; Brynjolfsson and Mcelheran, 2016; Waller, 2020). They do not rely on the individual experience and memory of whoever might have to make the decision – data-driven organisations are led by evidence and analysis not by ad hoc judgement and gut instincts. But they also use the detailed business experience and deep customer knowledge of their staff. They do this by digitally capturing experience and knowledge, and then making it available to other decision-makers who are confronted with similar decisions to make. The sheer size of the datasets that they use mean that they have to use software to look for useful patterns in them. In data-driven organisations it is not just high-level managers that make significant decisions, there are data and decision-making tools available to support other staff as they choose between the options to progress along their own work journeys, options that are too complicated to predefine in business processes models. Finally, data-driven organisations link decision-makers and decision-making together so that decisions are made by the right people and the right groups of people. Good decision-making involves deciding what decisions need to be made, who makes these decisions and how they do it (March, 1994; Buchanan and O'Connell, 2006).

In data-driven organisations most decisions use digital data to generate options to choose from and then they use digital tools to help people to choose from these options. They may have business process models to follow as guides, from procedure manuals, rules of their training or 'frozen' into the software that they use in their jobs. But nothing can be completely foreseen, so non-standard and irregular situations will always come up. People are employed for their ability to make decisions in these circumstances. If all choices and decisions can be foreseen, then a business process can be automated.

Every staff member goes through the journey of a day's work, a week's work or a longer period, and they make decision after decision after decision. In many cases, these decisions cannot be predefined and added into a business process model. Product designers choose between materials for their products; customer service staff choose different suggestions to suit different customers; software developers choose between different features for their code; marketers choose between different communications channels and different content for reaching different customer segments. Our jobs are like any day in the rest of our lives, they are one decision after another.

Data-driven organisations use data to help people to make these decisions by using patterns in that data. This includes patterns that help decision-makers to understand which solutions work best for which problems, and patterns that help decision-makers to define which problem they have in front of them. For example, a pattern that describes a large number of past problems, their solutions and how well each solution worked is useful for choosing solutions to problems, like recording the events of many customer journeys provides a deep understanding of the work-arounds, fixes and tricks that customers use to get the best out of a product. Or a pattern that describes the characteristics of a large number of different problems can be used to classify those problems, which is useful for recognising which problem to solve. An example of this is when firms group together Frequently Asked Questions to provide a quick way to find answers to common customer queries.

Data-driven organisations have six characteristics that we will cover next (Anderson, 2015; Brynjolfsson and Mcelheran, 2016; Waller, 2020):

1   Data-driven organisations collect data – the right data.
2   Data-driven organisations make data useable by all decision-makers – so who is the right decision-maker?
3   Data-driven organisations are a work-in-progress – and it shows.
4   Data-driven organisations are flexible and agile.
5   Data-driven organisations analyse data in different ways and for different reasons.
6   Data-driven organisations use patterns to automate where they can.

Data-driven organisations collect data – the right data

It sounds obvious but using data to make decisions means that data needs to be generated and collected. As more and more business processes and relationships are being digitised, more and more data is being generated, and everything we do online with organisations, and everything that uses software, can be recorded. Any software uses and produces digital data as a fundamental part of how it works, and what we click on in a website, what we tap on in an app, how we use games, spreadsheets and any other software can all be potentially recorded. Data records how we use the websites, apps and other software. Data-driven organisations do not store all of the data that they collect but they do try to keep the parts that they will need. I once had a conversation with a manager who worked for a very large loyalty card programme. Her problem was that she could potentially record every single tap on every single screen for all the millions of the users of her company's loyalty app. She was interested in finding out how to separate the useful data from the useless data. She did not have the space to store it, it would have been much too big, and she knew that she only needed part of that data to help with her decision-making. If it were cheap and easy to collect all the **data exhaust** that customers and other stakeholders generate as they work with an organisation, then that is what organisations would do. But data storage still costs money even if it is much cheaper than it used to be. Also, once it is collected, all that data needs to be filtered and sifted to find the useful information that it contains – not all data is useful and much of the work of data scientists includes filtering out what data is not needed, checking its quality, and getting it ready for analysis. Collecting more data would make this much harder, in fact choosing what data not to record is the first stage in filtering data into useful information (Abbasi et al., 2016).

Also, there will always be a missing piece of the data puzzle and organisations frequently need to get missing data from outside, from third parties. All organisations have a special view of their customers and other stakeholders. Retailers see their customers' shopping lives, hospitals see our health lives, our banks see our financial lives. The data that each organisation has access to only gives it a single viewpoint on our lives. Retailers do not see the details of what happens to us when we visit a hospital, although they may see us preparing to go to visit relatives by buying flowers near the hospital, or they may see us buying prescribed medicines from the retailer's pharmacy after treatment in the hospital. They may even see us buying more and more self-treatment medicines, like pain medication, in the weeks leading up to the hospital visit. But our relationship with a retailer will not generate the sort of detailed diagnosis and treatment data that the hospital and its wider healthcare system has access to. Similarly, a healthcare system does not have access to the details of our long-term diet, even though that might be useful for diagnosis and prevention (Shaw and Allen, 2017). In the same way, our bank will see where we spend our money and when, but it will not have access to the data that describes what we bought, just that we spent a few pounds at the Tesco store near a hospital. Every organisation has access to different data, they each have a different view of our life journeys, depending on what their role in our life is.

This is why organisations share data. They try to fill in the missing pieces of the data puzzle by getting data from other organisations that have a better viewpoint – a complementary perspective – of our lives. For example, retailers are very good at collecting data that describes what we do on their websites and their apps, and even in their stores, but they do not know much of what we do with their competitors, even though it is of great interest to them (Hall et al., 2017). As a result, retailers buy anonymised data from third-party sources like credit card firms because credit card firms see things from a complementary perspective (Helm, 2020).

Data-driven organisations make data useable by all decision-makers

Jad Naous, the VP of Engineering and Product at real-time analytics company Imply, pointed out that everyone is becoming an analyst, what he called an 'operational analyst' (Naous, 2019). Everyone must make decisions in their jobs: no job is completely covered by policies and procedures, or described by a business process model. It is impossible to write software that completely covers all circumstances and situations that come up. Much of our time at work is taken up by following procedures that Jad calls 'rote work'. But as we talked about earlier, there are always a huge number of decisions to be made. Jad gave three examples of how the role of analysis is changing, in its organisational level, its timeliness and in who does the analysis. First, decisions in data-driven organisations are being moved lower and lower down the organisational hierarchy. It used to be that data and analytics were too expensive for anyone but senior management and their own analysts to get hold of. But it has become much cheaper to collect and analyse data, and companies are sharing analytical capabilities with people who work in operational roles rather than only in strategic roles. Second, the timeliness of data analyses has gone from initiating special projects where data is taken away and processed to continuous analysis located near to where that data is created. Third, the availability of easy-to-use cloud software means that data analysis can be done by whoever does the job and needs to make the decision, rather than a specialist.

But if everyone is an analyst, then how can an organisation pick the right person to make a decision? Data-driven organisations make full use of cloud computing technologies for their data storage and data processing needs. So, anyone with an Internet connection can have access to the data and the analysis tools needed to make a decision, and a decision-maker can be located anywhere. If anyone in a retail firm has access to customer data, then which decisions should store managers make and which decisions should be made at headquarters? Like any models, business process models let us look at what is modelled and evaluate it. Models are simplified views of the thing that is modelled, they let us play around with whatever we model, and potentially reengineer and redesign it. In this case business process models help us to think about the organisational structure in terms of what decisions are made and who makes them. Business process models, together with VFA models, also help us to think about splitting up organisations and combining them with other organisations or working with external partner organisations in ecosystems (see Chapter 7).

In terms of the structure of an organisation – who has the power to make which decisions – we can use the characteristics of the decision itself to help us pick the decision-maker. Decision characteristics are important aspects of the decision, which help to filter out some potential decision-makers and point to others. They help us to define what capabilities and resources the right decision-maker will need to make a specific decision (Table 6.2). Some decisions are defined by their spatial effect, or the level of their consequences, for example, decisions that cover large geographical areas, or decisions that apply to many organisational levels. Some decisions need a specific skill set like engineering or medical training. Sometimes the key characteristic for handling a decision well is a strong relationship with the key stakeholders involved in the decision – who understands these customers well? Who will act on the decisions? Sometimes the timescale is important, for example, decisions that must be made quickly, or decisions that need a very long-term view, like planting forests. Lastly, it may be that the responsibility for a decision or the effects of that decision already forms part of someone's role. If someone is formally responsible or accountable, either in law or in their contract of employment, then they will need to agree to how a decision is made even if they do not suggest it or even make it themselves.

Table 6.2   The key characteristics of different decisions

Decision characteristic	Examples
Level, scale and focus of the decision's effects and actions	Strategic, operational, or a specific organisational focus
Skillset required	Finance, engineering, legal or another skillset
Key relationships required	User relationships, ecosystem partners, other information sources or action capabilities
Timeliness of response required	Real-time analysis, frequent checks, immediate response, occasional, triggered by specific events, recurring pattern
Responsibility or accountability assigned	Legal or contractual requirement

Adapted from conversations with organisations

The best person to make a decision is not necessarily the person who is paid to take responsibility, like senior management. Maybe their responsibility is actually to recruit, train and empower the right person to make the decision. Neither is it necessarily correct to say that customers should make the key decisions. Self-service has its advantages, but customers do not always know all the options that are available. They certainly do not know about all the customers that have made the same decisions in the past, or how those decisions turned out. If we think of decisions as assembling options to choose from and then choosing from them, then the best person to make a decision is the person or group of people who can do that the best. This will be the person with the 'big picture', which is the best view of the problem, the options to be chosen from and their consequences. It's important to be aware, however, that decision-making is not just a simple process of assembling options and then choosing between them – real-life decision-making is much messier and much more complicated. There are many ways of thinking about decision-making including:

- An overall movement along a route from defining a problem, to diagnosing the issue, to deciding and then designing a chosen solution and its components.
- Cycling backwards and forwards along a route that re-examines past decisions before finally passing points that cannot be gone back on, like the purchasing stage of the Customer Decision Journey model (see Chapter 4).
- Seeing the whole of the problem and chosen solution as one system that fits together well.
- Experimentation — trying options to test them out and see if they work or if they suggest other options (Mintzberg et al., 1976; Mintzberg and Westley, 2001).

Ultimately a decision-maker must choose an option to solve a problem and those options must come from somewhere. In this book, the metaphor of the 'big picture' is used to explain how this relates to using data analytics technologies to make decisions. Having the 'big picture' means not just 'seeing' but 'understanding'. Seeing the whole problem and its context, the whole situation. This might involve understanding how a project or a customer got into the situation that needs fixing. Seeing the 'big picture' means having access to a broad range of alternative choices that fit the specific decisions to be made and understanding the implications and knock-on effects of each, such as the costs and consequences of alternative solutions and how each might work out, with different future benefits and risks. In Journey-based Thinking terms, understanding the big picture includes the backstories of the stakeholders that the decision concerns, the full range of options to choose from and the downstream consequences of each option (Shaw et al., 2019). Depending on the decision to be made, the big picture might include the full situation a customer is in, knowledge of a user's personal perspective or the context of a company strategy. In other words, it means having a 'broad perspective' as well as the 'long view'. For example, a drink might sell poorly in one country because of cultural barriers, but the Sales Manager of another country might see the same drink as an obvious winner because she knows her country will love it. Imagine a production bottleneck that limits a factory's output, like a loading dock that has a maximum throughput for taking finished products away. What if the logistics manager knows that further down the supply chain there is a limit on what can be transported from the factory, for example a weigh bridge that all vehicles have to be weighed on before they leave the manufacturing site? If the throughput of the weigh bridge is greater than that of the loading dock, then it makes sense to increase the throughput of the loading dock. The downstream weigh bridge will block any increased throughput from the upstream loading dock.

The 'big picture' idea applies to all stakeholders, even decision-makers outside an organisation. It can even be provided as a service. For example, if a customer looks at flights in a selection on an airline's website, then is the customer the best person to make the decisions? Especially if they decide without knowing about similar flights on other airlines' websites. Comparison sites offer a big picture as a service to their users. For example, Expedia and Skyscanner give travellers this sort of big picture, Google Shopping allows you to compare similar products, and Compare The Market does this for insurance products.

Data-driven organisations are a work-in-progress – and it shows

Not many organisations are like Google, Amazon and Facebook who have been around for some time but who embraced the systematic use of data in making decisions right from the start. The technological capabilities that enable data-driven organisations are relatively new, so most data-driven organisations are either new start-ups or starting to become data-driven. These organisations provide us with lessons in how to turn into a data-driven organisation as well as how to behave like one.

The digital technologies that data-driven organisations rely on are still evolving, and for organisations that are becoming data-driven these technologies are still in the process of being adopted. For example, marketing departments were early adopters of methods for targeting customers using loyalty card data: finance departments have a long history of using financial and accounting data and this provided a firm foundation for increasing their data gathering and analysis activities. Strategy departments have always looked for data from company-wide IT systems and external market analysis firms. Also, manufacturing organisations such as Motorola used **continuous improvement** approaches like Six Sigma since the 1980s. But other parts of organisations like human resources departments have been slower to make data-driven decisions a normal part of hiring talent, performance assessment, people development and workforce management – although that is now changing (Ferrar and Green, 2021; Green, 2021). Even the wholescale digitisation of factories as part of **Industry 4.0** is still developing and spreading through manufacturing organisations (see Chapter 9). Most organisations are just starting their journey to becoming more data-driven (Waller, 2020).

First, organisations must prioritise where they use a data-driven approach. Businesses should not try to record and analyse everything; it is best to focus on a few key areas that can be showcased as quick wins to generate support and momentum. Sometimes the first data to collect is the data that will help you prioritise where to collect data. Okay, that sounds strange. But think about it – if an organisation is going to change to being data-driven, systematic, analytical and automated, then shouldn't this also apply to how it makes that change? The way to prioritise is to go back to an organisation's business model, the fundamental description of how it generates value (see Chapter 5). Some organisations just focus on customers and how to make customer journeys into the smoothest, fastest, cheapest and most amazing experiences possible (see Chapter 4). If frictionless customer journeys are the thing that is holding an organisation's business model back, then that is the place to start. But it depends on the business model. Some organisations might prioritise other stakeholders and their work journeys; some organisations might prioritise using data analytics to help retain high quality employees as well as customers.

Start by looking at your business model: is there something that is slowing how it functions? Or could something be freed up to make it generate more value? For example, some organisations make detailed **customer journey models** and rank the top ten problems that customers face after they purchase. Other organisations have already got great customer satisfaction scores, but they need more customers, so they prioritise the places where they lose potential customers before they complete the purchase stage of the Customer Buying Process model. In both cases, investigating the top ten reasons for losing potential customers, or for not getting them in the first place, generates evidence to decide which specific problems to tackle first. It does not have to be ten problems, just enough to know that the most important issues are included when the data is collected, and each issue is ranked. Some organisations study their business model and see that other stakeholders are their weak spot. For example, many organisations who are considering a data-driven approach realise that they do not have the right mix of analytical skills and data science skills (Marr 2020; Moritz and Zahidi, 2021). And some organisations see gaps in their suppliers or other organisations that are part of their ecosystem (see Chapter 7).

However, there is an even easier way to prioritise where to start being data-driven. If you are stuck, maybe because your job does not contain any of the above stakeholders or issues, then think about what matters in your role. How does your role help the functioning of the organisation's business model? Focus on that and ask yourself the questions:

1   What is going badly? Where is the waste, the errors, and the problems?
2   What could go better?

If you know the job well then just have a think and ask yourself these questions. If you are just starting a job or if you don't work in the part of the organisation that you are analysing then ask the people who do – especially internal customers, the people who work downstream in the same business processes. Start with a qualitative analysis and let that focus your quantitative analysis by telling you where to collect data. Collecting data helps you to understand what the top ten priorities are. Before you start counting you need to know what to count. The key is to use the organisation's business model to measure things and then to use these measurements to prioritise what to do. Chapter 10 will explain how you can use this mixture of qualitative analysis and quantitative analysis in a cycle to prioritise, plan and then execute a data and decision-making strategy.

Second, data analysts need to be fully connected to the rest of the organisation, they can't be isolated in a lab somewhere. All analysts need to understand what they are analysing to see opportunities to be analysed and to understand the context of their analysis. A key skill that sets **data scientists** apart from regular analysts is their mixture of business knowledge, mathematical and coding skills. Understanding and communicating with the business that they are analysing is hugely important for noticing what should be analysed and understanding how to analyse it, sense-checking their results, and finally explaining results to decision makers (Bowne-Anderson, 2018). We have already covered how data driven organisations prioritise where they start to collect and use digital data. But acting on those priorities requires a good understanding of how the business works or at least a rich set of collaborators who will provide that knowledge when asked. Understanding how the business works provides context, like the background and foreground in a photograph tells you the heights of the people in it. Understanding the context of a problem or opportunity, the business situation it is in, or the wider business process that it is a part of is critical for understanding why an analysis is worth doing in the first place. It is also required for evaluating the results when they are produced. For example, an analysis of a market might divide customers up into several segments. Some segments will be richer and more numerous than others, but they are not necessarily the ones to target first. A detailed understanding of how an organisation would go about reaching these different groups of people and providing exactly what they need might highlight some customer segments that are rich but inherently unattractive, perhaps because they are fussy and return most of the things they buy, or because they are expensive to deliver to. It's important to sense-check the answers an analysis provides in order to avoid errors. Sense-checking against actual business situations is also a valuable quality management skill for all stages of the analysis process.

Connecting a data analysis with the wider organisation provides an inbuilt sense-checking capability from before an analysis project starts, all the way through to when it generates insights and starts a new analysis cycle. The way to do this is to bring the data scientists closer to the part of the organisation that they are analysing. This includes:

1   Physically locating analysts in the same offices and buildings as other departments.
2   Rotating analysts through different departments if they are few in number.
3   Giving managers a much greater awareness of what is being done by data-driven firms in their industries and in their organisational functions.
4   Upskilling normal business analysts with more sophisticated data science skills such as more powerful AI analysis tools and an overall awareness of **data strategy**.

One new job role that data-driven organisations are using more of are '**analytics translators**'. These are different to normal business analysts. An analytics translator is the bridge between the hard-core data scientists and the rest of the business. This is sometimes called having a 'light quant' or a 'translation layer' in a business (SAS, 2011; Davenport, 2015). Analytics translators have the business understanding to see where the tools of data science can be used in a firm as well as the ability to communicate and explain it to all the relevant stakeholders (Shaw, D.R., 2018). Successful analytics projects are made up of lots of different skill sets and business functions. The wider the impact of any project, the more people you need to get engaged. There is a need for a role that bridges data scientists and the rest of the business. The work of analytics translators includes:

1   Noticing where data analytics could help the organisation.
2   Prioritising ideas for data science projects.
3   Writing the business case to assess the benefits versus the costs required.
4   Explaining the project to data scientists, how the technical requirements support the business requirements.
5   Keeping the project moving, for example, navigating unforeseen blind alleys and unexpected opportunities.
6   Selling the project outputs, for example, insights for better decisions and actions.
7   Implementing the analytical recommendations of the project (Henke et al., 2018).

These tasks need someone who really understands the organisation and its stakeholders. Someone who knows how data generates value through better business decisions, and who knows the right people to convince and to get involved. Someone who can explain the technical side as well as the business side. Finding a data scientist with all these communications and people skills, a deep business knowledge and an entrepreneurial imagination is rare.

There are examples from shared service organisational models that suggest how to connect data analytics to the rest of the organisation. Shared service models are a very common way of organising Human Resources (HR) departments and other support functions, like Finance and Procurement, especially in large or international organisations. Shared service models are when a business function is organised so that it is not spread out across an organisation but instead concentrated in a central place whilst still keeping some people locally within the offices it supports. For example, an organisation that has local HR departments in each country, city or factory that it operates. These 'satellite' HR staff based in local departments avoid cutting the HR department off from the rest of the organisation and the knowledge of how it functions (CIPD, 2021).

Data-driven organisations are flexible and agile

If all types of decisions can potentially be supported by digital data and digital decision-making tools, then what happens when situations change? Every decision depends on the situation that the decision is made in, the context of the problem and the circumstances of the analysis. But these things change all the time. Customers, staff, and other stakeholders change, what might be a problem for one customer might be an attractive benefit for another. Some customers like the simplicity of a basic product design and some have more specialised needs; some customers will find a store's location easy to travel to and some will not. Every customer is different – a solution for one customer might not fit the tastes of another. Even a single customer buys different things on different visits to a store or a website. Once a customer's initial needs are satisfied, they will need something else, and then something else and so on. If I'm thirsty then I'll need a coffee, but straight afterwards I will not need a coffee. I will need something else. It is the same with all stakeholders, as they progress along their life journeys. The problems, needs, opportunities and decisions that occur will change. It is also the same with analytics projects.

Data analyses start with high priority problems then look for lower priority problems. First, they solve the most frequent and damaging problems in customer journeys then they move on to the others. In manufacturing and other processes, it is the same, once one bottleneck is removed the next bottleneck becomes the problem. There is always another bottleneck. Also, the world keeps changing, competitors change their products, customers have different events in their lives that change their values and needs. Staff also have events and business partners change their strategies. When situations change then either the data that describes the situation must also change, or the wrong decisions will be made. Data-driven organisations avoid this by using **real-time data**, by continuous improvement and by **agile management techniques**.

Real-time data is a 'live' recording of whatever it is that needs to be analysed. It enables timely actions from analysing the data and it avoids missing important information. It does not have to be a second-by-second recoding, it could be just the contents of a shopper's basket every time they visited a store, or the number of products that a factory produces per day. It could be monthly, weekly, daily, hourly or every nanosecond. The data frequency depends on the purpose of the analysis. Gathering data at a much greater frequency than the events that you are analysing is a waste of data storage space. Gathering data at less than the frequency of what you are analysing will risk missing what happens, like when you zoom in on a Google Maps satellite image and eventually the picture you are looking at becomes too blurred to understand. Gathering data at too low a frequency can also give the wrong impression, like when old black and white films make wagon wheels appear to spin backwards because the frame rate of the film camera is too low to capture all the positions of the wheels. The granularity of the data must be slightly smaller than the insights that the analyst is looking for. A faster film speed would show the wheels in enough positions to show them spinning forwards. If the purpose of the analysis is to understand something that changes every millisecond, then to capture any changes, data needs to be recorded at a frequency that is higher than a thousand times a second. An example of this is how driverless car systems like the Waymo Driver use cameras and other sensors to monitor the road ahead on a continuous basis (Waymo, 2021). As long as the data is updated frequently enough to be relevant, like for spotting obstacles, and there is enough time to analyse that data and act on it, then the data is real-time enough.

Continuous improvement is a characteristic of organisations where most of the staff and other stake-holders believe in and aim for improvement in all that the organisation does. They see every business process as something that can be made better, not just once but again and again and again in continuous improvement loops. These are **cybernetic loops** that try an improvement, measure the consequences, analyse the results, and then repeat the loop (Beer, 1979). Like a driverless car continuously scanning the road ahead in the example above, or like the Open Systems Change (OSC) model in Chapter 3. Improvements are usually in small increments, like reducing substandard products on an assembly line by fractions of a percentage, but sometimes they make large leaps as well. Continuous improvement projects aim to make products, services and the business processes that produce them work faster, cheaper, better and with less errors.

Data-driven continuous improvement has its roots in techniques like Kaizen, the Japanese manufacturing strategy (Varian, 2007) and it is based around repeating cycles of data capture, data analysis and improvement. One example of a data-driven continuous improvement approach is A/B testing. A/B testing compares small changes to web pages, other services and even products, to see which work the best (Kohavi and Thomke, 2017; Thomke, 2020). A common example of A/B testing is when one part of a web page needs to be improved. For example, the size or colour of a 'click here to buy' button. Different visitors to a web page see different versions of the button at random until statistically enough people have seen each version of the button for it to be clear which design is best at getting them to buy. Website visitors work well for A/B testing because there is a vast stream of them for many small page design changes to be tested on. But A/B testing can also work for testing any changes where there are enough chances to statistically test them like web pages, all cloud-based digital services and any mobile app. These examples are all connected to the company that provides them by the Internet or a phone network, so the results of the small test changes can be recorded, then further changes can be made and tested. Think of all the changes that are made to free browser games to gradually polish them and improve their usability and attractiveness so that users will click on the premium version button or buy in-game upgrades. This is not so different to the market researchers that ask viewers of long-running TV soaps for feedback every week. For decades, feedback from large numbers of viewers has been used to guide teams of script writers as they work on next week's episode and longer story arcs.

A/B testing is a type of business experiment, which has its roots in a range of methods developed in the second half of the 20th century (Taguchi and Yokoyama, 1994). These methods were part of the Total Quality revolution that used statistics to improve product manufacturing quality, and which included Six Sigma approaches. Taguchi and others developed ways of designing experiments for systematically and efficiently testing out innovative ideas for improving product and service designs, or for reducing waste and errors in production processes. Testing out ideas costs time and money; there is always a risk of failure with complicated business processes. Smart business experiments used the increasing availability of data to run more experiments, faster and in a cheaper and more automatic way (Davenport, 2009). An example might be using slightly different subject lines on email marketing campaigns. If thousands of people receive emails in a short time period, then varying the email lets organisations test different versions and see how well they work. LinkedIn tries hundreds of experiments a day and companies like Etsy run dozens of experiments at the same time (Anderson, 2015). These two examples are online, so the experimenter gets fast feedback data about how people react to different designs of email subject lines or web pages. The process of doing the experiments like these can also be automated. The fast availability of feedback data and automating the tests make it quick and easy to test intuitive ideas as well as to systematically check a wider range of designs.

Agile management techniques are a way of managing people and processes to take advantage of new information. Frequent feedback from tests, checks, measurements and other data provides opportunities to make changes to how an organisation does things. Things like product and service design, or the design of business process models and business models. But frequent feedback would be wasted if the organisation could not change fast enough to use such insights (Saha et al., 2020). So, the organisation of data-driven organisations must itself be agile. Agile management techniques originally came from agile software development practices that use frequent user feedback to continuously improve the design of software, and agile software development practices themselves had their roots in the agile and lean manufacturing practices of the late 20th century (Desouza, 2006). Agile management techniques moved the focus from software development to product and service development and then to all aspects of what organisations do. Agile management principles include:

- Focusing on what the user needs – the user journey, where a user is any type of stakeholder.
- Forming highly autonomous teams – where decisions are fast and frequent because they are made by the team rather than at higher levels of the organisation.
- Forming cross-functional teams – the required knowledge is available for decisions.
- Having a single product owner to decide its features – including all the associated services that are needed.
- Very frequent meetings in a daily 'scrum' – where a team is regularly coordinated and updated, and problems are decided on.
- Focused bursts of work called 'sprints' – where the results of the last feedback data are acted on, e.g., weekly.
- Starting with a Minimum Viable Product – where the first version of the product is just good enough to ship out for users to give feedback data on, and to start the cybernetic cycle.
- Focusing on task priorities, called a 'backlog', rather than a timetable of tasks – because tasks and their order will always change after feedback from users.

These principles work best for iterative improvements, where small improvements come in a continuous stream. Large improvements to the design of products, services and processes will be split up into multiple teams, which slows the improvement cycle, or they just cannot be physically changed fast enough. For example, building a factory takes too long to be done in an agile way, at the level of the whole building project. But redesigning, testing and refining the products that the factory makes can be agile if the machines that make the parts of the product can be adjusted quickly enough. It could be said that slower and longer timescale projects are naturally agile because they happen slowly enough for us to act on them as they happen. Like a crane moving a giant steel girder, if it moves slowly and frequent position checks make targeting adjustments quite easy, although the girder is only placed once. Even if you only do something once it might be slow enough to get it exactly right, if you can make corrections. With data-driven organisations, it is now becoming possible for faster and shorter timescale activities to be agile because feedback data is becoming available soon enough, and agile management practices help companies act on that data fast enough to make a difference.

Data-driven organisations analyse data in different ways

Data can be analysed in many ways for many different purposes. Table 6.3 divides these into five fundamental uses of data based upon how it is used in information systems. These are sometimes listed as descriptive, diagnostic, predictive, and prescriptive uses of data (Wedel and Kannan, 2016).

Table 6.3   Five fundamental uses of data

Use of data	How this use is different from the others
I Analysis	Describes 'what is'.
	Data divides up what is recorded and only describes it, no causal relationships (like X caused Y) and no predictions are made.
II Explanation	Describes 'what is', 'how' this is so, 'when' it occurs and 'where'.
	Explains but does not predict what will happen.
III Prediction	Describes 'what is' there now and 'what will be' there.
	Predicts what will happen but does not give well-developed explanations of causes to justify itself.
IV Explanation and prediction	Describes 'what is' there, 'how' this is so, and 'why', plus 'what will happen', 'when' it will happen and 'where'.
	Predicts what will happen and explains the causes.
V Design and action	Describes 'how to do something'.
	Provides explicit instructions (e.g., methods, techniques, instructions) for doing something.

Adapted from Gregor's taxonomy of theory types in IS research (2006)

The above uses of data lead data-driven organisations to package their analyses in different ways. Here are some ways that the outputs and insights from analyses can be used. They were originally suggested by Jim Davis, the senior vice president and chief marketing officer of SAS (Harris and Davenport, 2017). Davis suggested:

- *Basic standard reports* – regular descriptions of what happened in a factory, in a department, to customers, or with a business process, e.g., performance of assembly lines or teams of sales people.
- *Ad hoc reports* – special one-time reports describing specific aspects of what happened in more detail and in ways that fit the needs of the person who asked for the report, e.g., performance of assembly lines or teams in specific situations, which might help diagnose causes of current problems.
- *Query drill down reports* – special reports that look deeper into an issue by going into lower levels of data, which has been aggregated, e.g., dividing regional-level sales figures for retailers like Starbucks or McDonalds into individual restaurant-level figures to find out which restaurants performed the best and worst.

- *Alerts* – notifications of events that will happen and actions that need to be taken when they do, e.g., prompts to buy more mobile phone data just before it runs out or reminders of meetings in a calendar.
- *Statistical analysis* – descriptions of what has happened in a wider population based on a statistical analysis of a sample. Statistics are used to get the 'big picture' even when you only have data on part of the populations analysed, e.g., understanding what most customers think of a product based on feedback from a much smaller number of customers than the total.
- *Forecasting and predictive modelling* – descriptions of what will probably happen using probability and statistical model techniques, e.g., when Amazon and other firms predict what customers will order so they can have products ready in stock.
- *Optimisation* – descriptions of a range of options for changing things that show the benefits and drawbacks of each, e.g., the costs and benefits of a range of product innovation options.

Data-driven organisations use patterns to automate where they can

If all the rules that describe how a business process will turn out can be written down in some sort of pattern, then that business process can potentially be automated – patterns like a recipe for baking a cake, a flow chart for replacing a vacuum cleaner's filter, or instructions for assembling a LEGO® model. If you can completely describe the decisions that need to be made in the business process that produces a product – or that provides a service – then this description can be turned into software. The only two reasons for having a manual process are that either the process has a real-world activity that cannot be controlled by software, or the decisions that need to be made in the process are too complicated to completely describe beforehand. Software control can be divided into inputs and outputs, and we can study this in terms of three problems. The first two problems are problems with the software itself. Software needs digital information as an input to make decisions and it needs the ability to act on those decisions as an output. The physical world and the software world need to join somehow. The third problem is that the decisions themselves need to be completely described within that software for it to make those decisions.

Let's look at the first problem: automation software needs digital data to make decisions. It used to be that most of the work that organisations did was paper based. Automating this work would have meant turning all that paper into digital datasets. But now, everything that we do online, on our phones, tablets and laptops, anything that we already use software to accomplish is already digitised. There are problems associated with connecting different software systems together but over the last few decades most work in organisations, most of their business processes, has gone from being paper based to software based. Software automatically produces data that records how it has operated. So, any downstream activities can benefit from upstream digitisation by learning from this recording. Furthermore, many new types of sensors and other data sources provide descriptions that paint extremely rich data pictures of the business processes that need to be automated. For example, an Internet of Things refrigerator can collect temperature data and other information about how it is used every day, and millions of phones with atmospheric pressure sensors can provide highly granular pressure data, across a huge area and in real-time (BBC, 2019).

The second problem is that automation software needs the ability to act on these decisions. Data is required to make a decision but then the decision needs to be acted on, the software needs to control an 'actuator'. Sensors sense things and actuators do things: lights light up, displays show words and pictures, motors move things and buzzers make a noise. Even if the action is just to notify a human customer or call centre operator, the software must be able to act. Here again the digitisation of our work lives and personal lives enables actuators to do what is required. Software notifications that use emails and messages are now easy to make because we work in online environments. We receive emails from human colleagues and automatic emails can also be sent by software, like out of office replies. Other online environments such as collaboration tools like Slack and Trello or meeting tools like Zoom, Skype and Microsoft Teams are naturally accessible to software because they are themselves software that are connected to the Web. Separate software systems must be able to work together but the basic problem of giving software the ability to act is solved in online environments because everything is already connected. Other solutions to this connection problem include the common use of devices like phones and tablets, which connect people to online environments wherever they are and whatever they are doing. But the most important step forward in giving automation software the ability to act is the recent huge increase in software's capability to deal with complicated decisions.

The third problem is that the decisions themselves need to be completely described within that software for it to make those decisions. The software needs to contain a pattern that describes most if not all the decisions that will be needed. Decisions about which option to choose in each situation, for most situations that are likely to occur. No automation software can deal with all the situations that will occur; it just needs to cover enough to be useful. Similarly, the resource limitations of organisations mean that there will be options that organisations choose not to offer in certain situations, because it would be too expensive to do so. These need to be made by the software developers after consulting relevant experts in other parts of the organisation. They are the equivalent of limiting a new car to a specific range of colours to reduce costs or making deliveries only at certain times of the day, and to certain places. As we will see in Chapter 10, very often data can be analysed to find a useful pattern that helps with both types of decisions, which option to take and which options to offer. For example, product and service options for a customer to choose from, or options for a product designer to offer or not offer. Patterns that tell us which option to take in each situation would include information that links the characteristics of a single customer with the product that they are likely to prefer. This pattern could be used to make product recommendations to that customer. Patterns that tell us which options to offer for all situations and all customers would include information that describes all potential customers and the profitability of separate subgroups. Here the pattern shows the financial outcome of targeting different subgroups. Ways of using the patterns that are contained in data will be explored in more detail in Chapter 10.

Automating how people and machines work together

Marc Andreessen was the co-builder of Netscape, one of the first web browsers, and an early investor in Skype, Facebook, Twitter, Zynga, Foursquare and many other famous organisations. He once said that 'software is eating the world' (Andreessen, 2011). What he meant was that most of the tasks that people do are either becoming substantially automated by software or organised by it. These tasks include decision-making, business process activities, service production and managing relationships between team members or with external partner organisations. Coding tasks into software makes them more flexible and easier to record as data, and this data can in turn be analysed to learn how to improve how the tasks are done. For example, if a set of tasks never changes, like the recipe for a meal, then it is relatively easy to code the instructions into software and automate the process. 'Do this, then this, then this'… and so on. The series of tasks involved, i.e., the flow of work or 'workflow', can be organised by special workflow software. Workflow automation software such as Monday or Zapier acts like a project manager and initiates tasks by people or by other software. Then it monitors the completion of the tasks (Monday, 2021; Zapier, 2021) (see Chapter 8). Robotic Process Automation (RPA) is a related type of automation software. RPA is different workflow automation: there is some overlap, but RPA automates individual human activities, whereas workflow automation strings together the activities done by humans or software.

RPA carries out routine tasks like simple responses to emails or typing a password and getting information from a system, or anything that can be fully described by simple rules (Boulton, 2018). For example, UiPath's RPA technology reads text and images that human workers would see on screen and uses computer vision and other technologies like speech recognition to operate the software in the place of a person. This includes reading documents and operating the other software applications that people would use if they were doing it (Gross, 2019). Other RPA suppliers include Automation Anywhere, Blue Prism and many more (Gartner, 2021). RPA tools commonly learn to operate software by watching humans do it. They learn by observing the software's graphical user interface using 'screen scraping', and by monitoring how users' use their mice and keyboards (Lhuer, 2016). One of the advantages of RPA is that it replaces human labour costs and avoids human error in a top-down way. But RPA bots only replace some of the human parts of a job. The original software applications and IT systems that the people used remain where they are. This avoids the detail and costs of a full software development project to automate the job from the bottom-up, by writing software to do everything from scratch. However, RPA project implementations can run into various types of difficulties including finding that the work required is not as standardised and simple as first thought. Also, if the information inputs and tasks that the RPA bots deal with need to change then it can be costly to retrain the RPA bots. Other difficulties include problems with staff getting used to working with bots, and when the fraction of tasks that are simple enough to be automated using RPA is much smaller than originally thought (Edlich and Sohoni, 2017).

Chapter summary

The structure of an organisation is based on who makes which decisions and this is changing as more people in organisations get access to more information and more decision-making tools. It is changing from being top-down, internal and centralised to being more distributed, which means that decisions can be made by lower levels of staff and external people, like customers. These decisions include not just the initial design of business processes but the decisions that must be made each time a business process is acted out.

Organisations are becoming more data-driven. More people have access to the information needed to make the best decisions, and that information is being used in different ways. Data-driven organisations use data and decision-supporting technologies to make decisions in much more systematic, informed and detailed ways than in the past. They use agile management techniques and digital collaboration technologies to be able to act on these decisions in a timely and flexible manner. Data-driven organisations also automate more decision-making processes using patterns that they find in data.

Further reading

Beer, S. (1979) *The Heart of Enterprise*. New Jersey: John Wiley & Sons Ltd.

Hammer, M. and Champy, J. (1993) *Reengineering the Corporation: A Manifesto for Business Revolution*. New York: Harper Business.

Marr, B. (2020) 'The future of jobs and education', Forbes. https://www.forbes.com/sites/bernardmarr/2020/12/11/the-future-of-jobs-and-education (accessed 8 April 2022).

Mintzberg, H., Raisinghani, D. and Theoret, A. (1976) 'The structure of "unstructured" decision processes', *Administrative Science Quarterly*, 246–275.

Mintzberg, H. and Westley, F. (2001) 'Decision making: it's not what you think', in P.C. Nutt and D.C. Wilson (eds.) (2010) *Handbook of Decision Making*, New Jersey: John Wiley & Sons.

Moritz, R.E. and Zahidi, S. (2021) 'Upskilling for shared prosperity', World Economic Forum and PWC. https://www.pwc.com/gx/en/issues/upskilling/shared-prosperity/upskilling_for_shared_prosperity_final.pdf (accessed 8 April 2022).

7

HOW TO BUILD AND GOVERN A BUSINESS ECOSYSTEM

KEY IDEAS

- Business ecosystems are collections of stakeholders including separate organisations and individuals that work together to mutually create value for each other.
- A business ecosystem's information platform enables its stakeholders to work together by letting them share information and capabilities.
- Supply chains mostly move and transform materials, information and other resources in a single direction towards a single group of consumers. Business ecosystems include supply chains, but they move resources in all directions and between all stakeholders.
- An ecosystem's business model describes the roles and contributions of the ecosystem's stakeholders, like an organisations business model does.
- An orchestrator is the organisation that controls the ecosystem's platform. The platform enables the orchestrator to form a 'big picture' of how all stakeholders work together.
- A 'big picture' enables an orchestrator to influence all stakeholders that have access to less information. It does this by selectively recommending useful options that support the ecosystem's business model.

LEARNING OBJECTIVES

After reading this chapter you will be able to:

- Describe the challenges and opportunities that business ecosystems present to the organisations in them.
- Explain the difference between the business model of an ecosystem and the business model of a single organisation.
- Define what an ecosystem orchestrator is and explain its role.
- Explain why ecosystems rely on information sharing platforms.
- Describe how ecosystem platforms generate complexity for ecosystem orchestrators.
- Explain how ecosystem orchestrators deal with complexity in their ecosystems.
- Explain how ecosystem orchestrators influence their ecosystem's stakeholders even when they do not own them.
- Describe how an ecosystem orchestrator finds, persuades and recruits new organisations to its ecosystem.

This chapter explains how some organisations are starting to work with other organisations in business ecosystems by using emerging data technologies. Business ecosystems are diverse collections of separate organisations, which work together to share resources and capabilities on a vast scale that crosses the boundaries between industry sectors. Business ecosystems include supply chains but are different to them. Each business ecosystem's information platform enables organisations to work together by sharing information and capabilities, which supports the ecosystem's business model.

This chapter describes the role of an ecosystem orchestrator in building and managing ecosystems. This is the organisation that controls the ecosystem's platform, which enables it to influence the whole ecosystem without directly owning any of the organisations in it.

What is a business ecosystem?

The last few chapters have focused mainly on how an organisation's stakeholders work together to support a business model. In this chapter we go up a level and look at whole business ecosystems. These include lots of organisations' business models and how they operate together in an ecosystem (Figure 7.1). As with any system you can always go up a level and down a level. Organisations have business models, and so do departments, teams, individual people and products. Every ecosystem also has a business model to describe how it creates value for its stakeholders, and why this keeps on working.

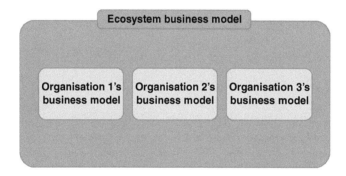

Figure 7.1   An ecosystem's business model includes the business models of the organisations in it

Natural ecosystems and business ecosystems

Usually, we talk about an ecosystem of organisations, but the ideas in this section can also be applied to all levels of analysis. It depends on what you are focusing on. It is easy to see the separate parts of an ecosystem when it is big enough to include supply chains in different industries, rather than when an ecosystem is made from people in a single department, or an ecosystem of one person and their immediate colleagues. All these levels of analysis are systems and if that system sustains itself by mutually satisfying its stakeholders with what they require, then it is an ecosystem.

One idea from the researchers into natural ecosystems is that ecosystems are recycling pathways for scarce resources, like nutrients and energy (Shaw and Allen, 2017). For example, rainforests seem to be wet and full of rich collections of nutrients, but actually, they just recirculate nutrients really efficiently. The daily rain showers in a rainforest reuse water from past rain showers. Water and other nutrients are passed from one organism to another in circular pathways that recirculate them (see Figure 7.2). This is why when an area of rainforest is cut down it frequently turns into savannah or desert. If you break the cycle, then the water and nutrients are lost – water drains off and valuable nutrients are lost as top soil blows away. The recirculation pathways are made up of interlinked chains of organisms just following the 'business models' of their genomes. For example, in Figure 7.2 worms convert fallen leaves into poo and the nutrients in the poo are eventually drawn back into the tree with the help of fungi. The worms, the fungi and the tree are individually just doing the 'job' that is programmed into their genome, but together they process nutrients and move them back to the tree for reuse. This natural ecosystem consists of the pathway from one organism to another and back to the tree. It is the circular pathway that is the ecosystem not the individual worms or trees. Organisms can even be swapped out for alternative species if they perform a similar enough role. What counts is that they perform their role in the ecosystem's circular pathway.

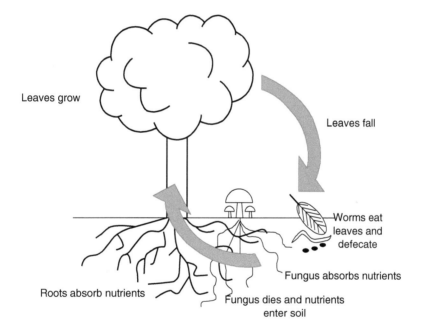

Figure 7.2   Example of an ecosystem's circular pathway

Adapted from Shaw and Allen, 2017

For organisations the implications of recycling a scarce resource are huge. Any organisation is limited by some scarce resource that limits its business model and forces it to operate at no more than the maximum that the availability of that resource permits. For example, the availability of batteries limits the supply of electric vehicles even though the demand from customers is much higher (Kobie, 2020). Or the limit might be some other business variable like a global shortage of computer chips (Sweney, 2021), just plain old customer demand or lack of fuel. All business models run at their maximum until they hit a limit, just like any other system. If firms can extend that limit by reusing and recycling the limiting resource, then they can increase the value that the business model creates. Part of the reason that organisations are starting to form business ecosystems is because they enable them to reuse resources that limit their business model.

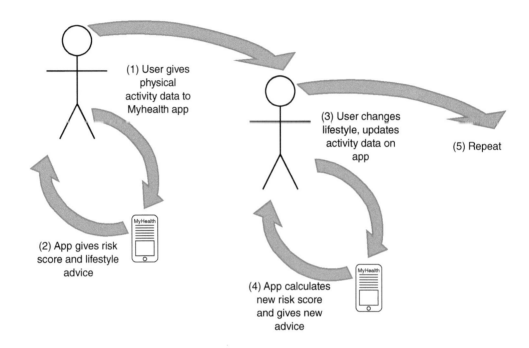

Figure 7.3   Reusing scarce customer attention by continuing to be useful

Based on Shaw and Allen, 2017

For example, many thousands of organisations compete for the scarce resource of customers' attention. In the research on innovation ecosystems, the example of a health app illustrates this (Shaw and Allen, 2017). The app provides a free risk score for several major diseases based on some simple health questions that the user answers (see Figure 7.3). But as well as a risk score it also gives the user some advice about lifestyle that they can follow before it recalculates their risk score. The benefit to the user is that they might reduce their risk of some major diseases if they follow the advice, which encourages them to keep using the app. In this example the app recycles the attention of the user. The benefit to the app company is that each time they use the app they contribute more data, and they make themselves available for more advice – including marketing messages or health improvement advice – both of which might benefit other ecosystem stakeholders such as advertising firms, brands that provide health related products and services, or government health agencies that wish to promote more healthy lifestyles or gather data on users' lifestyles.

You can see examples of the development of recirculation ecosystems in the circular economy strategies promoted by the Ellen MacArthur Foundation (EMF, 2021) and in circular business models (Atasu et al., 2021). By working together in business ecosystems, organisations can reuse resources to minimise the impact on natural ecosystems or they can grow the value that their business model creates. Other ways to think about ecosystems, like the mutualism ideas from Chapter 2, help us to think about the different ways that organisations can work together in communities.

Orchestrating business ecosystems

Network orchestration is a way to analyse how to build and manage a business ecosystem that focuses on the role of a single firm working with many other firms. Business ecosystems have many organisations in them but usually we only work for one of them. I have spent more than 17 years researching network orchestration in a range of industries including electricity industry regulation (Shaw et al., 2006), football with Manchester United (Shaw, 2007) and the ports industry with the UK's Department for Transport (Shaw et al., 2017; Shaw et al., 2019). In this time the word 'ecosystem' has partly replaced the word 'network', as organisations work closer and closer together using new digital technologies. The use of the word 'network' comes from a time at the start of the millennium when it was obvious that organisations were working together in new ways that were enabled by the Internet and the World Wide Web, but it was not obvious how this worked or how it was developing. The word 'ecosystem' represents a much more interdependent way of organising organisations (Jacobides et al., 2018; Birkinshaw, 2019).

An ecosystem orchestrator is a single organisation that influences an ecosystem of other organisations for a common purpose. Purposes include managing the value creation process of the whole ecosystem (Dhanaraj and Parkhe, 2006; Moller and Svahn, 2006); setting a unifying vision for ecosystem members (Moller et al., 2005); developing and implementing government policy (Janssen and Estevez, 2013; Janssen and Helbig, 2018); sourcing and managing resources for the ecosystem to use including defining members' roles (Lorenzoni and Lipparini, 1999; Goerzen, 2005; Shaw, 2007); and helping information and knowledge sharing across the ecosystem (Lorenzoni and Lipparini, 1999). Orchestrators have a different role to the other organisations in the ecosystem, they direct and influence activities rather than 'do things' directly. Orchestrators design and implement the ecosystem's business model, so that stakeholders mutually satisfy each other. Using Osborne and Gaebler's words, orchestrators separate the 'steering' activities like policy-making and governance from the 'rowing' activities like manufacturing and logistics (1993). For example, Li and Fung and the Fung Group of companies create whole supply chains for specific purposes on behalf of their clients. Instead of manufacturing clothes and other consumer goods themselves, they create a supply chain for each project. They join together all the design, materials sourcing, product manufacturing and logistics firms that are needed to do all the work that gets the goods into a retailer's stores (LF, 2021). This requires a deep understanding of which organisations have the capacity, availability and quality that is needed for each project. Li and Fung's ecosystem shares this information with Li and Fung who then create each supply chain as required.

However, an orchestrator rarely owns the organisations that are members of its ecosystem, and it does not necessarily directly control them. But it still needs the ability to influence them (Hagel, 2002; van Heck and Vervest, 2007). An orchestrator organisation influences the firms in its ecosystem using the same tool that it uses to connect the network in the first place, the network's digital platform.

Platforms link ecosystem stakeholders together

Platforms allow stakeholders to work together to share each other's resources and capabilities according to the ecosystem's business model (Iansiti and Levien, 2004; Iyer and Davenport, 2008; Janssen and van der Voort, 2016; de Reuver et al., 2017). They are frequently based on an information technology, like social media networks are, but they can also be based on a common standard for working together. Any sort of agreement that helps people to organise how they work together is a type of platform, including laws, codes of practice and even agreements on which side of the road to drive on. Pre-defining some variables to change them into constants reduces the variety of things that need to be checked and managed because they change (Beer, 1979). Even agreeing to regularly meet at a certain place, at a certain time and talk about a certain topic is a type of platform because it cuts out all the other options and makes it simpler to organise the meeting.

A platform is a way of integrating all ecosystem stakeholders, organisations as well as individuals. It enables them to share resources and capabilities. For example, in my research on creating platforms to make maritime ports more efficient and more resilient, there are a huge range of different stakeholders involved, all with different information needs. Port operators need to know about ship arrival schedules, vessel sizes, needs for tug boats and pilots, the cargo on board, maintenance needs, fuel requirements and weather forecasts. Ship operators need to know which terminal or berth to go to, berth sizes, unloading and loading times, maintenance needs and fuel availability. Importers, shipping agents and logistics companies need to know about ship arrival schedules, the cargo's onward land transport schedule and customs requirements (see Shaw et al., 2017). Other stakeholders include harbour masters, shipping lines, terminal operators, cargo processing firms, warehousing and storage firms, passenger ferries and cruise liners, local inhabitants, road transport firms and logistics firms (Shaw et al., 2019). We can think of this collection of stakeholders as a single global ports system, but there are so many people and organisations, and they are so spread out across ports around the world that it is a very fragmented system. Some stakeholders work in the same organisation, like Associated British Ports, which owns several ports, or a shipping line with many vessels, or they work together in supply chains and have at least heard of each other. But most stakeholders do not even know each other exists. Even if they are aware of one another, then there may be no way to regularly share information or translate it from one organisation's information format to another's. For example, the units of measure, metrics or even the language that organisations use might be difficult to translate or incompatible.

These information gaps cause problems when stakeholders want to share information in order to become more efficient and resilient. For example, arrival times for cargo ships from the other side of the world are very uncertain. At the Port of London along the River Thames, if the intended unloading berth is not available, ships can potentially use unused berths elsewhere on the river to wait. But knowing about the availability of berths owned by separate firms depends on sharing information between the many firms that operate the berths along the river. Information sharing helps efficiency and resilience because it fills information gaps (Shaw et al., 2019).

Platforms help organisations to share information and other capabilities (Brown et al., 2017; de Reuver et al., 2017). They are a mix of information system bridges and organisational bridges, and they are the fundamental tool of an ecosystem orchestrator. Without a platform there can be no orchestration. The role of a platform is to bridge the information gaps between stakeholders to help them work together. By bridging information gaps, an orchestrator creates their own ecosystem. Gaps are anything which stops information flowing and/or stops it being understood. Information system platforms use IT to join organisations together, for example the Internet, the World Wide Web, email systems and social medial platforms. Organisational platforms are additions to organisational structures that join organisations together. For example, workshops that include cross-functional attendees or networks of firms and government agencies, which gather together in diverse groups (Shaw et al., 2019).

Figure 7.4 shows examples of how the Maritime Resilience Planning team (MRPt) within the UK's Department for Transport set up a range of organisational platforms to bridge interorganisational gaps that were hindering resilience planning activities. These platforms were aimed at helping information sharing and joined-up working between organisations, to help increase the resilience of ports to accidents, attacks and other crises. The ports system is made up of government agencies, many other organisations and the platforms that span them, all working on different system levels. Panel (a) shows levels in the global system of ports, from all ports in all countries in the world to a single port. Panel (b) shows the levels in a single ports system: the level of the whole port, the organisational stakeholder level and the level of specific capabilities that support stakeholders' business processes, such as the capability to unload or to inspect a cargo. Levels are just different perspectives for looking at a system and the levels above a single port level include many perspectives such as:

- Levels of spatial scales ranging from near to the port to far away – these are bridged by transport platforms such as rivers, coasts, rail lines and roads.
- Levels of political, organisation and legal domain scales ranging from within the same country to degrees of political understanding – these are bridged by treaties like EU membership.
- Levels of commercial agreement scales ranging from shared organisation rules to degrees of agreement in how to work together – these are bridged by contracts.

As with any system, each level is a different perspective. Panel (c) shows the original government and private organisations involved in resilience planning activities to protect ports. There were many gaps between these organisations in the local land around single ports and around groups of ports – the various emergency services, local government services and sub-national agencies were not joined up. Panel (d) shows the organisations that were created to bridge these gaps, including networks of diverse stakeholders and regular workshops, forums and meetings. These 'organisations of organisations' were organised on several levels including Local Port Resilience Forums, which linked stakeholders in a port to the Local Resilience Forum (LRF), LRFs which linked together local organisations from just outside the port (for example emergency services), and groups that were focused on much larger scale crises like flooding along a whole coast.

Platforms linking stakeholders together produce complexity

Platforms have different sides. If a platform joins a single type of stakeholder together then it has one side, like Facebook originally only joined friends and social contacts together. Then Facebook added another type of stakeholder, advertisers, to make two sides. The number of sides a platform has depends on the number of types of stakeholders. The more sides that a platform has then the larger the variety of resources and capabilities that they can contribute to the business model of the ecosystem that the platform supports. Variety and diversity are very useful because they increase what an ecosystem can do; they increase the range of its business model. For example, by adding advertisers to its ecosystem, Facebook gained revenue flows.

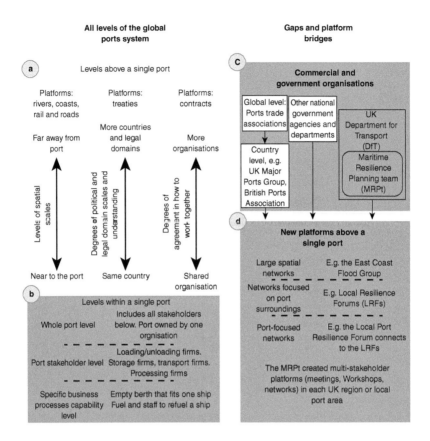

Figure 7.4   Examples of platforms to bridge interorganisational gaps

Adapted from Shaw et al. (2019)

But linking together diverse stakeholders also produces complexity problems because it creates dependencies. Dependencies are the different things that could happen depending on the different needs and situations of stakeholders. For example, all the people and organisations in a single port have different aims and objectives, different priorities, and even different ways of communicating with each other. For platform orchestrators, there is a serious danger of information overload from the sheer amount of information that stakeholders might give out or ask for when using the platform, and there is uncertainty about how their needs will change. Dependencies cause uncertainty because 'this' depends on 'that', which depends on 'something else' and so on.

Orchestrators are like spiders at the centre of their webs. They build and operate the platform that their ecosystem runs on, which gives them access to all that happens on it. For example, when planning how to increase the resilience of ports ecosystems, information sharing is key. Organisations in a single port depend on each other for providing services, people, cargo and information (Shaw et al., 2017). When a crisis hits one part of the system, like a damaged crane or a blocked road, it will have a cascading effect on many other parts (Hsieh et al., 2014). But the stakeholders in a port or the wider country's system of ports can potentially help each other by lending each other spare equipment, suggesting workarounds, and suggesting alternative ports (Akakura et al., 2015). If a tidal surge floods a whole port, then vessels can be potentially diverted to another port (Shaw et al., 2017).

The key to resilience planning is having the right information. But organisations that operate in ports each have huge amounts of data from device sensors and their IT systems, all of which might be useful for spotting crises and planning how to deal with them. Individually, they also have detailed knowledge of alternative routes, substitute equipment, spare parts, replacement staff and other resources to use if they have to. But there are complex barriers that make it hard to lend equipment or to help each other's customers. Specialised equipment is frequently impossible to move, e.g., container cranes; sometimes specially trained operators are needed, or maybe machines cannot be moved around quickly. Another problem is that if customers start to use new ports because their regular port is out of action then they might never return. Without the right platform, there are even barriers to sharing information, for example ports firms worry that the government and competitors might use any information they share to block planning applications for developing the port (Shaw et al., 2019). But sharing information between stakeholders can help orchestrators to deal with the information overload and the complexity of ports (Comfort et al., 2001; Welsh, 2014).

How orchestrators deal with complexity problems

Orchestrators deal with complexity problems by filtering out as many of the complex permutations and dependencies as they can. Information overload, the uncertainty of what might happen, and the overwhelming permutations of what actions they could take can all be managed by picking which issues to focus on and prioritise, and which to filter out. An orchestrator can use its platform to build up the 'big picture' of its ecosystem members, and then use the same big picture to filter the information that it receives to avoid information overload. It is this big picture that lets an orchestrator prioritise where to focus its resources, where to act and how to advise its stakeholders.

In my research on the UK ports system, the big picture perspective for the whole ports system is a special focus of interest that captures and integrates information from all the platform's users (Shaw et al., 2019). In the ports case, the MRPt in the Department for Transport was the orchestrator and the platform was the collection of meetings and groups in Figure 7.4d. They had a much wider focus of interest than any of the other ports' stakeholders. Their focus covered the whole UK ports system, including every port, every stakeholder and all the transport and communications infrastructure that enabled them to operate smoothly. Even the senior management of companies that ran multiple ports did not have this perspective. All organisations except the MRPt were focused on their individual work, which was much more about what happened in the port itself rather than the whole ports system. For example, I interviewed a ferry operator that had their receptionist watch TV traffic reports for traffic delays on the motorways that led to the port. Ferry crossings of the North Sea were on a tight schedule and the ferry operator needed to know if trucks would be late. But traffic delays were not part of a ferry operator's normal work, so a staff member had to watch TV traffic reports.

Trade associations like the UK Major Ports Group and the British Ports Association focus on more than one port but even they did not consider the whole UK ports system. Another special feature of the MRPt's integration perspective was its responsibility. The MRPt was responsible for resilience planning, not for profitably running a company or for helping trade association members to run their ports profitably. The MRPt was responsible for the healthy functioning of UK ports for the benefit of all stakeholders, including companies and any other users of ports, such as passengers. This responsibility gave it a view that was special not just in scope but also in terms of its interests. This special responsibility helped the MRPt's staff to see connections between information that other stakeholders would miss. This is the difference between looking and seeing. If you are responsible and accountable for something, then you see things that will not be seen by someone who is not responsible for that; you will be sensitive and pay attention to different things. The Japanese film Rashomon highlights how people see very different things when they look at the same event from different perspectives – in the film a murder is seen by four witnesses who all describe it in four different ways (Roth and Mehta, 2002). In my research I saw how each port operator would know how much salt they had in their own stores for putting on icy port roads during winter, but only the MRPt would regularly check to see if ports varied in their readiness and if they could potentially spare salt to share amongst each other.

All orchestrators are exposed to complexity, this is an unavoidable consequence of using a platform to access diverse resources and capabilities. But the 'big picture' that an integration perspective gives an orchestrator can also be used to filter complex information flows. For example, the MRPt was able to rank problems by their disruptive effects on the whole UK ports system. This enabled them to prioritise how they responded in a systematic way. An orchestrator's system-wide picture helps it to define priorities for all other stakeholders. It enables orchestrators to recommend where platform users should focus on, what they should prioritise and where they can learn from and help each other.

The complexity of a system is generated by the number of possibilities that the system generates (Allen and Starr, 2017). These are the number of potential options that could be taken, the number of potential linkups between stakeholders, the number of 'what-ifs', or to use a Journey-based Thinking view, the number of routes that different stakeholders could take on their journeys. It is the sheer number of permutations that makes complexity extremely difficult to deal with. But complex possibilities can be managed by filtering, and one role of an orchestrator and its platform is to do this for their ecosystem's stakeholders. Social networks do this by using members' profile data, behaviour data, current connections or other measures of likely compatibility to recommend new friends or business contacts. All stakeholders in an ecosystem can potentially connect with all others to share resources and capabilities in the form of goods and services, but some connections are much more beneficial than others for the individual stakeholders concerned, and the overall balancing of the ecosystem's business model. The MRPt's business model was designed to increase the resilience of the UK's ports system. This frequently meant helping port stakeholders to plan alternatives and workarounds, for example, when a fire stopped a key road from being used, or a bridge collapsed and blocked a train line. Resilience planning deals with planning alternatives for any sort of crisis at any scale, from a key staff member falling ill so they cannot work, or a flood that removes the capabilities of a whole port from the ports system. The 'big picture' that only the MRPt had access to enabled it to filter out complex permutations for ecosystem stakeholders as well as for itself. When crises hit, it could suggest to stakeholder firms where to borrow spare parts, consumables like fuel, or even terminal berths or warehousing space. The MRPt had the system-wide information and the specific interests that enabled it to recommend better options than were known to a single logistics firm or even to a company that owned many large ports, like Associated British Ports or Hutchison Ports (Shaw et al., 2019).

How orchestrators govern and manage business ecosystems

In some ways, every stakeholder orchestrates the capabilities and resources of whoever they work with. It doesn't matter whether a stakeholder is an organisation of people or a single person, every business model relies on external contributions. But ecosystem orchestrators are different because they have a much more diverse network of capabilities and resources to draw on. They also have a special perspective, which includes access to the big picture of how their ecosystem operates. This shields them from complexity and can be used to recommend options to all the ecosystem's stakeholders. It is this recommendation power that is the basis of network governance and their control of the platform.

By operating the ecosystem's platform, the orchestrator can use its big picture view to see which options best fit the aims and objectives of the platform users, and it can see which stakeholders would benefit from being introduced so that they can join-up and work together to mutually help each other, for example, in customer–supplier relationships or in more complicated arrangements. An orchestrator can see which relationships are possible, but it does not have to make every introduction or suggest every way of joined-up working. It can choose which relationships to start off and how they might function by making stakeholders aware of some but not all possibilities. Platforms help orchestrators to manage by letting them recommend to stakeholders how they can work with each other for mutual benefit. This lets orchestrators influence those stakeholders because orchestrators can choose which joining-up options to recommend and which to not recommend. This is how orchestrators influence their ecosystem members without having direct power over them. They make stakeholders aware of options that will get them what the stakeholders value and at the same time support the ecosystem's business model (see Table 7.1) (Shaw et al., 2017).

Table 7.1   The main orchestration and platform ideas with examples

Orchestration and platform ideas	Description	Ports system examples
Complexity problems	Platforms produce complexity by making the ecosystem orchestrator the centre of all that happens between its many users, like the spider at the centre of a web. This might produce information overload for the orchestrator	Ports systems have huge numbers of diverse stakeholders with many different aims and objectives, capabilities and priorities. How can a small government team like the MRPt influence them to work together and plan for more resilient ports?
Big picture perspective	The capability to have a whole system viewpoint and see links between diverse occurrences, which together might affect the health of an ecosystem's business model. This provides a 'big picture' view, which can be used as a filter to prioritise what is important	The MRPt was interested in anything that affected the capabilities of organisations to move goods and people onto, through and out of UK ports. For example, fires that stop roads being used or rail lines that are blocked by collapsed bridges. A capability can be a key staff member off sick or a flood that stops a whole port from working

(Continued)

Table 7.1   (Continued)

Orchestration and platform ideas	Description	Ports system examples
		The MRPt's big picture view enabled it to see the effects of different choices on the whole system. For example, relaxing maximum ferry passenger numbers when transporting UK citizens when a volcanic ash cloud stopped European flights. It also meant that the MRPt knew of more workarounds and other alternatives than other organisations. For example, where to borrow fuel for emergency vehicles during a fuel tanker drivers' strike
Option facilitation	Knowing about more options than any other stakeholder enables orchestrators to recommend options to stakeholders	The MRPt suggested to stakeholders who they could work more closely with and how, then introduced them
Selective orchestration	Selectively recommending options to stakeholders so they do what the ecosystem business model needs	The MRPt wanted more resilience planning, which required information sharing between stakeholders who did not usually meet or did not usually talk about ports. So the MRPt created networks, groups and workshops with themes, objectives and purposes to support this

Another example of a platform owner that uses its operation of the platform to get a special perspective on its users is Amazon. Retail companies of all sizes use Amazon's Marketplace as a platform for selling all sorts of products to consumers. They use Marketplace to meet and interact with customers, and as they do this Amazon learns a lot about things like what buyers are looking for, how buyers behave and what works and what does not. Some of this it shares with retailers and some of this it does not (Kelion, 2020). It has even been accused of using some of this data to launch products that compete with the sellers on its platform that it originally learned from (Mattioli, 2020).

Creating and growing a business ecosystem

Part of the role of an ecosystem orchestrator is building and growing their ecosystem. This involves the ongoing process of replacing staff, customers and other stakeholders that leave because the ecosystem business model no longer gives them what they value. It also involves building the ecosystem in the first place. Creating and growing a business ecosystem can be understood by using two of the theoretical lenses that I introduced in earlier chapters: the first is Value Flow Analysis (VFA) (Chapter 2) and the second is Journey-based Thinking (Chapter 4).

First, VFA diagrams help us to see how ecosystems are created and grown in a similar way to how they help us with creating and growing organisations. Every organisation has an ecosystem if it has external stakeholders. The VFA diagram of an organisation's ecosystem is just a higher-level view of the organisation's business model. The organisation level and the ecosystem level of a VFA are just two views of the same system. Both describe the business model of how the ecosystem, or the organisation works, how stakeholders mutually satisfy each other. In any VFA diagram, the outer VFA of an organisation's business model is its surrounding ecosystem. The qualitative difference between an ecosystem business model and an organisation's business model is ownership that gives direct control. Some business model strategies prioritise ownership and control and some prioritise openness and access to external capabilities. Business models that focus on single organisations being in control are likely to have a lower variety of stakeholders to draw on than business models that focus on a diverse ecosystem of partners. This is because there is a limit to what one company can manage and control. Ownership takes up time and resources – anyone who buys a house, a car or a pet will know this. Organisations that collaborate with other organisations use open business models in the sense that they open up their business models to external resources and capabilities (Chesbrough, 2006; Chesbrough, 2007). For example, Proctor and Gamble started to source ideas for products from external partners in addition to its own research and development staff (Huston and Sakkab, 2006), and Qualcomm went from manufacturing mobile phones and base stations to making chips and selling licenses to the technologies it developed to other manufacturers (Chesbrough, 2007).

Ecosystem business models are reliant on influencing rather than just direct control. Also, indirect influencing and separation between the organisations in an ecosystem enables them to be more diverse than a single organisation that has lots of owned or partially owned partners. This diversity is echoed in the two views of natural ecosystems that we have already used to think about business ecosystems. These are the recirculation of scarce resources along pathways of linked business models, and how communities of business models work closely together and compete along different dimensions of mutuality (Chapter 2). In both cases natural organisms mainly do not directly control each other, they are separate organisms. Also, it is the diversity of resources and capabilities that organisms contribute that gives natural ecosystems their ability to produce new things and to some extent be resilient. Business ecosystems also have a diverse set of stakeholders to draw on, which makes them inherently more able to innovate (Shaw and Allen, 2017).

Creating a business ecosystem starts with designing its initial business model, the first collection of stakeholders that have the minimum resources and capabilities to mutually satisfy each other. For example, the VFA diagram in Figure 7.5 shows the basic business model of retailers like Tesco, which is to buy products in bulk from suppliers and display them in store for consumers to buy. After that, growing the business ecosystem means adding to its business model by studying the stakeholders in the business model to find their **unmet needs** or **reusable capabilities and resources**. Unmet needs are things that a stakeholder values but that they do not currently get (Shaw, 2007). They can be additional products or services, or they might be small changes to the products or services that they buy already. Unmet needs might even just mean rewards for participating in a business model that are brought to them in a different way. Customers and other stakeholders might not know their need or they might not know that something to satisfy their unmet needs exists.

Satisfying unmet needs is an example of the big picture perspective of orchestrators. They have strong relationships with stakeholders that enable them to understand what many stakeholders of the same type need. For example, they can learn from old customers what new customers who are similar might need but are not aware of. Learning from one set of stakeholders to help another set works for all orchestrators, but ecosystem orchestrators have a very diverse set of stakeholders to learn from and then draw on to supply those unmet needs. This is where reusable capabilities and resources come in. If an orchestrator knows that any stakeholder would really value something then they do not necessarily have to produce it themselves, they could just find a partner to supply it. Reusable capabilities and resources are capabilities and resources that are already being provided in the orchestrator's business model and that can be supplied to other stakeholders. For example, the supermarket Tesco has used its loyalty card data to sell analyses to its suppliers like Procter and Gamble, Coca-Cola and Kimberly-Clark (Rohwedder, 2006). Satisfying unmet needs and reusing capabilities and resources are examples of ecosystem growth. The relationships between the business model's stakeholders become more complicated. This is shown by the dotted flow arrows in the VFA diagram (Figure 7.5) (some flows of resources are not shown). Two other ways to grow an ecosystem are by connecting to new supplier stakeholders, who can supply unmet needs with their own capabilities and resources, or by adding new customer stakeholders who need the spare capabilities and resources that current stakeholders have. For example, Tesco Bank in the past used banking capabilities from NatWest bank and also the Royal Bank of Scotland to provide customers with new banking services (Rodgers, 2011).

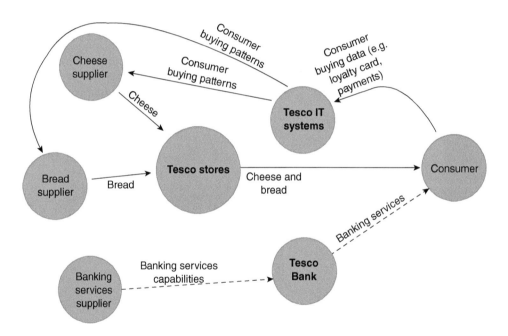

Figure 7.5   VFA diagram of the basic business model of a retailer and new connections that grow its ecosystem

Second, Journey-based Thinking helps us understand how ecosystems are created and grown by focusing on the stakeholders' journeys. Analysing customer journeys is a powerful way to uncover unmet needs. These include needs that some customers already know about but cannot get or needs that they are unaware of but would really value, like useful advice for assembling and using furniture for the first time, or recipe ideas for ingredients. Other examples of unmet needs are add-on services like deliveries, extended warranties, diagnostic and repair services, or spare parts. Analysing customer journeys uncovers new unmet needs because journey analyses are a systematic study of what is required to smoothly get a customer to their objective, as well as a way of suggesting even better objectives. It is critical to do a journey analysis for each stakeholder at the same time as an ecosystem business model is designed. Do this before the ecosystem is created by starting any relationships with suppliers, recruiting staff or selling to customers. Remember that all stakeholders are customers because, as we see in a VFA diagram, all relationships are two-way relationships. Journey analyses will explain how each stakeholder carries out their individual roles and how they should work together in a joined-up way.

Journey analyses show how to grow an ecosystem because they highlight missing capabilities and resources so new stakeholders can be recruited to supply them. Journey analyses of ecosystem stakeholders will suggest new stages that they would value. Things that must happen in these stages can be enabled by inputs from other stakeholders. These inputs will be attractive to the person whose journey it is if they make the journey easier, quicker, cheaper or more attractive in some way, such as when Amazon brought out the Dash handheld barcode reader and microphone. Instead of having to search for a product online, shoppers could use the Dash wand to automatically order a product from Amazon by reading a barcode or by speaking into the microphone (Davis, 2014; Cellan-Jones, 2016). More recently this service has been superseded by Amazon's Alexa AI working through its Echo smart speaker – customers can just ask Alexa to organise a delivery. Amazon has also started to deliver groceries in major cities around the world with its Amazon Fresh service. The Dash wand, the Alexa AI and Echo smart speaker combination, and the Amazon Fresh delivery service are all examples of tracing the journeys that customers are on and finding stages that are missing. Amazon added this mixture of products and services stages to gradually make the journey of ordering and receiving goods easier for customers, as well as more valuable for its business model.

Journey analyses compliment VFA diagrams because they use a completely different perspective. Journey analyses focus on the help that is required to complete a stage, in the context of progressing towards a final objective, whilst VFA diagrams focus on the many stakeholders who provide that help.

Three examples of what happens as you grow an ecosystem

Creating an ecosystem starts with designing the ecosystem's business model in a VFA diagram and then designing the journeys of all the business model stakeholders. Then an orchestrator grows the ecosystem by recruiting stakeholders with the appropriate capabilities and resources and influencing them to join and play their role in the business model. Ecosystems grow by adding new stakeholders and by adding new flows between stakeholders. The orchestrator is also responsible for building and operating the platform that enables stakeholders to work together, and the orchestrator to monitor how well they do this, which includes getting the information that is needed to influence them. Here are three examples of what can happen.

Super apps are an example of using Journey-based Thinking to grow the number of products and services that an organisation provides to any single customer. Connie Chan explained them as high frequency but low margin services, like mobile phone apps for food delivery and taxi services. These types of apps have frequent interactions with customers, which help them to build up a picture of those customers' lives, which in turn helps them to understand what other services they could sell to those same customers (2019). Every digital service generates a 'data exhaust' (Shaw, 2020). This is information about customers' lives and the other products and services that they might need. When it is coupled with a trusted ability to suggest products and services to the customer, it's a winning combination. Super apps understand their customers' lives, they have their customers' trust, and they have their attention. They are perfectly placed to be a gateway to extra services that can all be provided by partners in a super app's ecosystem. Mobile payment apps like Alipay and WeChat are examples of super apps. Another example is the way that Amazon learns which extra services to suggest to Amazon Prime users based on data it gleans from their relationship with Prime.

A second example is the way that job platforms have grown and developed over time to help two stakeholder groups in new ways (Coolican and Jordan, 2020). Early job platforms just acted as a way to match work that needed doing with people who could do it. On one side of their platforms, they let job finders find out about jobs and then apply; on the other side they helped recruiting organisations to publicise jobs and quickly find a short list of best matching candidates. But gradually they have added services for job finders such as payments, collaboration and insurance, and services for organisations such as training, vetting and credential checking.

A third example of how ecosystems grow is out of sector competition. This is when an organisation uses a strong understanding of the needs of a customer, a strong and trusted relationship, and the capabilities of external partners to provide products and services, that until then were provided by organisations in other industries, such as if a mobile phone company started to provide car insurance because telecommunications and insurance are separate sectors. Insurance firms would never consider the mobile phone company to be a competitor until it used its access to different customer data and business partners to compete (Atluri et al., 2017).

Building ecosystems of companies and products using the Internet of Things (IoT)

An increasingly common way to connect stakeholders up into an ecosystem is by using the Internet of Things (IoT). An IoT device is anything with a chip and a wireless connection. Any IoT device can potentially share data and capabilities with any other IoT device. IoT refrigerators, toasters, cars and phones can all be connected together to share data and work with each other.

All devices have sensors and actuators. Sensors sense things; they gather data, like the cameras, microphones, touch screens, accelerometers and other sensors on a mobile phone. Actuators make things happen, like screens, audio speakers, vibrators and other actuators on a phone (Porter and Heppelmann, 2014; Porter and Heppelmann, 2015). Wireless connections and different types of sensors and actuators are now so cheap that they are common in not just cars and expensive machinery but TVs, heating systems, air conditioning systems, refrigerators, kettles, toasters and all manner of home devices and business machines. When the devices that people use at home and at work connect together then so can the people who use them as well as the organisations that make them (Lamarre and May, 2019).

All IoT devices can potentially share data with other devices that might find it useful. For example, the Waze app mixes together real-time traffic and road information from many different Waze users, to help other Waze users to avoid traffic jams (Waze, 2021a). IoT devices also have capabilities that they can share. A device's capabilities are whatever the device does as part of its function – toasters toast things, refrigerators cool food. The Waze app shares traffic speed data by updating the location of each phone or by warning users about accidents or jams. When different products work together, they are much more useful than a single IoT product because the total information that they have access to is much richer and so are their combined capabilities. Different IoT products with complementary capabilities can potentially work together to produce a much better user experience. For example, Waze data can be used to help a city's traffic flow in real-time or to support city planning decisions (Waze, 2021b).

Linking different IoT products together also links the firms together that manufactured those devices. This is because every IoT device is already connected to its manufacturer for software updates and for information collection purposes. If devices from different manufacturers connect together then this connects the manufacturers to each other. Phone apps are part of the IoT because they are connected to the Internet through Wi-Fi or their phone. The Internet connection allows devices and software to record how they are used so that the manufacturer, or the software firm, can learn how to improve the software or the product it runs on. All software-as-a-service (SaaS) software is connected to the software supplier because the software is running on the software supplier's cloud as well as the user's laptop, tablet or phone. So, data can be shared to describe how the IoT device or software is used, and to control it, which means that capabilities can also be shared, and different devices can work together in a coordinated way.

But if you want to build an IoT ecosystem, how do you choose which IoT products to link up with, and which firms to partner with? There are many products and firms in the world – how do you find the right ones? The answers to these questions comes from analysing the customer journey of the people who use the IoT product. If you make toasters, then it is people making toast. If you make refrigerators, then it is the people who use your refrigerators. The same goes for cars, phones, factory machines and other IoT devices. If you make a detailed description of your user's journey, then you will notice other devices and pieces of software that help that user on their journey. These are the devices and pieces of software that your device needs to work closely with. So, their manufacturers and providers are the stakeholders who you need to recruit to your ecosystem. The three user journeys in Table 7.2 show how similar as well as different devices can share useful information because they have their own parts to play in users' journeys.

Table 7.2 Data is shared to fill gaps and then generate and choose options along three user journeys

User journey example	Selected stages in each example journey				
	Stage 1	Stage 2	Stage 3	Stage 4	Comment
Cooking a fresh pasta dish in a kitchen	(a) Consult recipe app or recipe website for meal ideas (b) Choose recipe and get instructions (c) Recipe app checks with refrigerator for availability of ingredient options (gap)	(a) Remove fresh pasta from refrigerator (b) Refrigerator adds a reminder to shopping app to order more pasta	(a) Start to heat pasta in a pan on the cooker's hob (b) Cooker monitors temperature of pasta water and reduces heat when it starts to boil	(a) Cooker beeps when timer runs out and pasta is ready (b) Cooker tells smart light bulbs in dining room to turn on (gap)	Notice how what were isolated devices from different manufacturers can share information to be helpful

(Continued)

Table 7.2   (Continued)

User journey example	Selected stages in each example journey				
	Stage 1	Stage 2	Stage 3	Stage 4	Comment
Travelling to work in a smart city	(a) Check navigation phone app for easiest route (b) App checks journey progress of other app users (gap)	(a) Unavoidable disruption adds one hour this morning (b) Ask app for alternative routes	(a) App suggests walking, bus and rail options (b) Choose underground rail option (c) Start journey	(a) App notifies user of station closure (b) Choose best alternative station (c) App shows new walking route	Notice how information from sources around the city lets the app support user decisions in real-time to adjust the route
Assembling products in a smart factory	(a) Six identical assembly lines start to assemble components into products (b) The lines operate for an hour	(a) News of a supply disruption reaches the factory (b) The supply of components then reduces by a sixth	(a) Management must decide which line to close	(a) Collect data from all assembly machines on all lines (gap) (b) Compare data to decide which line has machines needing maintenance	Notice how unforeseen disruptions and high-level decisions are managed using shared data from many devices to make a maintenance opportunity

Having found devices that could help users along their journeys, the next question is how do you recruit their manufacturers? How do you persuade them to join the ecosystem you are building? Organisations with deep pockets like Apple and Google can just buy them up, which works for eliminating competitors as well as gaining capabilities (Azevedo, 2020; McLaughlin, 2020). But that's not the only answer: another way is to analyse the journey that these stakeholders are on. If you can explain how joining your new ecosystem will help them progress on their own journeys, then they might be persuaded to join you. The user journeys of your new recruits also tell you how to design the platform that your business ecosystem depends on. Ecosystem platforms include information systems platforms and organisational platforms. Both types of platforms bridge the gaps between stakeholders. If you understand the user journeys of the organisations and people that you want to recruit, then you will understand these gaps. The details of these gaps provide the specification for the bridging job that your platform needs to do. For example, Amazon's Alexa AI is a platform for bridging gaps like being able to operate a computer with just your voice to order products, find information, set timers or control a wide variety of household gadgets (Amazon, 2021).

Table 7.3 takes the three journeys from Table 7.2 and describes the information and capability gaps that can be bridged by features of an IoT platform. In all three examples data must be collected from a variety of sources and analysed to support the decisions of the cook, the commuter and the factory production manager.

Table 7.3 Information and ability gaps that need bridging and the platform features that can do this

Ecosystem example	Information and capability gaps	Platform features required to bridge gaps
Cooking fresh pasta in the kitchen	1 Knowing if the ingredients for a meal are in the refrigerator and within their use-by dates 2 Ability to turn lights on in another room when your hands are full of serving dishes	1 Sharing food availability and use-by information between refrigerator and recipe app or recipe website 2 Capability for cooker to tell smart light bulbs to turn on
Commuter travelling to work in a smart city	1 Real-time traffic flow speeds on routes to work 2 Real-time journey times for other transport modes 3 Instructions for reaching other transport modes (map) 4 Real-time status of passenger flows on other transport modes (e.g., stations)	1 Collecting movement data from other navigation phone apps 2 Sharing real-time operational data from transport company systems (e.g., rail company) 3 User can be updated through their phone
Assembling products in a smart factory	1 Information from the supplier's logistics systems that either predicts or speedily reports delivery disruptions 2 Data from sensors on all the individual machines on all six assembly lines, which predicts when machines will break down, or reduce their effectiveness	1 Sharing real-time locations of all delivery shipments 2 Aggregation of data from all sensors of all production machines 3 Capability to analyse sensor data in real-time

Chapter summary

When an organisation maps out the journeys that its customers are on, it gains a much deeper understanding of how it should help its customers progress towards their objectives, and even how to suggest better objectives. But many of the things that customers need to make smoother progress, or to enjoy the experience, will not be something that the organisation can supply. These are unmet needs, things that customers need even though they might not even be aware that these things exist. Maybe the organisation and its current partners do not have the resources and capabilities to fulfil these unmet needs with new products and services. Maybe the organisation needs to add new partners to its ecosystem who do have these resources and capabilities. This illustrates how an organisation's ecosystem could grow using a customer demand perspective.

Supply chains focus on transforming resources for a single set of consumers, and in a single direction. Business ecosystems include supply chains, but they share resources in all directions and between all stakeholders. To do this they rely on digital platforms to help them share information and work closely together. The controller of a business ecosystem's platform is the orchestrator of that ecosystem. Orchestration is a very complex role because orchestrators need to balance all the different needs and capabilities of the ecosystem members that use the platform. Only this will maintain the ecosystem's business model.

Ensuring the success of the business model is made even more complex because orchestrators seldom own all the ecosystem's members. Without ownership, how can an orchestrator recruit members to join, and then control them when they do? The solution to these problems comes from the orchestrator's control of the ecosystem platform itself. Ecosystem members rely on the platform to connect up and work together, and an orchestrator can use this information to build up a 'big picture' of its ecosystem members' needs and how other members can satisfy them. This big picture can be used to prioritise where to focus resources and where to act. This includes suggesting to stakeholders how they can work with each other for mutual benefit. Orchestrators recruit and influence ecosystem members by using the platform to tell them about options that will get them what they value, and at the same time, support the ecosystem's business model.

Further reading

For more on complex systems and natural ecosystems please see Allen, T.F.H. and Starr, T.B. (2017) *Hierarchy: Perspectives for Ecological Complexity*, 2nd edn. Chicago: University of Chicago Press.

Birkinshaw, J. (2019) 'Ecosystem businesses are changing the rules of strategy', *Harvard Business Review*, 8.
Chesbrough, H.W. (2007) 'Why companies should have open business models', *MIT Sloan Management Review*, 48(2): 22. https://sloanreview.mit.edu/article/why-companies-should-have-open-business-models (accessed 7 April 2022).
EMF (2021) 'What is the circular economy?', Ellen Macarthur Foundation. https://www.ellenmacarthurfoundation.org/circular-economy/what-is-the-circular-economy (accessed 7 April 2022).
Porter, M.E. and Heppelmann, J.E. (2014) 'How smart, connected products are transforming competition', *Harvard Business Review*, November. https://hbr.org/2014/11/how-smart-connected-products-are-transforming-competition (accessed 7 April 2022).
Porter, M.E. and Heppelmann, J.E. (2015) 'How smart, connected products are transforming companies', *Harvard Business Review*, October. https://hbr.org/2015/10/how-smart-connected-products-are-transforming-companies (accessed 7 April 2022).

SECTION 3
SKILLS TO HELP ORGANISATIONS RESPOND

8

HOW TO UNDERSTAND WHAT CUSTOMERS REALLY NEED

KEY IDEAS

- Customer journey models include the journeys of many past customers, so they can suggest how current customers can reach objectives that they never thought of as well as objectives they have already chosen.
- Customer journey models describe all the decisions customers need to take and all the capabilities and resources that they require on the path to reaching their objectives.
- Customer journey models help customers to make informed decisions. Journey models can guide them by suggesting options to choose from and explaining the outcomes of each choice.
- Customer touchpoints are opportunities for organisations to interact with customers and gather data 'snapshots' of each customer's individual journey.
- There are many different data sources for recording customer touchpoints including websites, apps, organisational IT systems and human staff. Each data source provides a different perspective on customers and their situations.

LEARNING OBJECTIVES

After reading this chapter you will be able to:

- Describe the information that is contained in customer journey models.
- Explain how customer journey models can be used to help customers.
- Explain how customer journey models can be used to help organisations by helping their staff as well as their customers.
- Describe the difference between customer touchpoints and the stages of a customer's journey.
- Describe the types of data that are the raw material for building customer journey models.
- Explain which data sources are used to gather data to build customer journeys and the differences between them.

> Q: Why improve customer journeys?
>
> A: There is nothing more important than successful customer journeys.

In this chapter we will build on the ideas in Chapter 4 and look at how to find out what customers really need to make successful journeys. This chapter explains how journey models are a series of linked decisions, which customers must make to reach their personal objectives, and a source of even better objectives that customers had never thought of before. In this chapter we explain how customer journey models are used to guide customers in making informed decisions, and how they are constructed from customer data that is gathered every time a customer 'touches' an organisation, like when customers phone up a call centre, ask staff questions in a store, or look at web pages. We describe some of the many different data sources that can be used to record customer touchpoints and explain how each data source provides very different customer journey data.

Improving customers' journeys

A major benefit of analysing customer journeys and making customer journey models is that they can be used to improve customers' experiences of those journeys (Lemon and Verhoef, 2016; Rosenbaum et al., 2017; Richardson, 2010; Tueanrat et al., 2021), whether they are buying products from a supermarket, using a social network, finding and consuming a digital service, or downloading and using a mobile app. All parts of a customer's life can be modelled as journeys and the model can be used to improve:

1   How customers enjoy the experience.
2   How useful it is for customers.
3   How easy it is for customers.

These three aspects of customer journeys overlap but enjoying the experience is particularly important for recreational services like holidays, music and food. Products and services that help customers to accomplish things like mowing a lawn or collaborating with colleagues must be very useful. Finally, all products and services must be easy to find, choose, buy and then use. We have all had experiences of products and services that were not very enjoyable, like bad restaurant visits, or buying devices that did not work well or were hard to use. The patterns to be found in customer journey data can be used to improve those journeys in two ways. The first is by guiding customers to help them navigate through all the choices that they are confronted with, so they pick the best options for their individual needs. The second is by systematically removing journey barriers, which are anything that stops a customer progressing towards their goals. Barriers are the parts of the journeys that give bad experiences or make things difficult and less useful for customers. Examples of barriers include unpleasant or boring situations, complicated instructions and products or services that do not work as they are supposed to.

Guiding customers to help them make informed decisions

One way of thinking about customer journeys is as a series of choices, one after the other (Iyengar and Agrawal, 2010). Each stage of a journey is separated from the last stage by the decision to choose it: decisions like which routes to travel, where to get advice and suggestions. Ultimately customers make their own decisions, organisations can only offer them options to choose from: options like several versions of the same phone with different memory sizes, different ways to pay for the phone and different delivery options. Helping customers as they make the many decisions along their journeys has three benefits. First, it makes it easier for customers to get where they want to go. Second, in the pre-purchase stages of a customer's buying journey it can subtly influence the customer to purchase an organisation's own products. Third, in the post-purchase stages it can guide the customer in how to use the product or service successfully. This is very important because successful and satisfied customers tell their friends, and they come back for more.

Informed decision-making is a way of guiding customers, which is consistent with the idea of informed consent to treatment in healthcare systems like the NHS. This is when a patient is given 'all of the information about what the treatment involves, including the benefits and risks, whether there are reasonable alternative treatments, and what will happen if treatment does not go ahead' (NHS, 2021). The basis of informed consent comes from the principles of biomedical ethics (Beauchamp and Childress, 2001).

The main idea behind guiding customers to make informed decisions is that they should understand as much as they are able to about the options that they have, and the personal implications of each option for them. A similar approach is followed in career guidance counselling when careers advisers give job finders three progressively more in-depth types of support to help their decision-making. These types of support are Information only, Advice and then Guidance (IAG) (Shaw, 2009). For example, a job finder will initially get general information from online and documentary sources, then more specific advice from a careers advisor and finally some personalised guidance during an in-depth meeting. Personalised guidance explores all of the job finder's available options and how they might develop into career goals.

A Journey-based Thinking approach includes three key perspectives, which help informed decision-making:

1   The past journey: decision-making is based on the capabilities that a customer has available to do something next. A customer's capabilities are based on their history of how they got to their current situation and the resources that they have available to use. Their main resource is the information that they have for making decisions, so supplying them with better information helps to guide them.
2   The current situation: decision-making is a choice between a customer's potential next moves. It is a choice between the options that they have access to and that they are aware of, options to use their capabilities and their resources. A good way to help a decision-maker is to improve the quality of their options – not by giving them more options, which leads to information overload, but by giving them a better set of options to choose from than they had before (Iyengar and Agrawal, 2010).

3   The future journey: decision-making builds into a series of choices, which together form the stages of a route on a future journey towards a specific goal, like choosing between branches at every junction on a path. Goals can be jobs, qualifications, states of well-being, actions a person can make, skills a person can develop, or other personal objectives. A good way to help a decision-maker is to help them to clarify their route forward. What do they need to do next and what are the likely outcomes of each route, good or bad?

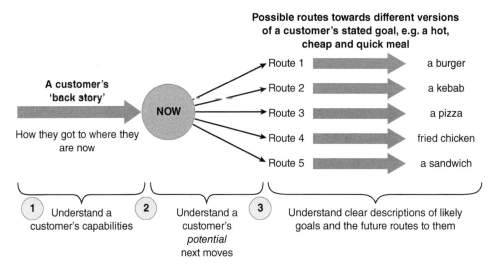

Figure 8.1   The three key perspectives of informed decision-making

Figure 8.1 shows the three types of information that are required for guiding customers to make informed decisions (1) the capabilities and resources that a customer can use; (2) the options for using these capabilities in different ways; and (3) how choosing each option starts that customer on a different route towards a different goal.

These ideas can be used in designing mobile apps, websites or any other type of digital services. They are particularly useful for self-service designs, like restaurant menus, which rely on providing options that customers choose from. For example, a good design for every screen in a mobile app must include enough options to be useful to different users, but not so many that it is overwhelming. Every screen holds choices for the user, like branches in a path. A good understanding of the capabilities and resources that a customer can use is necessary for suggesting options that are realistic and usable for that customer. A good understanding of how each option starts that customer onto a different route towards a different goal is necessary for suggesting options that fit the customer's stated goal, like buying food that is hot, cheap and quick to get hold of.

Getting the right data to guide decisions and actions

In planning any project, including projects that model customer journeys, it is best to start with the desired outcomes and work backwards to see what data is needed. If you start with thinking about data and how to use it then it is easy to get lost. There are many ways to use any data. The Big Data Information Value Chain (BDIVC) model is very useful for thinking about how to get data for improving customer journeys (Figure 8.2) (Abbasi et al., 2016). The idea is to start with a high-level description of the decisions and actions that would be possible using a useful information pattern in a dataset. Then, think about the data and data sources that are needed to find that pattern.

You can use the BDIVC model to specify data sources for decisions and actions that would be very useful to an organisation. Start on the right of Figure 8.2 by describing the actions that might be needed, and then the decisions that need to be taken to decide which actions to choose. Then use these decision options to define the information pattern that would help you to guide them. For example, in Figure 8.2 the decisions are about which product to recommend to which types of customers. If you knew the pattern of which types of customers usually bought which types of products, then you could use it to guide your product recommendations to other customers. Information patterns are made from information so describing a pattern tells you which information you need to make it: in this case what customers bought plus profile information about those customers. Defining the need to make a pattern then helps you figure out where to get it from: in this case customer loyalty card data. Notice that the left side of the chain explains the difference between information and data. Information is precise and just what you need for some purposes (building the pattern). But data is just a dump of raw material from a data source that is full of unwanted things that need to be filtered out. Also, going back and forth along the chain is very helpful for assessing how well the BDIVC links fit together and for considering alternatives.

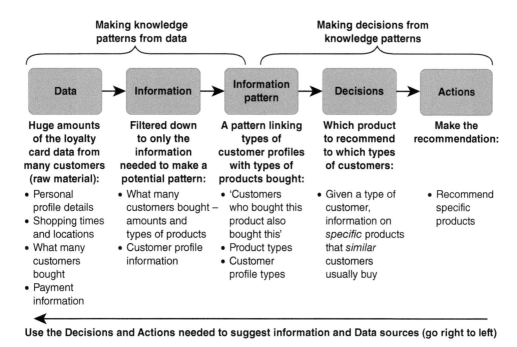

Figure 8.2   The Big Data Information Value Chain with a loyalty card data example
Adapted from Abbasi et al., 2016

A customer journey analysis will suggest many potential decisions and actions to start using the BDIVC model in this way. In the loyalty card data example in Figure 8.2, key decisions include choosing what to recommend to each individual customer. This could be at the stage before they go to the checkout page of the online store, or it could be at the stage of receiving the regular emails that all loyal programme members get. When organisations find patterns that link different types of customers with the sorts of products that they usually buy, these help them to make buying recommendations. The pattern would be made up of customer profiles as well as records of past purchases. The information that describes their past purchases is what a loyalty programme naturally records as people shop. All this information could come from data gathered in the normal operation of the loyalty programme, including the customers' profiles in their loyalty programme accounts. But patterns like this are also used by retailers to decide what to recommend to customers who do not participate in the loyalty programme. As long as the customers who do participate statistically represent all the store's customers then even customers that do not participate will be similar enough to one type of customer in a pattern for recommendations to be made.

Choosing the right data sources

'Data' is a very dangerous word because it could mean a recording of anything. Customer data includes information about a customer, what they have looked at and bought in the past, where they are in their life right now and what their potential future interests are. It could be from social media sources, from banks, credit card firms, the government, healthcare providers, and many other sources (see Table 8.1). It could be data that identifies them as individuals or data that only describes something about groups of people without identifying individuals. It could be an actual record of what a customer did, or it could be data that describes what has been inferred from other data – data made from data. All these are types of data and with data that identifies individual people it is critical to respect customers' data privacy.

Table 8.1   Examples of data sources for customer journey analyses

Where to get the data for customer journey analyses
Retailer loyalty card schemes
E-commerce and all online activities
Order tracking and other logistics data, e.g., RFID chips, sat nav data
Financial services
Healthcare organisations, e.g., health monitoring equipment, medical scan data and medical records
Social media data
Still images and video, e.g., camera on mobile devices and laptops
Internet of Things (IoT) devices
National, regional and local government level services, e.g., personal tax, local planning applications
Mobile app data, e.g., location data from a taxi app like Uber or Lyft

To get the right data for an analysis, first you need an Analysis Question (see Chapter 10). An Analysis Question provides a way to focus the analysis project and to evaluate the outcomes of the analysis project. How well was the Analysis Question answered? Next follow the instructions in the last section for using the BDIVC to specify the data and data sources that you need to make some decisions and actions.

Table 8.2   Overview of types of some customer data and their sources

Type of data	Description and examples	Source of data
Personal profile data – who customers are. Accumulates and changes relatively slowly	Contact data like name, phone number and address	When customers register for an account, they are asked a whole list of questions
	Physical data like age, gender, height and weight	More questions can be asked as part of ordinary interactions with them
	Data about tastes like food and music preferences	Behavioural data can be recorded and added to personal profile data
	Data about hobbies and interests	
	Permissions data that record a person's data privacy preferences	
Past journey behavioural data – what customers have done in the past. Accumulates but does not change	Records of anything that customers have done with an organisation, e.g., website activity, mobile app activity, what they bought, all phone, email and messages. Also includes staff experiences	Data from customer touchpoints like website cookies, account logins and social media data
		Marketing databases, e.g., emails for newsletters
		Financial and payment systems
		Delivery and returns systems
		All contact centres and other customer relationship channels
		Interviews with staff in physical stores
		The recorded customer journey data from past customers with similar past journeys
Current situation data – where customers are now in their lives. A snapshot of their current situations	A customer's current situation is where they are in their wider life journey right now. Some stages in customers' lives are very common, like marriage, births, new jobs and buying cars. Recognising which life stage a customer is in right now enables an organisation to recommend options for the next stage	Live online activity, e.g., website activity, mobile app activity
		Recent data, which might be still up to date, e.g., recent emails and messages
		Data on other customers that are similar and might have been in similar situations
		Estimates of the current situation based on the above. Unless the customer is in live online contact with the organisation then their current situation is always a prediction based on the above data, i.e., data made from data

(Continued)

Table 8.2   (Continued)

Type of data	Description and examples	Source of data
Next option choice data – what customers might do next. Changes when they choose an option	Next option choice data is a choice of options that are personalised for each customer or for a small customer segment. Sometimes called 'Next Best Action techniques'	Personalisation is based on the above data, i.e., data made from data. This includes other customers that are similar and therefore might like similar things
		Options are generated with recommendation engines, like Amazon's 'people who bought these products also bought these products'
Goals and aims data – the outcomes that customers want to eventually get. The end point of their needs – updated when they get better ideas for what they want	Goal and aims are the personal objectives of each customer	What customers say their objectives are in their personal profile data
		The objectives of similar past customers
		Goals and aims are also generated from the above data, i.e., data made from data. This includes inferences from what they look for on websites and other things that they do

Table 8.2 gives an overview of the types of customer data that is available and some sources for it. This applies to business-to-consumer (B2C) organisations, business-to-business (B2B) organisations, not-for-profit organisations and government service organisations. All these organisations provide something that people need even if they do not pay for it directly. An understanding of each customer's profile, their past, their current situation and their future goals and aims greatly helps organisations to satisfy their customer needs by guiding them. Guiding in this case means supporting them in making decisions – primary decisions like buying specific products and services, or complementary decisions like choosing how to get the information they need to make the primary decisions. All customer journeys are chains of decisions; each journey stage is separated from the adjacent stages by choices of which stage to take next. Each journey is a series of many decisions and even retail journeys have a chain of decisions before the actual decisions to buy. Retailers use different ways to guide customers including Next Best Action techniques, which prompt sales and customer service people with actions, as well as customers. For example, questions that call centre operators should ask (Bain, 2020). Many organisations use **recommendation engines** to generate selections of products to show to customers on web pages. For example, when you see 'customers who bought this product also bought this product', prediction systems like these are an example of data being made from data. For example, a simple pattern that predicts when someone needs car insurance renewal can be made by adding one year to the date when the old insurance cover was taken out, or when a car owner asked for a quote. More complicated prediction techniques include looking for reoccurring patterns of the products that similar types of customers buy together. These are called 'associated product analyses' and they can be used to recommend extra purchases to customers based on what customers who have similar profile data and similar buying data have bought in the past.

Some of the data that is required for an analytics project is already present in the organisation and some has to be bought in from external partners. It depends on what decisions need to be made.

Either way, the first step in getting hold of any data is to carefully specify which data is needed. This must be done before looking for it in an organisation's internal database, or consulting external data suppliers like Experian, Equifax, Kantar, Google, Facebook or others. Organisations get customer data from customer **touchpoints** (Table 8.2). Customer touchpoints are when customers interact with an organisation and the interaction is recorded. Customer touchpoints are not the same as customer journey stages because customers continue to live their lives and progress along their individual journeys in between touchpoints. Touchpoints are more like snapshots or limited glimpses of the few events in customers' lives that an organisation is part of. Much of a customer's journey is invisible because it occurs well before the first touchpoint with an organisation or in between touchpoints (Hall et al., 2017).

Using websites as a data source

Interactions with an organisation's website are touchpoints and websites are important data gathering tools, as are mobile apps and social media. Websites can also be used to collect customer profile data and get a good view of what happens in the stages of customer journeys. The vast range of topics that organisations put on their websites each provide a chance to learn about customers – and websites can do this for millions of customers (Table 8.3). Website data includes anything to do with a topic

Table 8.3   Types of customer data that can be captured from websites

Type of website data	Description and examples	Area of website data gathered from
Personal profile data	Data about individuals and groups of website visitors	Registration pages, personal account management pages
		Initial account preferences – marketing and privacy – and updates
		Identified by logins or cookies
Past journey behavioural data	Past purchases, comments and other interactions with the site	Checkout pages and payment systems
	Past click-journeys through the site including dates and times Time spent on each page, order of click-journeys	Product pages and other pages with different topics
		Identity data is gathered using cookies or login information
	Indications of levels and variations of interest in specific topics covered by different web pages	Data that does not identify individuals is also gathered by recording visits to each web page and what visitors do on each page
	Changes in volume of visits, the mix of visitor profiles over time	
Current situation data	Live data from product pages and other pages with different topics	Based on where on a website and when the visitor used their touch screen, mouse or keyboard last, as well as which web page is currently showing on screen

(Continued)

Table 8.3   (Continued)

Type of website data	Description and examples	Area of website data gathered from
Next option choice data	A choice of options that are offered to the customer in the form of actions to take on the current web page. For example, a menu to click on, text boxes to fill in or opportunities to upload files. The choice of options decides the next page that a visitor will see, and the other actions taken by the organisation, e.g., linking with a bank to take payment, or scheduling a delivery	Based on the above data and similar data from past customers Options are generated with recommendation engines that use recording of the choices of past customers to suggest similar choices to similar customers, like Amazon's 'people who bought these books also bought these books'
Required outcome data	The personal goals and objectives of each customer, e.g., a specific product or piece of information to help a visitor with a query Other outcomes that might fit that customer based on an analysis of similar past customers	What customers say their objectives are in their personal profile data Equivalent information from similar past customers Inferences from the above data

that an organisation puts on a web page. Topics include product categories and individual products, customer queries, an organisation's background and news about an organisation. The topic of the page is a theme for communicating information to customers. More importantly, it is also a theme for gathering information back from customers using responses, cookies and login details. Responses include text typed into forms and comments, where people click and even which page they go to next, which can be either on the same site or on another site. Browser cookies identify the same person when they revisit the site, so they can be used to build up a record of what customers do over several visits. Login details identify people, but they also link up with useful profile data. Websites use cookies and logins to record how long a person spends on different pages and in which order they visit those pages. This is their 'click journey' through the site. Click journey data can be used to predict what they will do next as well as what other topics on the site might interest them, e.g., similar products and topics to what they spend the most time looking at.

Mobile phones are another way to gather valuable data about customers and where they are on their journeys (see Table 8.4). Mobile app data cover similar topics to website data, but these topics are more focused on the specific tasks that the app is there to help with, although websites also guide users through tasks like ordering products or finding out information, and a phone's browser can also provide access to websites. Data about mobile phone users is personally identifiable either through the sign-up profile for the app or by using each phone's unique identifying number, its **IMEI number**.

Phone data is particularly useful for getting information about the location of a customer when they use the app or a mobile website, because phones always know their own location. Another valuable characteristic of phone data is that it is more likely to be recorded in real-time. This is because people carry their phones with them, and always have them switched on and ready to use. Real-time data is data that is recorded and used at the same time. For example, when a customer gets lost and immediately looks at a navigation app to see their location for guidance. The app knows the customer's location moment-by-moment and is ready to help right away. This sort of real-time assistance can apply to getting lost in any type of search or customer journey, not just in physical travel. Phone apps also have access to ancillary phone data, which potentially includes descriptions of all the other apps on the phone and access to any other data on the phone that the customer has given permission to use, such as contacts and their numbers.

Table 8.4 Types of customer data from mobile apps and how the app collects it

Type of app data	Description and examples	How the app collects the data
Personal profile data	Data about individuals and groups of app users	App registration process, app account management sections
		Initial account preferences, e.g., marketing and privacy preferences. Updated preferences
		Individuals identified by login, cookies or mobile device IMEI number
Past journey behavioural data	Past user activity including purchases and other interactions	Checkout pages and payment systems
	Past use of the app including locations, dates and times. Time spent in each section of app, order of tap-journeys	Product information sections and other sections of the app with different topics, e.g., specific tasks
	Indications of levels and variations of interest in specific topics covered by different app sections, e.g., things that are hard, take time or need multiple visits to an app	All data is either linked to individual users using app login information or to the phone's IMEI number
	Changes in the volume of users, the mix of user profiles over time	
Current situation data	Where the user is now in their life journey, i.e., what the app is helping them with right now and potentially their exact and changing location	Based on the specific app screen, the position on that screen that was tapped on and when it was tapped on
	Live data about how the users are using the app	Location data triangulated from the specific mobile phone masts used by the phone

(Continued)

Table 8.4   (Continued)

Type of app data	Description and examples	How the app collects the data
Next option choice data	A choice of options that users are offered to tap on The choice of options decides what the app will do next, e.g., taking payment or scheduling a delivery	Based on the above data and data from similar past customers. Data comes from a variety of touchpoints not just the app Options are generated with recommendation engines. Like websites these use recordings of the choices of past customers to suggest similar choices to similar customers
Required outcome data	The reason why customers use the app, e.g., buying a product or getting advice Specific reasons that will satisfy an individual user, e.g., which product or advice	What customers say their objectives are in their personal profile data Information from similar past customers about which objectives satisfy types of users, e.g., specific products and advice versus specific users or specific problems Inferences from the above data

Using social media as a data source

Social media is another valuable source of customer data. Figure 8.3 shows how social media is used to gather data about customers at all stages of their journeys and how this can be fed back to support all sorts of activities. Social media data can be used not only to guess what customers are thinking and doing at different journey stages, including what stage they are at. It can also be used to influence them.

The rows of Figure 8.3 are arranged from top to bottom according to the six main stages of McKinsey's Customer Decision Journey model. This is one of many models that provide a framework for understanding customer journeys (Court et al., 2009). The idea is that most customers go through these six stages as they look for purchases. Columns a. to d. in Figure 8.3 are arranged according to which parts of an organisation would find the data useful. The resulting matrix of cells shows how different data is generated at different journey stages and is relevant for different parts of an organisation. As always, this data includes behaviour data and profile data: data about what people say and do on social media and who they are as 'types of people'.

Column a. describes data that is useful for staff who are concerned with monitoring how the brand of the organisation is thought of by customers and potential customers. At the top of column a. is data that tells staff which people are aware of the brand – have they heard of it? What do they think of it, and most importantly would they *Consider* it on a long list of potential purchases? As we go down column a., social media data can tell us which customers are *Evaluating* their long list of potential purchases to decide on a short list, and which products are still on it. Then as people post about their new purchases, we can learn who eventually *Buys* and which products they buy. Most importantly, we can use social media data to learn about their *Experience* of using the product, after they buy, and what they tell other potential customers as a result. For example, very satisfied customers will become *Advocates* of products, by praising products and organisations on social media, and then maybe they will *Bond* with them by choosing to repeat their purchases and posting that they have done so.

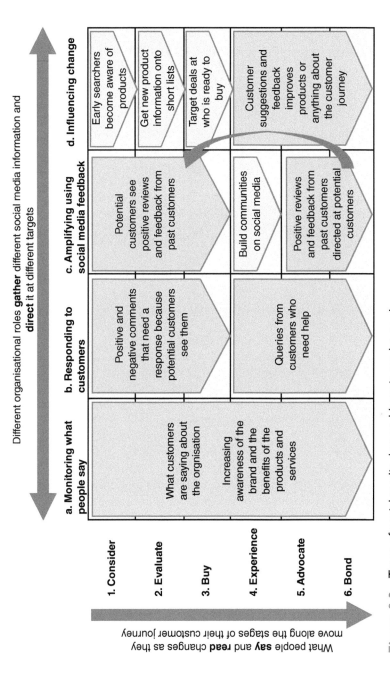

Figure 8.3   Types of social media data and how it can be used

Based on Divol et al. (2012)

Column b. describes data that is useful for staff who are concerned with crisis management and customer service. At the top, before the *Buy* stage, social media data can be used to quickly alert an organisation about crises, like when airline passengers tweet about being unfairly removed from planes or other public relations disasters. It is critical to monitor social media networks that an organisation's potential customers use for news about crises. This lets organisations see what its customers see so that timely action can be taken. The bottom of column b. holds data that can alert an organisation to problems or opportunities that occur after a product is bought. These can be anything from product assembly problems, or even difficulties in getting it out of the box. All posts, tweets and other social messaging are linked to specific people, so when a customer alerts an organisation about their problem then the organisation can respond with appropriate help and advice directly to that person. This is particularly useful for publicly showing how supportive an organisation is of its customers.

Column c. describes data that is useful for staff who want to increase referrals and recommendations, to foster communities and to increase brand advocacy. Referrals and recommendations from past customers on social media can be relayed to potential customers in the early stages of their journey – most importantly, at the point where they are deciding which products to filter down to a short list, or to actually buy. Connecting happy past customers from the bottom of column c. to potential customers at the top is particularly valuable because customers trust other customers more than they trust organisations. Communities of past customers that share information and stories about products on social media are well worth fostering because they are highly trusted. Critically, they might understand product users better than an organisation's staff and they provide significant extra resources for dealing with customer queries. For example, questions and answers on Reddit, Quora and other social media are very useful sources of solutions for highly specific problems that might not be dealt with on an organisation's Frequently Asked Questions web pages. YouTube is also full of video demonstrations of how to accomplish tricky product assembly and troubleshooting processes.

Column d. describes data that is useful for staff who want to understand how **customer sentiment** – customers' feelings and attitudes towards brands and products – and their behaviour changes over time. Customer sentiment for a whole market changes in response to advertising campaigns and cultural changes, and the top of column d. covers this. But column d. also covers social media data for understanding how the sentiment and behaviour of customers change as they progress down the column, through the stages of their buying journey. Understanding which stage individual customers are at is critical for targeting them with the appropriate marketing communications. For example, product launches are best targeted at people who are *Evaluating* a short list because they are near to buying but still choosing between options. Hearing about product launches too early in the buying journey risks products being forgotten or superseded by other later launches. Also, deals and offers need to be targeted at people who might buy because they will be wasted if they are received by people who will buy anyway, or would never buy, or have already bought the product. The bottom half of column d., after the *Buying* stage, holds customer suggestions data. This is valuable data that can be used to improve a product or anything about a customer journey.

Examples of business objectives and tasks, and which social media data can help with them

Social media data provides a record of what people post and comment on about an organisation, its staff and its products. It also includes information on who people aim their social communications at – like their friends –and who the senders and receivers are in terms of their demographic characteristics, their location and their patterns of past social media behaviour. Counting the things that happen on social media by collecting data enables a firm to support many different business objectives. Figure 8.4 shows examples of three business objectives, some of the tasks that help to fulfil them and the sort of social media data that can be used to carry out these tasks.

For the objective of increasing visitor traffic to a hotel website, the volume of traffic from different social media can be counted to see which social media is used by people who are more likely to click through to that website. LinkedIn users are very different from Instagram users, and they use these social media sites for different purposes. Understanding patterns of which social media is used by the type of people who need hotels is useful for deciding which social media sites to target with posts about the hotel's attractive features and holiday deals. The business users of LinkedIn might not be appropriate for increasing holiday visitor traffic, but they would be great for increasing mid-week business and conference visitor traffic. Different customer channels are best used for different purposes, just like different social media sites. Social media data can be used to compare social media to other channels that organisations use to interact with customers, channels like TV, radio, email, apps, call centres and physical stores. Different channels work best for the different stages of the customer journey and the different activities in Figure 8.3.

Examples of business objectives		
Increase website traffic by attracting more visitors	Understand what people are saying and doing because of product designs and marketing communications.	Increase sales by influencing choices at all stages of the customer journey.
Examples of tasks that data can help with		
Increase number of site visits, their length and engagement during a visit.	Improve brand strength and customer experience.	Increase lead generation, sales and profits.
Examples of date: what to count and then monitor for trends and changes		
Number of fans, followers, shares Click – through rates Volume of traffic from appropriate social media Share of return visitors, Page views, unique visitors, time spent on the site or specific pages Top keywords used in search engines Frequency of brand mentions on social media Number of social media conversations about brand and competitors	Sentiment changes trends: positive or negative Sentiment differences for each social media Number of brand advocates Number of reviews and positive ratings Trend in number of customer service issues Number of customer issues fixed via social media versus total number Search engine performance, e.g. search results placed high or low	Number of sales leads and trend Cost per lead and lead conversion rate Support cost (per customer in social channels) Share of repeat customers (from social media vs other channels) Sales revenue (direct or 'assisted') Transaction value per customer Customer lifetime value

Figure 8.4   Examples of data that can be gathered by counting what happens on social media

Posting on social media is very useful. For example, counting which posts website visitors click on the most to reach a website and what social media users say in response to posts provides a picture of what they think about the topic of each post as well as a general idea of your organisation's brand. Frequency counts of social media mentions, likes, shares, retweets, repins and other data can be made daily, weekly or for any period that is relevant to a business objective. Then each frequency count can be repeated for the next period and the next to build up trend data to see if the count is going up or down over time. Trends give feedback about an organisation's activities, like product and service improvements or social marketing campaigns. Anything that can be counted once can be counted again to watch the trend, and trends can be used to understand customers' changing feelings about the organisation and what it does. Even the timing of social media posts and marketing emails can have a strong effect on how successful they are, so gathering data on how the time of day affects the number of views of a post or the number of emails customers open is very important. For example, some types of customers have more time to read newsletter emails or posts over the weekend, so sending them on Friday night or Saturday morning works best for them.

All customer touchpoints are data sources

Any interaction between an organisation and a customer is a potential source of data because any interaction can be recorded. For example, if an organisation can persuade a customer to give their email address in return for regular newsletters it can record when these newsletters are opened. This will measure the interest of the customer and whether the email address is real. Newsletters also contain a **Call To Action** (CTA), which is designed to get readers of the newsletter to do something. A CTA tries to provoke readers to do something useful for the organisation because it would also be useful for them. CTAs include registering to receive further information, going to a specific page on a website, downloading an app or just giving an opinion on something.

Chatbots are another example of something that looks like a useful service to help customers but is also a valuable data gathering tool. All services are two-way – chatbots need to ask questions before they provide specific advice. So, they gather detailed information about individual customers' situations as well as general query areas that affect many customers. Chatbots are like those flow chart diagrams that guide you through a complicated series of steps with a few branches along the way – they ask questions at the branches to see which way you should go but every branch in the route is fully planned out and explained. Anything that can be fully described as a set of rules can be made into a flow chart or a chatbot. For example, laws about parking in a city are human rules, they are clearly described, simple and they change relatively slowly. Contrast this with the mechanisms that produce weather. These mechanisms are well understood but they work together in such complex ways that predicting the weather can be very tricky. But human rules on parking fines are simple enough that their application can be described in a flow chart or chatbot for almost any parking situation. This enables the DoNotPay app to use the rules of parking fines and appeals in London and New York to guide people through the process of appealing against their fines using chatbots (Cuthbertson, 2016).

Websites, mobile apps, social media and other customer touchpoints are all chances to record customer interactions. But the sheer amount of data that would generate is too much to store so most of it is not kept. Organisations must design their customer touchpoints precisely so that they gather the required data for their Analysis Questions, which we will cover in Chapter 10.

Tools for managing customers' journeys

Table 8.5 shows some online tools that are used to manage customers' progress along their journeys. These tools are grouped into three groups: Customer Relationship Management (CRM) tools for managing how customers progress along their overall journey, tools for designing and managing websites, and tools for managing content on social media.

In the early stages of a customer's journey, CRM tools help organisations to manage customers' progress by persuading them to purchase from the organisation. After the purchase stage, organisations continue to monitor and support customers to help them successfully use what they purchased, and to understand their problems and to spot opportunities to help them. This is done using a mixture of **digital channels** such as email, social media, websites and mobile apps. There are many cloud-based tools for optimising how all these channels are used by organisations, including tools that monitor the operation and use of mobile apps like MetricFire, Google Analytics for Mobile Apps and AppDynamics. These app monitoring tools are a bit like the analytics functions of the website tools in Table 8.5. These monitor how users use the different parts of a website, including the numbers of visitors, where they go and what they do. App tools also monitor how well the app software functions as it works, which helps to highlight problems and suggest solutions. This is very useful because the apps on mobile devices can be updated using their Internet connection to correct software problems that might cause errors, slow the app or confuse users.

Many of these tools can be connected together to move data between each other and to automate how and when they operate. The way to decide which tools to use, as always, is to use your customers' journey model to guide which stages to focus on, which in turn helps to decide what data you need. It helps in deciding what stages of the customer journey need improving (see Chapter 4 for examples of how to model journeys). A qualitative description of the stages of a customer journey model will provide a framework for adding more quantitative data from these tools, to provide detail where you need it. All the tools in Table 8.5 are cloud-based so they are all inherently connectable, but automation tools like If This Then That (ITTT) and Zapier can send data and instructions to various tools according to pre-defined triggers. As its name implies, ITTT tells other tools and devices to carry out whatever simple tasks they are designed to do when pre-defined events happen. For example, they can be told to send a notification email using an email app when a new customer fills in an online form in another app or on a web page, and simple tasks can be linked together to build more complicated and automated activities.

Another aspect of these tools that is very different to many software tools is that using them does not require much if any software coding skills. They are **'no-code' tools**, which means that they have templates that users can choose from and customise to build websites, social media management tools, mobile apps and whatever else the tool is for. Many of them are also free to use for low levels of use or for introductory periods. Finally, the tools mentioned here are just a few of the many that are out there. More examples include Heyoya, which lets customers add voice comments; various chatbots that can both ask and answer questions; and heat map tools for displaying concentrations of activities, like where web pages are clicked on the most. It is easy to find more by searching for 'tools like Zapier', 'email marketing tools', or using the phrase 'online tools that' with whatever you need the tool for.

Table 8.5   Online tools for monitoring and managing the progress of customers' journeys

Tool name	Description
Customer Relationship Management (CRM) tools: used to monitor and support progress along customer journeys	
Shopify https://www.shopify.co.uk	CRM tool plus an online store tool including product pages, payment and delivery functions
Hubspot https://www.hubspot.com	CRM tool for all stages of the customer journey
Other CRM tools	Zendesk, Zoho CRM, Salesforce and many more
Mailchimp https://mailchimp.com/	An email marketing tool with other automated marketing features Automates the large scale sending of emails to customers to help them along the stages of their journeys, including newsletters and special offers
Zapier https://zapier.com	Automation tool that uses pre-designed templates to let you connect other online tools together and automate without the need for writing code. E.g., collect data from tools that let customers fill in forms, like Google Forms or Typeform, and then add it into a spreadsheet tool like Google Sheets
If This Then That (IFTTT) https://ifttt.com/	Automation tool that uses simple templates and rules to create automated series of activities, which respond to triggers. Also connects devices like phones and apps and online services like Twitter and Amazon's Alexa
Other automation and connection tools	Microsoft Power Automate, Zoho Flow, Actiondesk, SnatchBot
Website tools: used to design and produce websites, and monitor what visitors do	
Wix https://www.wix.com **GoDaddy** https://uk.godaddy.com **WordPress** https://wordpress.com **Zoho Sites** https://www.zoho.com/sites	Websites are immensely valuable tools for helping customers to progress along their journeys. There is a range of online website building and operating tools that use pre-designed and customisable templates to avoid the need for coding. They have different abilities to connect with other tools like social media. Zoho offers a large range of online business tools including website tools
Google analytics https://analytics.google.com	Tool for monitoring what visitors do on a website, including time spent on pages, which pages they visited and where they came from to get to the site
Social media tools: used to manage the production and publication of content, and monitor its effects	
Hootsuite https://hootsuite.com	Social media management tool. Schedules the posting of content, replies to messages, monitors trends, manages adverts and analyses the effects on the audience
Buffer https://buffer.com	Social media management tool with similar but less extensive features to the above

(Continued)

Tool name	Description
MeetEdgar https://meetedgar.com	Social media scheduling tool
DivvyHQ https://divvyhq.com	Content marketing tool for organising and automating communications to customers and for collaboration between staff, as well as with external partners
Loomly https://www.loomly.com	Social media tool focusing on brand management
Other social media management tools	CoSchedule, Sprout Social, Zoho Social

Chapter summary

Understanding, analysing and improving customer journeys is the start and end of what makes organisations successful. There is nothing more important because helping customers to be successful by being indispensable is both the purpose and 'fuel' that drives organisations, especially if we recognise that all organisational stakeholders are types of customers.

Customer journeys require a series of linked decisions that only a customer can make. But customer journey models can guide customers to make the best decisions for them. This is because customer journey models contain knowledge about many past customers' journeys, like how to get to a customer's objects as well as suggestions for entirely new objectives that can still fit that customer's needs. They help customers to make informed decisions by suggesting options to choose from and explaining the outcomes of each choice.

Data for building customer journey models is produced by recording customer interactions at all stages of customers' journeys. This data comes from many sources including websites, apps, an organisation's IT systems, other organisations and human staff.

Further reading

If you are interested in helping customers, staff and anyone else to progress along their personal journeys then you might be interested in design thinking. Design thinking is a way of designing products, services, processes, organisations and anything else. What sets it apart is its focus on the people who will use and take part in the thing that is being designed. A good source of information is the company IDEO (https://designthinking.ideo.com).

Hierarchy Theory also helps us to think about customers' journeys and the systems of stakeholders that support them: Salthe, S. (1991) 'Two forms of hierarchy theory in modern discourses', *International Journal of General Systems*, 18(3): 251–264.

HOW TO DESIGN AND PRODUCE WHAT CUSTOMERS NEED

KEY IDEAS

- Journey models can be used to improve production journeys, which are the work journeys of the workers and machines that produce products and services.
- Production journeys can be improved using journey models to make them more efficient and successful, just like customer journeys.
- Two main types of production journeys are design journeys and manufacturing journeys.
- The purpose of a production journey is to produce products and services that help customers' journeys, so improving production journeys starts with a customer journey model.
- Many different data sources help us to understand the production journeys of workers and machines, including factory machine software, all an organisation's IT systems, all devices that workers use and even the products and software that has been sold to customers.
- Each data source provides a different perspective on each individual production journey as it progresses.

LEARNING OBJECTIVES

After reading this chapter you will be able to:

- Explain what production journeys are and who progresses along them.
- Describe the similarities and differences between customer journeys and production journeys.
- Describe how production journey models can be used to improve a product's design and how it is manufactured. Explain how this can also be done for services.
- Explain how organisations use production journey models to guide their workers. Describe how this can benefit workers as well as the organisation.
- Describe the sorts of data that are used to build production journey models. Explain the differences between these data sources.

The last chapter used a customer perspective. It explored how to use customer journey modelling to understand what customers really need and how to help them. This chapter follows on from that by tackling how to produce products and services that satisfy those customers' needs. It does this by applying Journey-based Thinking ideas to product and service production journeys. Production journey models are descriptions of how products and services are designed and then produced. Modelling production journeys can be used to improve the work journeys of the people and machines that make products and services, which in turn improves the journeys of customers that buy and use them.

This chapter explains what production journey models are and how to model two types of production journeys – product design journeys and product manufacturing journeys. It explains how both types of production journeys can be improved by using data feedback techniques like A/B testing and Minimum Viable Product (MVP) strategies, and it describes some of the many data sources that can be used to do this. Then it explains how production journey models can be used to help workers and machines in their roles and give workers a better experience.

Designing the products and services that customers need for their journeys

In the last chapter we talked about how to use customer journey modelling and Journey-based Thinking ideas to understand customers' experiences of their journeys and what is needed to help them reach their goals. But customer journey modelling can also be used to design and improve the products and services that help them reach their goals. All types of stakeholder journeys, including customer journeys, are ways of process thinking. Process thinking is a method of thinking about the world in terms of how it is changing. It considers everything to be fundamentally evolving and unstable. Everything is in the process of becoming something else, change is more fundamental than stasis, which produces novelty rather than uniformity (Rescher, 2000; Styhre, 2002). Process thinking is particularly useful for analysing how different customers can be helped along their personal journeys by products and services, which are themselves the outcomes of their own production journeys. Production journeys are produced when workers and machines work through the stages of their own work journeys to design and produce products and services. Table 9.1 has some examples of different types of journeys.

Table 9.1   Different types of journey models can be used to analyse how people and machines work together

Customer journey models – for analysing how customers reach their personal objectives with help from all the journeys below (see Chapter 8)

Staff work journey models – for analysing how the activities of staff members support business processes but are different for each person. or each iteration of a business process

Machines, electronic devices and software journey models – for analysing how software works within business processes but operates differently for each machine or run of that software

Product and service life cycle journeys – for analysing how products and service designs are created, improved and eventually phased out

Product and service production journeys – for analysing how product units are manufactured, and how a service is produced

Journey-based Thinking and business processes

Journey-based Thinking helps with the design of all business processes, including those that produce products and services. It comes from research into customer journeys in retail marketing (Lemon and Verhoef, 2016; Rosenbaum et al., 2017). The main difference between business process thinking and Journey-based Thinking is that business process models are objective whereas models that describe customer journeys, and the journeys of any other stakeholder, are subjective. Business process modelling comes from research into improving production processes in organisations (Curtis et al., 1992; Shaw et al., 2007). Journey-based Thinking comes from research into services and value creation (Ramirez; 1999; Vargo and Lusch, 2004; Lepak et al., 2007), and focuses much more on subjectivity, how every person experiences their personal journey in a different way, even if a journey is enabled by business processes. All stakeholders experience different positives and negatives; this is how all stakeholders each experience a different journey route to the same goal. Even journey analyses of machines can be made from an individual machine's perspective. After all, each car of the same make and model has a different maintenance history in its log book. Business processes need to take account of differences between each time they are enacted. But they start from a general perspective, the perspective of producing a service, whereas Journey-based Thinking starts from the individual perspective of whomever makes that journey, a service-needs perspective (Shaw, 2007), the perspective of consuming a service.

Work journeys produce products and services that help customer journeys

Just like customers, all the workers and machines in an organisation can be thought of as travelling along their own work journeys. It is these work journeys that produce the products and services that customers use. Machines, electronic devices and software also follow their own work journeys, journeys that are based on their roles in an organisation's business processes. The difference between a business process that a worker or a machine follows, and the journeys of those workers and machines is that business processes are general, top-down ways of thinking. Journeys are bottom-up ways of thinking about how individual workers and machines progress towards their own goals. Business process models and journey models meet in the middle, but they start from different perspectives, top-down as opposed to bottom-up. Journey models analyse the subjective experiences of each single worker or machine progressing along a personal journey; business process models try to standardise the activities of all workers and machines. Journey models and business process models are two ways of planning and analysing activities.

However, the personalisation of journey models has a limit. Even modern digital technologies cannot record the individual differences between the working days of large numbers of workers or machines, as they unfold second by second. But that level of detail is not necessary because organisations could not respond with that degree of flexibility. Even if a supermarket used a loyalty app to understand what each one of its millions of customers needed to buy in their weekly shop, it could only sell them products that it stocked. All organisations are limited in what they can do by their organisational capabilities. They cannot infinitely customise everything that they do even if they know exactly how every customer's needs differ from all the others. So, they have to standardise at some point. A top-down perspective is useful for standardisation and for a global viewpoint, whereas a bottom-up perspective helps to analyse individual circumstances and backstories, which is useful for searching for the root causes of production problems, or for assessing the quality of raw materials and data by seeing how they were sourced.

Journey-based Thinking can be used to analyse the life cycles of product designs as well as how those products are manufactured. Products start with an initial design stage, then a first version stage and then the designs go through stages of improvement until each design is phased out in favour of a new version. Individual product units also follow journeys on factory assembly lines as they start off as raw materials and become finished units, which are then delivered to customers. Unlike products, services are produced and consumed at the same time. They are produced by the collective activities of workers and machines progressing through specific stages in their own personal journeys. The secret to designing product and service production journeys is to start with a model of the customer journeys that the production journeys are there to help with (see Chapter 8). A customer journey model describes how customers produce service-needs as they progress along their journeys. Service-needs are the requirements for the next stage – they are the thing that a service satisfies, its reverse. Thinking about service-needs helps us to understand how to fulfil these service-needs with products and services, which will enable a journey to move forward towards the journey-maker's objectives (Shaw, 2007). Thinking about product and service designs in terms of how they help customer journeys makes it easier to make sure that they actually do help.

Helping retail customers' journeys

All customers travel along different journeys, so the key to supporting them is to understand the various routes each type of customer takes. Table 9.2 shows how the routes of every individual customer vary in lots of ways, even though most customers go through similar main journey stages. Within each main stage there is a large variation in what happens to each customer, so each customer journey ends up being subtly different. Customers start from different personal situations, they have different needs and tastes for what they want to buy, and they end up purchasing different product variants or service options. But that is just the first half of a customer's journey. The after-purchase stages of a customer's journey are arguably even more important than the pre-purchase stages. After a customer buys something it becomes even more important that they have a smooth and frictionless journey, and a great customer experience. This is because an after-purchase journey that is useful, easy and a great experience will help to convince them to buy again from that organisation and recommend it to their friends on social media.

All journeys are full of decisions that customers need to take. The reason why all customer journeys are different is that customers make different decisions. Indeed, one way to think about customer journeys is as a long chain of decisions, one after the other. That is why another common framework for modelling customer journeys is McKinsey's Customer Decision Journey model (Court et al., 2009). Retail customer journeys and business-to-consumer (B2C) customer journeys have strong similarities to business-to-business (B2B) customer journeys. They start with the recognition of a problem to be solved, then a search for solutions and the evaluation and choosing of a solution, followed by a purchase decision, and a start to using what was purchased. Government services can also be modelled this way. Table 9.2 also follows this broad set of stages and is based on McKinsey's Customer Decision Journey model. All products and services – B2B and B2C, commercial and non-commercial – can be modelled by starting with these high-level main stages and then gradually adding detail by asking the stakeholders involved what actually happens. Customers, staff, partners and other data sources can be used to gradually add detail to the model until it is detailed enough for the purpose of your analysis. The purpose of the analysis is defined in the Analysis Question, which we cover in Chapter 10.

Table 9.2   How the main stages of retail customers' journeys vary, adapted from Mckinsey's Customer Decision Journey model (Court et al., 2009)

Main stage	Description	Ways that routes through each main stage vary
1. Problem recognition stage When a customer becomes aware that they need something, maybe without knowing what it might be	An event or collection of events initiate a customer journey by creating a 'service-need' – the requirement for some customer problem to be solved. E.g., something breaks and needs to be replaced, the customer sees an attractive item of clothing in the street, or a nice car on TV, or some new product that they hear about from friends	• Various starting points and trigger events • Different problems that need solving, things customers would love to have rather than need, or new products and services that customers want
2. Information search stage When a customer assembles a 'long list' of options	The customer looks for potential solutions to the problem or products and services that might fit the service-need, compiling a list of possible solutions from many different sources. E.g., searches on Google, YouTube and social media like Pinterest, or conversations with family, friends, work colleagues and staff in stores. Generates many potential options, which people store as saved photos and notes, emails to themselves, website bookmarks, Pinterest collections and in other ways	• Many different sources used, online, offline, face-to-face • Little attempt to filter, a 'long list' not a 'short list' • Can last minutes, hours, days or even months, depending on what is searched for • Includes actual products and services as well as information needed to find them, e.g., suppliers, advice sources • Ideas stored in various ways
3. Evaluation of alternatives stage When a customer gets more information to filter a 'long list' into a 'short list'	The customer filters their long list to remove most options using advice from family, friends, staff in stores and experts. Advice is online, offline and in person More information is searched for to support this filtering depending on the product or service, e.g., pricing, dimensions, materials, quality, availability, physical look, the service agreement and other characteristics	• Filtering a 'long list' into a 'short list' • Follow-up searches for detail to help make the final choice • Many different trusted sources used • Various choice criteria are used
4. Purchase decision stage When a customer decides which product to buy	The customer decides on the exact product or service to purchase. For products, this is the exact product code. For services, this is the exact set of service options. Decisions include options about payment, delivery, warranty and insurance. These decisions also include how any contact with the supplier will continue after the purchase, e.g., agreement to be added to a marketing database	• Decide on the exact product code or the exact service variant • Decide on the after-purchase options, which determine what happens later
5. Purchase stage When a customer buys something This is the major division between the two main parts of the customer journey – pre purchase and post purchase	The customer purchases an exact product or service. In a store this includes queuing up at the till, paying, getting a receipt, bagging and walking out of the store. Online this includes going to the customer's basket, reviewing items, choosing payment and delivery options, and choosing from additional service and contact options, like warranty and insurance. It also tells the buyer about marketing communications options like whether to be contacted in the future about new products	• Purchase the exact product or service • Various ways to pay • Various delivery options • Various warranty and insurance options • Various marketing communications options

(Continued)

Main stage	Description	Ways that routes through each main stage vary
6. Post purchase experience stages Everything that happens after buying: starting to use the purchase, the ongoing relationship with supplier, and the end of use **This main stage has many more sub-stages than previous main stages because here, whatever is purchased joins with the customer's life journey**	6.1 Getting products into a position to use them Products get delivered and potentially installed, e.g., washing machines or cookers. Any consumables to use with the main product are purchased, like petrol, razor blades or washing powder. Or there may be set-up activities like charging a phone and adding a sim card	• Various ways to deliver and install, might need specialist help • Does not apply to services
	6.2 The first time a customer uses a product and service The customer follows instructions for using their purchase for the first time. The instructions that teach the customer are a training service, e.g., online or paper manuals, or videos. Problems that the customer might have are supported by customer service staff, including for example Frequently Asked Questions, a call centre, a website, videos or an online user group	• Requires a training service, which might be in a manual or in videos • Various problems that customers encounter • Various information sources for solutions and ways to diagnose and pick solutions
	6.3 Ongoing use of products and service The customer continues to use the product or service and searches for new ways to make use of it (including new problems that occur). Information sources to help this come from customer service staff, including for example Frequently Asked Questions, a call centre, a website, videos or an online user group	• Various problems that customers encounter • Various information sources used
	6.4 End of use (new customer journey?) The customer stops using the purchase because it breaks down or does not function well enough. Alternatively, they might no longer need it, or they might want to replace it, which triggers a new customer journey. This is also the stage where physical products start their own recycling, refurbishment/reuse, repair or disposal journeys	• Various reasons that the customer stops using the purchase • Various disposal options for products • Various new customer journeys to start

Segmenting groups of stakeholders by their journey routes

Journey-based Thinking enables customers and other stakeholders to be segmented not just by their destinations, like the products that they buy or their personal objectives, but also by the routes that they take to get there. In other words, they can be grouped together by similar starting positions and then as they go along their journeys they can be grouped by similar problems, queries or any other qualities that mean they have similar experiences. Route segmentation enables organisations to find common problems that occur on journeys and then prioritise fixing them by the scale of each problem and the impact on customers. Route segmentation can also be used to amplify positive experiences in journeys as well as to reduce negative experiences. It can do this by recognising when things go well for some customers and then replicating it for other customers in similar situations.

The way to segment customers' routes is shown in Figure 9.1. First, make a high-level customer journey model, as described in Chapter 4. This will provide a picture of the main stages that most customers go through: where they start from, like when they first notice that they need a product, or when they start looking for a solution to a problem, then how they move forward from there. For most B2B and B2C customers, the customer journey will follow the main stages in the Customer Buying Process (CBP) model (Kotler et al., 2009) or Mckinsey's Customer Decision Journey model (Court et al., 2009). For stakeholders that do not actually buy anything – like suppliers or co-workers – the stages will consist of some other series of step-by-step activities that most of them enact as they move towards their goals. In Figure 9.1, the main stages are numbered 1 to 6 like in Table 9.2's retail customer journey, but there could be as many as are needed to cover the parts of the journey that are being analysed. For example, they might only focus on the stages after the purchase is made. Notice that the substages in Table 9.2 show how the main stages of a customer's journey link with the work in all the production journeys that help that customer to progress.

Next, find out where customers experience problems in their journeys and then prioritise them. This will be in terms of bad experiences, not very useful advice and things that make it difficult for customers. Information on the types and scales of customers' problems can come from data sources like the customer service and call centre logs, complaints records or by talking with the relevant people in the organisation who deal with customer problems. Customer problems can be understood best by breaking the main stages down into substages to highlight the specific events that contain or cause the problems. All customers have the same general journey, but they experience the detail of the journey – the substages – very differently. This is because customers come from a variety of backgrounds, they are equipped with different knowledge, and they aim for different goals. This is shown in Figure 9.1 by the five parallel routes of substages followed by customers a, b, c, d and e. The routes of customers d and e are very similar for most substages but not all. The fours crosses in main stage 3 may represent a frequently occurring problem. The same might be true for three crosses at the start of main stage 6. The difference between the routes of these customers is in their experiences of small substages – what are problems for some customers are not problems for others.

The way to prioritise customers' problems is to balance the impact of the problems with their frequency. A minor inconvenience to a small number of customers is much less of a priority for fixing than a dangerous product failure that happens a lot. Many of the high frequency and high impact problems

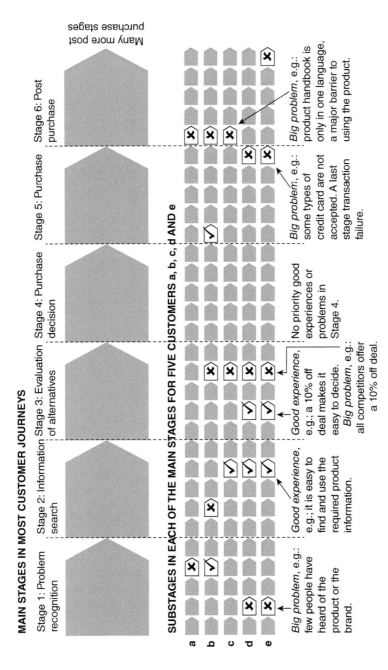

Figure 9.1 Different substages make up different routes through the main stages of customers' journeys

Customer journeys can be broken down into main stages and main stages can be divided into substages. Customers experience different routes for the same overall journey when they have different experiences at lower-level stages. Counting the good experiences and the bad experiences shows organisations where to prioritise actions that reproduce the good experiences and remove the bad ones with future customers. Understanding the types of customers who have these good and bad experiences provides a useful pattern for treating customers differently.

will already be well known to the organisation. The difficulty is in prioritising middle level problems. The best way to do this is to rank the types of problems as well as their impact using advice from a mixture of people in the organisation, people who together represent a spread of expertise and responsibilities. The aim is not to get a perfectly agreed set of priorities but a good enough list to get working on. This approach also helps to gather support for doing the work.

Sometimes the solution to a problem is not a general fix for all customers but a way of finding a specific type of customer who is prone to particular problems, or who reacts well to particular experiences, e.g., customers d and e in Figure 9.1. This is a way to segment customers by their routes because it highlights problems or good experiences that only affect a certain type of customer. Whilst problems should be removed, if they are high priority, good experiences should be tackled in the opposite way. When good experiences are found they should be replicated for more customers, either by understanding the types of customers that like them, or by understanding the types of situations that they happen in. For example, some customers might be very successful at using a product because of their experience of using something similar, or some stages of a customer journey might be smooth and problem-free because a well-trained team oversees it. Either way, an understanding of the reasons and context of a good experience is helpful for replicating it.

Helping staff journeys

Journey-based Thinking and customer journey modelling can also be applied to non-retail customer journeys because all stakeholders are a type of customer, for example, the work of staff in product design and manufacturing. Together, the work journeys of these people produce products and services for the official customers. The main stages of product design and product manufacturing journeys are shown in Table 9.3. The main stages of the design journey are similar to the retail customer journeys described in Table 9.2 because they are mainly concerned with searching for potential solution options, and then choosing from them in order to solve design questions. A product design journey is usually more fluid and iterative than a manufacturing journey because its objective is to create a design that does not yet exist. A product manufacturing journey is relatively fixed because the product to be manufactured has already been designed. However, product manufacturing journeys also change because staff who work on them will try to improve them. Indeed, every stage of a product manufacturing journey can be improved to reduce waste, errors and other costs, as well as to improve aspects of the product that the customer would value. The main difference is that product manufacturing journeys tend to be improved in lots of small incremental ways rather than with the large 'step changes' that the redesign of a product would make.

Service production journeys can be described in a similar way to product manufacturing journeys. First, there needs to be a clear description of what journey the service customer is on and how the service should play a part in helping them. Then, working backwards from this description, the roles of staff, machines, software and guidance information can be planned out so that from the customer's point of view, they all work smoothly together.

Table 9.3 The main stages of a product design journey and a product manufacturing journey

Product design journey		Product manufacturing journey	
Main stages	**Description of stages**	**Main stages**	**Description of stages (soft drink example)**
Frame the objective as a question, e.g., 'How can customer accomplish X?'	Specify what the design enables customers to do, based on what customers need for successful journeys and great experiences	Gather raw materials	Carbonated soft drinks have a number of ingredients including a sweetener or sugar syrup, carbon dioxide, water and the drink formula. They also need a bottle with a cap or a can. All of these need to be gathered, checked and brought to the start of the production line
Gather inspiration: get rough ideas	Observe and talk to customers and people who understand customers to get ideas about customers' service-needs and their problems that need solving, plus potential solutions. This is like the start of the Customer Buying Process model but applied to designing products, not choosing products	Prepare raw materials	Before filling, bottles and cans need to be thoroughly washed and rinsed
Generate ideas: get solutions	Use the inspiration gathered to help push past the obvious and come up with fresh solutions to the problem	Assemble/mix raw materials	Before filling, the ingredients need to be mixed and tested for balance in the amounts of sweetener or sugar syrup, carbon dioxide, water and the drink formula
Make ideas tangible: prototypes	Build prototypes for testing what works and what does not	Package product	The bottles or cans are filled and sealed with a cap or ring pull
Test prototypes and learn	Test the prototypes, get feedback and improve them	Label packaging and inspect	Bottles are labelled. Cans already have information printed on them. Containers are checked
		Package and stack in warehouse	The bottles or cans are packaged using plastic or paper and then stacked on pallets and moved to the finished products warehouse

Design journey example based on IDEO's design thinking process (IDEO, 2021). Product manufacturing journey example based on the author spending a year in a Coca-Cola bottling and canning factory in Poland

Improving product and service production journeys

Production journeys are the journeys that an organisation's staff, its partners and even its machines and software progress along as they produce products and services for customers. Modelling these production journeys helps to improve the journey experience for staff and for the organisation's partners, and it makes all of them more likely to succeed in their work objectives. Modelling the journeys of machines and software helps them to be more effective because it systematically analyses what they need to accomplish and what resources and support they require to do it.

All parts of production journeys can be modelled to improve their experience, usefulness and ease:

- How people feel about the experience – which helps staff retention and motivation.
- How useful the stages of the journey are for people and machines – for reaching their objectives.
- How easy the stages of the journey are for people and machines – without extra effort, uncertainty and confusion.

The experience of working in a production journey is as important for workers as it is for customers on their journeys. If workers do not like the experience they will not perform as well or they will leave. The design of production journeys must fit the personal objectives of the people that take part in them, and they must be able to get the raw material and informational resources that they need to do their jobs. These journeys must also be designed so that the roles of people and machines comfortably fit their capabilities. A person that is nearly well trained enough or a machine that is mostly powerful enough for a job will fulfil that role some of the time but not all the time. There is a natural variation in how each journey is enacted. This is similar to the way that every customer experiences a slightly different customer journey. So, production journeys must be designed to include people and machines with capabilities that can comfortably deal with most variations that come their way.

Encouraging more joined-up working

Modelling production journeys helps staff to join-up and work more closely together. Journey models describe the activities of individual staff members, external partner organisations and even machines and software. They give a timeline for what needs to happen, when, and who needs to do it. This mixture of 'what', 'who' and 'when' can be used to coordinate complicated activities where lots of people and machines need to work together smoothly over extended time periods. Putting all this information into one model also provides a chance for many different people to check it, to fill in information gaps and to reach a consensus about solutions.

It also enables backwards planning, where you start with the desired outcomes and plan backwards to where you are now. In Figure 9.2 there is an example from Mckinsey that illustrates how the journey of staff producing a customer experience links to the journey of the customer as they experience a service. It also shows how the places where the organisation directly interacts with a customer, customer touchpoints, are very limited snapshots of the whole of what that customer experiences.

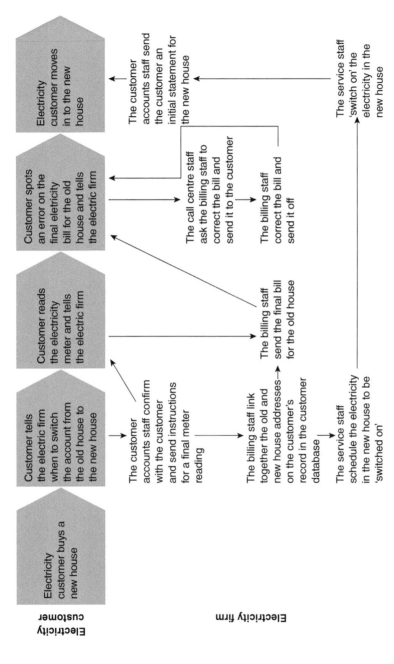

Figure 9.2 Different staff working together to help a customer to move house

Adapted from (Maechler et al., 2016)

In another energy firm example, Octopus Energy designed its organisational structure and IT systems to make sure that the person who answers a customer's call can solve 95% of the problems. Instead of separate departments using separate IT systems and working in silos, the firm uses cross-functional teams with the power to make decisions and fix problems themselves. The firm mapped out the stages of its customers' journeys including apparently minor issues like 'no-reply' email addresses. These shield operational staff from customer queries but are frustrating for customers who want to communicate with specific experts. They also mean organisations miss out on getting useful feedback from customers. Octopus uses customers' emails to get valuable information on how to improve the clarity and design of its communications. The company's focus on customer experience also enables it to learn of their unmet needs. This led to it renting out thermal cameras to customers who wanted to see where their houses were leaking heat, and then giving them advice on helping to reduce this waste (Gilliland, 2021).

Using data to improve product and service production journeys

Two commonly used ways to improve production journeys are Minimum Viable Product (MVP) strategies and A/B testing strategies. Both use feedback loops to make changes. They use data from the recordings of past customer experiences to improve future customer experiences. MVP strategies are part of a set of techniques called 'lean start-up methodologies', which came out of the lean manufacturing ideas of the Toyota Production System (Reis, 2011; Blank, 2013). A/B testing is another experimental approach that compares different versions of a journey in parallel (Chaffey and Smith, 2017).

MVP strategies use feedback data to improve products and services from a 'just good enough' start. The initial MVP might not meet all customers' needs but it offers enough features to fit their basic needs and to get some customers to use it. This produces feedback data and other operational data, which can be used to improve the product or service's design, as well as how it is produced. Feedback data comes from customers themselves or other ways of monitoring the design's performance for customers, like website and app usage data, customer satisfaction questionnaires or customer interviews. Information from customer support staff and sales staff also provides valuable feedback for product improvement. The difference with feedback from users of online software – or products that have an Internet connection – is that data can be gathered much faster, automatically and at a much larger scale. This also applies to online software like Hotmail or anything that we do on a website because it is connected via the Internet to the organisation that made the software. It is the same for Internet-connected products like the Amazon Echo and Google Nest smart speakers. Data feedback and improvement loops can be continuous and based on highly detailed data (see Figure 9.3).

Organisations use feedback data to continuously improve any designs, for example when the same customer uses an updated piece of software, or when another customer buys the next improved version of a product. What counts is getting a chance to implement improvements. Internet of Things products are connected to the cloud so their software features can always be updated, as can any online software, like online games. But physical products can only be updated when there is an opportunity to replace a part, like the brush head of an electric toothbrush, or if a product can be refurbished. If this is not possible then products can only be upgraded when customers buy a new version of the product. This

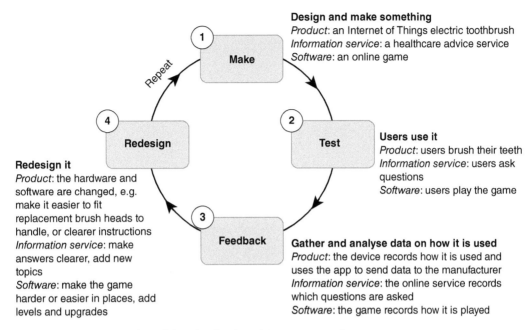

Design and make something
Product: an Internet of Things electric toothbrush
Information service: a healthcare advice service
Software: an online game

Make

Repeat

Redesign

Test

Feedback

Users use it
Product: users brush their teeth
Information service: users ask questions
Software: users play the game

Redesign it
Product: the hardware and software are changed, e.g. make it easier to fit replacement brush heads to handle, or clearer instructions
Information service: make answers clearer, add new topics
Software: make the game harder or easier in places, add levels and upgrades

Gather and analyse data on how it is used
Product: the device records how it is used and uses the app to send data to the manufacturer
Information service: the online service records which questions are asked
Software: the game records how it is played

Figure 9.3   Four examples of data feedback and improvement loops

has implications for the speed of the improvement loop because updates to software and information services can be made at almost any time, whereas buying a new product depends on how often customers replace that type of product. The important thing is to redesign the product or service, so it changes how customers experience the journey that they are on and helps them to progress towards their goals in a better, cheaper, faster and smoother way. It is only a better product or service if it improves the customer's journey.

For product organisations it is especially important to think about the services that they provide to go with their products to make a completely smooth customer experience. These include information services at all stages of the customer journey to help the customer choose the right products, an easy buying and delivery service that uses a well-designed website, a simple and quick to use product manual with a quick start guide, and a selection of ideas on how to use the product, like recipes for a microwave oven. Services that go well with products also include a full set of help services for customers' queries, like Frequently Asked Questions, a competent customer service team and a helpful user community.

Some examples of what A/B testing strategies are used to improve include web page design details, the fonts and formats of marketing emails, the targeting accuracy of online advertisements, and the text and graphics in mobile apps. Imagine two people are sitting side by side, each looking at the same product page on their phones. They are trying to find a great t-shirt for one of them. You would think that they will be looking at exactly the same thing on their screens, but maybe not. If a single web page gets a large number of people looking at it every minute, then small changes can be made to the page to test how they affect the behaviour of visitors. This is why A/B testing is also called 'split testing', because it splits the streams of visitors to a page – some visitors see one version of a page, and some see another. If small changes to the font, the colours or the images on a web page cause more people to buy a product then the changes will stay.

A/B testing can be used in any situation where some feature of a product or service can be changed, and you can get fast feedback on the effects of that change. Websites, apps and other online software are perfect for this because they are always connected to large numbers of users, who quickly react to the changes and generate feedback data. Parallel comparison tests like this can also be done when designing stores in different locations, or when setting prices for different groups of customers. Parallel comparison tests are not just for comparing design choices that cause more sales, they can also be used to compare ideas for reducing negative customer experiences like choosing how to assemble complicated furniture. They can also be used for increasing good customer experiences like using well-designed information pages that make it easy to choose between different versions of a product. This can be measured by gathering data on good outcomes like more sales or higher customer satisfaction ratings.

Manufacturing and logistics data can also be used to improve how people and machines function on their individual work journeys, in ways that improve their **productivity**, the quality of what they yield or their **availability** to work. Whether it is the journey of a person or of a machine, all journeys can be analysed on their own as well as part of a greater production journey. When analysing how to improve product and service production journeys it is best to start off by looking at the whole manufacturing process. This includes the work journeys of all the people and machines that work in it. Start at the end of this 'journey of journeys' and work backwards through the stages of that journey to look for problems and barriers that reduce productivity and increase waste.

The benefits of improving production journeys

Production journeys enable customer journeys, so improving production journeys will improve customer experiences. But it will also lead to substantial efficiency savings and quality improvements in whatever the organisation does. Some of these benefits include:

- **Productivity** – production journeys focus on the work journeys of an organisation's staff and machines and redesigning them is aimed at making them faster to carry out and use less resources.
- **Quality** – the quality of the outputs of production journeys is improved by analysing the stages of activities that go into making it, whether it is a product or a service.
- **Yield** – whilst related to productivity and quality, **yield** is a valuable way to measure the efficiency of a production journey. Yield is the number or amount of good quality outputs that are produced for a given set of inputs, e.g., X tonnes of scrap paper might yield Y tonnes of cardboard when it is recycled.
- **Machine availability** – individual machines that work in a production journey can be monitored to predict when they need maintenance. This increases the overall time that a machine is available to be used and it reduces unplanned maintenance in favour of planned maintenance. Sensors on individual machines collect condition monitoring data like productivity, the quality of its outputs and operating characteristics like temperatures, vibrations and evidence of wear.

- **People availability** – the availability of staff is fundamentally different to machine availability and relates to the idea that every stakeholder is a customer. If stakeholders do not get what they need from a business model, then they will leave or underperform. With staff this means increased sick days, reduced productivity through lower motivation and higher staff turnover. Data sources for monitoring this include staff satisfaction surveys, regular performance discussions with managers, and exit interviews.

Getting the right data to guide decisions and actions

Chapter 8 explained how a customer journey analysis will suggest many potential decisions and actions to be taken and how the Big Data Information Value Chain (BDIVC) model can be used to analyse them. The same approach can be used for improving production journeys. A production journey analysis will suggest areas to improve the journey based on how the people involved feel about the experience, how useful it is for the people and machines, and how easy it is to succeed in the role. Each improvement area can be described in terms of the decisions and actions that might improve it. Then the BDIVC model can be used to suggest the data that is required and sources of that data.

Choosing the right data sources

The data that describes production journeys includes information about the products and services being produced as well as the design of how they are produced. Customer journeys are designed by each customer as they choose their next stage, one after the other. Their choices might be influenced and guided by organisations but ultimately every customer designs their own life journey. But the journeys of products and services that move from raw materials and information into finished products and complimentary services must be carefully planned and coordinated, or the people and machines that enable production journeys will not work smoothly together. Imagine a factory that fills thousands of bottles with soft drinks every day. The production journey of a single bottle of cola depends on the work day journeys of all the people and machines that work to produce it. Delays will be caused if people do not arrive for work at the right time, or if the drinks are ready but there are no empty bottles available. For a bottle of cola to exit the factory on a truck with hundreds of other bottles it must go through many stages, including loading onto a pallet, wrapping the pallet with protective film and loading it onto a lorry. Before that final stage each bottle will have been moved around many times. And right at the start the cola mix and the bottles need to be prepared, and then the bottle needs to be filled. Every stage requires activities by people and machines like forklift trucks, pallet wrappers and bottle fillers. And each stage consumes many resources including the cola mix of water, sugar and cola concentrate, empty bottles, wrapping film, and electricity. If any of these people, machines and resources are not available at the right time then there will be a delay. If any activity is done wrong, by using the wrong resources or the wrong machine settings, then the resulting bottles of cola might taste bad or be substandard in some way. This will create other types of waste and delays. The work journeys of a complicated system of people, machines and resources like a factory need to be carefully 'choreographed', or there will be many delays, mismatches, errors and waste.

Production journey data includes information that describes every stage of the journey which produces a product or a service, as well as the journeys that design and redesign them. This data comes from manufacturing departments, service departments and the machines and software that they use. These sources strongly overlap with the data sources in Chapter 8 that record customer journey data (see Table 9.4). As with customer data, it is critical to respect workers' data privacy, as with any data that identifies individual people.

Table 9.4   Overview of data sources for product and service production journey analyses

Software on factory production machines
Organisational IT systems, e.g., finance, production, logistics, websites, sales and marketing, HR
All workers' PCs, tablets and work phones, e.g., product location and stock level apps used by staff in supermarkets
Financial services IT systems, e.g., banking systems and payment systems
Health monitoring equipment, medical scan data and medical records
Internet of Things (IoT) devices, e.g., assembly line machinery, farm and factory vehicles
National, regional and local government IT systems

Choosing data sources to improve production journeys can be complicated. Like with customer journey data in Chapter 8, start with the sort of decisions and actions you might need for each task and use the BDIVC model to specify the data sources you will need.

Table 9.5 shows an overview of the types of data that can be recorded from product and service design journeys and the sources of each. Design journeys plan out the roles of people and machines on the production journeys that actually produce the products and services. All design journeys must start with a clear picture of how the product or service will help the customer. This includes which customer segments are involved and how this help fits into their customer life journey (see Chapter 8).

The next stages of design journeys gather inspirations of problems and solutions that the organisation can help these customers with, then they try to solve each one (Table 9.5). The design journey has stages that are very similar to those in a customer journey because it starts with a problem definition, then it finds a long list of potential solutions, which it filters into a short list and finally chooses one. A major difference to a customer journey is that a design journey should include stages that build, test and learn from prototype products and services. Prototypes test whole designs or key parts of designs on real users to find ways to improve them before the design is finalised. This is different to MVP approaches that sell just-good-enough versions to customers in order to get real-life feedback. In each case the important point is to use feedback data to improve the design. Improved versions of the product or service can be introduced when it is commercially appropriate, which will usually be when the costs of changes to the design, manufacturing and associated services are paid for by increased or continuing sales. Evaluating the design reuses data on the initial design objectives from the first stage.

Table 9.5   Types of data that record product and service design journeys

Type of data based on stage and task	Description and examples	Source of data
Frame a question – the initial design objectives in the form of a question, e.g. 'How can customer accomplish X?'	Data that helps to specify what a customer needs to be helped to do. This includes the type of customer as well as the customer journey stage(s) that the product or service should help them with. For example, a simple toaster helps people to toast bread and other food. But some customers use a toaster for convenience when they are in a rush, or with frozen as well as fresh food. The toaster's design must reflect these different objectives and different uses	A customer journey analysis for relevant customer types and their life journeys (see Chapter 8) Includes the definition of relevant customer types (customer segments)
Gather inspiration: get rough ideas	Find potential solutions by looking at similar products and similar problems. Includes breaking the problem down into small parts and sub-stages to look for ideas	From customers: interviews, questionnaires, and data recordings of customers' past journeys From staff: interviews and questionnaires, including staff in the analysis team who really understand customers From other products: online search
Generate ideas: get solutions	Develop ideas from the last stage and choose the best ones. Requires evaluation based on the initial design objectives in the first stage and some feedback	Data on initial design objectives from the first stage, i.e., data made from data. Supplementary evaluation feedback from customers and relevant staff
Make ideas tangible: prototypes	Build working prototypes that are designed to test some or all of the features in the design	Data generated by building a prototype. For example, learning how easy and cheap it is to build, learning errors and problems that occur during building products or writing software. Manufacturing staff feedback
Test prototypes and learn	Use prototypes to get data on what works in the design and what does not. Might include MVP testing with real customers. Includes improving the prototype and potentially retesting it. Incudes scheduled redesigns and upgrades when commercially appropriate	Data generated by users of prototype, including relevant customer types. For example, feedback from users including interviews, questionnaires and data recordings of product use

Journeys that produce and manufacture things

Table 9.6 shows an overview of the types of data that can be recorded from production and manufacturing journeys and their sources. Analyses of manufacturing journeys start with an evaluation of the overall outcomes of the journey, i.e., how well does the manufacturing process perform in a specific period of time, like in one work shift or in one day? Data that records product manufacturing journeys are all aimed at evaluating whether enough units of product – or service instances – complete the journey on time, at the right quality and at the lowest cost. So, the focus in Table 9.6 is

Table 9.6   Types of data that record product and service manufacturing journeys

Type of data	Description and examples	Source of data
Data for evaluating the performance of the full manufacturing journey	Used to evaluate the overall outcomes of the manufacturing journey. This data is focused on the outputs of the final stage of the manufacturing process: how well the final stage produces products and services Includes outputs: volume and quality of products and services produced as well as a measure of their quality and the time and resources this whole journey consumed Evaluation is based on data that compares the planned (or best possible) performance scores versus the actual scores	The original design objectives that described the purpose of the design, based on the customer journey analysis of relevant customers and their life journeys (see Chapter 8) Actual performance scores: • Volume of products and services produced – production line counters, digital service software, payment systems, other IT systems (e.g., total units manufactured, total customer transactions processed) • Resources consumed by a stage (e.g., amount of raw materials) • Quality systems data (e.g., number and types of rejects) Planned performance scores: • The original journey design • Past performance data for the same journey
Data for evaluating a single journey stage	Similar to the above, an evaluation of each manufacturing journey stage is repeated for all stages Includes outputs and resources consumed by a stage Evaluation is based on data that compares the planned (or best possible) scores versus the actual scores for each stage	As above but for each stage. E.g., volume and quality data from individual production machines, production lines and staff. Also, data on resources consumed by each stage Full description of all the stages of the manufacturing journey
Required raw materials and resources data	Data describing the volume, quality and availability of the input resources required and what was actually available for each stage, including the first stage. This is used to assess performance	The raw materials, consumables and other inputs required to run the production line or the service centre (e.g., energy, water, information and materials)

first on the outputs of the final journey stage, i.e., the output of the whole assembly line or the service as experienced by the customer. This involves starting with the final stage and working backwards stage-by-stage. For each stage the key data to be gathered describes the volume and quality of products produced, or the number of customers serviced and their own evaluation of the quality of that service. Notice that the data which describes quality describes good quality as well as bad quality, i.e., waste. Quality is a notoriously subjective measurement, but it can be evaluated for products and services by using the original design objectives that described the purpose of the design. Product quality evaluations are a contrast between the original purpose of a design and what is eventually produced. Performance evaluations of a manufacturing journey are a contrast between the actual performance and the planned (or best possible) performance. This is the performance that the whole manufacturing journey or single stage is expected to be able to achieve based on the expected manufacturing capacity of the people and machines involved.

The inputs and outputs of each stage can then be analysed. Input data describes the resources that are actually consumed by a stage. These include materials, energy, information and the time spent by people and machines to successfully work on that stage. This includes the input resources that were required and that were available for a stage. This availability information is used to take into account what was achievable at the time, since a stage cannot perform well if it is starved of raw materials by a bottleneck (Goldratt and Cox, 2004).

Tools for managing production journeys

Production journeys are the complicated arrangements of people, machines and other resources, which help customer journeys to move along. They always need to be managed and they usually can be improved. For manufacturing products this means increasing productivity and product quality. For producing services this means increasing the quality of the service as experienced by the service's customers, as well as increasing their productivity. Managing production journeys also means having to deal with unforeseen disruptions that occur, such as breakdowns or delays in the supply of raw materials or labour. Tools for managing production journeys help by monitoring the activities of machines and people: how they worked in the past or how they are doing in real-time. They collect information to paint a detailed picture of how machines on factory production lines operate, or how the staff that produce a service work.

For product manufacturing lines, this means using the sensors and software that are part of the machines that fill bottles on a bottling line, label packages in a biscuit factory or work on any stage of a production line. In Figure 9.4 there are four machines on three lines, which take in raw materials and produce finished products. Each machine reports how it operates to a data room that holds racks of servers, which are like small PCs. The data room collects the data and prepares it for sending to the organisation's Enterprise Resource Planning (ERP) system. ERP systems run software that supports the different departments of an organisation, including human resources, finance, marketing, logistics and in this case, manufacturing. The ERP system receives operational performance data from all the organisation's factories, including a legacy network of old but still operational software. All this helps the organisation to build up a 'big picture' view of its performance in manufacturing, as well as in other departments.

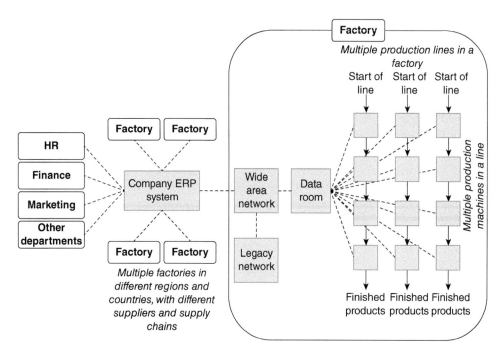

Figure 9.4   Data is combined from machines, production lines, factories and other departments

Adapted from examples by Polestar, 2021

For services, managing how staff work to produce a service requires information on how they collaborate together, which tasks and activities have been completed by different people and the quality of the finished job. Examples include checklists of what activities need to be done, when and by whom, or information describing how well customers think their queries have been answered by call centre staff. Service industries use software and machines to support production activities just as they do in manufacturing. For example, software in IT systems, laptops, web servers and people's phones, or in medical equipment, vehicles like tractors and ticketing systems. This software will generate useful journey description data in a similar way to the production line machines in Figure 9.4. Table 9.7 shows some online tools for monitoring the activities and collaboration of staff. Like the online tools in Chapter 8, there are many other tools that can connect these separate tools together so that they can share and combine data. Some tools, like Zapier and If This Then That (ITTT), also automate activities.

The online tools in Table 9.7 are very useful for gathering data and supporting how people work together but the data they gather can also come from other sources, for example from online sources, by filling in paper forms or by staff asking questions. Other sources include:

- Mystery shopping – where a staff member or external contractor impersonates a customer to 'stand in their shoes' to understand their experience of consuming a service.
- Focus groups – where a panel of customers discuss their experiences of using products and being a customer of an organisation.

- Follow-up survey – where customers are asked what they thought of a service just after they consume it.
- In-app survey – where app users are asked what they thought of the app just after they use it.
- Website popups – where users are asked what they thought of the site just after they use it.

The above data sources can be used to understand customers' overall satisfaction levels and then answer more detailed questions about the experience, how easy and how useful it was to them (Grigoroudis and Siskos, 2009; Stewart and O'Connell, 2017).

Table 9.7   Examples of tools for monitoring staff activities and helping collaboration

Tool name	Description
Monday https://monday.com	Online tool for building workflows without coding. Connects with other online tools to share data using pre-designed and customisable templates. The software is designed to automatically organise and coordinate activities including project management, sales and customer relationship management, marketing, design and software development
Slack https://slack.com	Online tool for managing projects and organising people, based on direct messages. Easy to link with other online tools
Trello https://trello.com	Online tool for managing projects and organising people, based on cards that list required activities and who should do them. Easy to link with other online tools

There are also many online tools that are based on the formal project management methodology Prince2. www.prince2.com.

Look at the 'big picture' to spot problems and then 'drill down' to find causes

All this data can be used to see the 'big picture' of how staff and their machines perform and how planned performance compares to actual performance. For example, a planned production journey for an international organisation might be to service 100 customers per day, or to produce 100 cars per hour. This plan might be a robust prediction based on what usually happens. If the actual number of customers or cars is less than 100 then there is a problem. Assembling a 'big picture' from the bottom-up means that the organisation has detailed performance data at all levels of the organisation, from the bottom to the top – the region level, the factory level, the production line level and the machine level. This sort of data can be used to 'drill-down' from top level problems to lower levels looking for causes of performance losses on the level above. Maybe one machine's breakdown at the machine level held up an entire factory at the factory level. The same drill down approach can be applied to different time periods to compare days of the week, night versus day shifts, or different groups of workers. It can also be used to see if different departments might contribute to problems because the ERP system holds data on how these departures performed as well, and how their work affected the overall productivity of the organisation.

The data that these tools gather can also be used to simulate how all these activities would run if things were changed. This is useful for testing out potential improvements and for checking if responses to disruptions are practical. Data recordings of how production lines, machines or teams of service staff work together help to describe their capabilities and capacities, their work rates and the quality of outputs that can be expected in different situations. Understanding all these characteristics is required to check the implications of small changes to some of them, like switching people around in teams or upgrading a machine to a higher throughput.

Chapter summary

Journey models can be used to improve the journeys that produce the products and services that help customers to progress along their own journeys. This is because all people and machines are each on their own journeys as they move through their lives, and all journeys are linked to other journeys.

Two main types of production journeys are design journeys and manufacturing journeys. Design journeys construct the plans of production journeys. Then production journeys follow these plans to produce services and manufacture products. Every product and service design should start with a detailed understanding of how the product or service will help the user on their own customer journey. So, customer journey models are indispensable inputs to design journeys just as designs are required for starting production journeys.

Production journey models record the work of journeys – the stages and activities – of the workers and machines involved in production activities. This includes the software, IT systems and all the devices that workers use. These people and machines are rich data sources for modelling production journeys so that they can be improved. These data sources help to build up a 'big picture' for spotting high level problems, then they provide more detailed information for 'drilling down' to find the causes.

Further reading

Chaffey, D. (2021) 'Blog articles on AB and multivariate testing'. https://www.smartinsights.com/archive/conversion-optimisation/ab-multivariate-testing (accessed 7 April 2022).

Patel, N. (2021) 'A/B testing: definition, how it works, examples & tools'. https://neilpatel.com/blog/ab-testing-introduction (accessed 7 April 2022).

Richardson, A. (2010) 'Using customer journey maps to improve customer experience', *Harvard Business Review*, November. https://hbr.org/2010/11/using-customer-journey-maps-to (accessed 7 April 2022).

10

ELEMENTS OF A DATA AND DECISION-MAKING STRATEGY

KEY IDEAS

- Emerging data technologies present several potential dangers in how data is chosen and analysed, and in how insights are used.
- A qualitative approach reduces these dangers by providing context by using systems and process perspectives, and subjective thinking.
- Using data starts with asking the right 'Analysis Question'. An Analysis Question helps to focus a data analytics project and provides a way to evaluate its outputs.
- Looking for patterns is the objective of a data analytics project. Patterns are arrangements of information that help to answer Analysis Questions.
- Patterns help us to see differences between the 'Things' that we analyse, to understand why there are differences, and then to use this understanding to develop useful tools.
- Patterns in datasets are found in two different ways: by grouping similar Things together (clustering and association) and by quantifying the relationships between the characteristics of Things (regression and classification).
- Machine learning is an automated method for searching for patterns in data. Techniques include supervised, unsupervised and reinforcement learning methods.

LEARNING OBJECTIVES

After reading this chapter you will be able to:

- Describe the dangers that emerging data technologies present in terms of hidden assumptions and how they might hurt stakeholders.
- Explain the potential biases that analytics projects might be open to.
- Define heuristics and explain how they help us.

(Continued)

- Explain how a system-wide and processual view of stakeholders can help to solve business problems. Explain how a subjective view of stakeholders can help.
- Explain why information patterns are useful.
- Explain why using different patterns of information in a customer dataset is like looking at customers from many different viewpoints.
- Describe the differences between clustering patterns and regression patterns. Explain what they can each be used for.
- Explain the differences between supervised, unsupervised and reinforcement machine learning techniques.

This chapter explains some of the dangers inherent in the newness of emerging data technologies, including the unforeseen consequences of using the new data sources, new types of data and new data analysis tools that are increasingly used in new business areas. These dangers can be reduced if we are aware of the assumptions that underly how these technologies are made and used. Qualitative tools like Value Flow Analysis (VFA) (Chapter 3) and customer journey mapping (Chapter 4) can make us more aware of these assumptions by complementing the quantitative tools of hard data science like software coding and mathematics.

Next, this chapter describes the elements of a data analysis and decision-making strategy including the definition of an Analysis Question to focus the start of a data analytics project, the role of data patterns in analytics projects and how data patterns help to answer the Analysis Question. Then it explains the types of patterns that can be found in data and the overall types of machine learning techniques that are used to search for them.

The case for 'qualitative data science'

Hard data science needs to soften up. News stories about data privacy and data ethics are very common. Sometimes the stories are about biased decision-making or a lack of transparency; sometimes they are about how organisations use data to take advantage of customers and other stakeholders. These issues generate strong concerns for customers and government regulators, and they are particularly important for future leaders and managers to be aware of because they present very real legal issues, which can impact people's careers. They are part of a qualitative side to data science that is commonly neglected by computer scientists and mathematicians because their training focuses more on the hard quantitative tasks of manipulating data rather than the softer qualitative issues of what the data represents, and the business context of why the tasks are being done. It is easy to focus on the methods for transforming and filtering digital data to look for patterns, rather than how these methods affect the bias, practicality and even the fairness of how these patterns will be used in an organisation. A simple example is when data on white males is used to train an artificial intelligence (AI) model to choose job applicants. Non-white females or non-binary applicants will not be recognised by the AI model in the same way as white males. This is harmful to all concerned and there are many similar examples in the news. Quantitative approaches are very precise but only have a narrow focus, whereas qualitative approaches have a much wider reach whilst being fundamentally imprecise (Fitzgerald and Howcroft, 1998).

A qualitative view of the dangers of data science techniques is particularly important for business students and managers because it is most likely that they will be the team members who are tasked with designing the data analysis project at the start and selling the results to the wider organisation afterwards. A qualitative perspective is particularly useful for people with a quantitative background, like computer scientists, engineers and mathematicians, because it includes points of view that are not core on such courses. A qualitative perspective also helps to address people's concerns about important issues in our society like fairness and ethical business practices. For example, how organisations and society in general use data to treat people who are not male, not white or not from certain western countries, or how organisations can help their staff to flourish in a way that helps the organisations do well.

It is easy to assume that data science is mostly about coding and mathematics, but these quantitative skills are just the methods that we use for finding patterns in datasets. There are many crucial stages before that, for example deciding on the questions that a data analysis project needs to answer; then looking for, gathering and preparing the data, and checking its quality. After patterns are found there are then many more crucial stages, for example evaluating the quality of the patterns in the data model; explaining and selling the use of the data model to the rest of the organisation; and evaluating the whole process.

The dangers of data science's new datasets, tools and insights

In business, in the news and on social media, there is widespread interest in emerging data technologies and in the new opportunities that they bring (Agarwal and Dhar, 2014). These technologies capture and manipulate digital data at much larger scales and faster speeds, and with much greater precision than was possible in the past, and they include big data analytics, machine learning and other types of artificial intelligence (AI). Their impact on organisations makes them a game-changer for business. However, there are concerns about how these technologies are being used, especially in the assumptions underlying the data, the analytical techniques and the consequences of how analytical outcomes may benefit or hurt stakeholders (Abbasi et al., 2016; Galliers et al., 2017).

These concerns are based on the complex capabilities with which data science provides organisations. For example, researchers have questioned how data scientists choose datasets and how this might lead to biases like 'algorithmic discrimination' (Newell and Marabelli, 2015). A dataset is only a sample of all the data that could be recorded to describe some phenomena (Kitchin, 2014) and all data is unavoidably biased by the way that it is collected because we can never fully capture every aspect of what we record. Data about what people like to eat could include questionnaire responses from pupils in several schools, or people who go to a shopping mall on one day, or everyone who responds to a global online questionnaire. But it will not include responses from every human being on Earth; no organisation has the resources for that. Every method that we use to record data misses out some of what could be recorded, whether it is a questionnaire, a face-to-face interview, a video recording, a photograph, or a song recording. Questionnaires and interviewers could always ask more people and more questions; cameras could always use different angles, or shots that take in a wider view, or focus in closer on the subject. Similarly, microphones could pick up more of the detail of musical instruments and singers' voices, if they worked on different sound frequencies and were closer to the artists. Not everything that happens can be recorded. So, decisions need to be made about the granularity, extent and criteria of the recording (Ahl and Allen, 1996). Granularity sets the smallest distinctions that the recording process will distinguish, and extent sets the largest distinctions. The criteria of the recording process is whatever the instrument that generates the data is built to sense, for example answers to questions sensed by a survey, light sensed by a digital camera, or finger touches sensed by the touchscreen of a phone. Instruments can only sense what they are built to sense. Surveys cannot sense light, digital cameras cannot sense finger touches and so on. In addition to sample biases, which miss out some part of whatever is recorded into data, there are many other biases that alter how we analyse data. Some of these include:

- Memory biases, which interfere with our brains' information storage and retrieval.
- Statistical biases, which include the assumption that all that happens is distributed on a normal distribution (a 'bell curve').
- Confidence biases, which make people think that they are more able than they actually are.
- Adjustment biases, which hinder how people adjust their decisions in relation to additional information.
- Presentation biases, which bias the way information is taken in and used (Arnott, 2006).

Another problem is that bias in a pattern found in a dataset might be impossible to evaluate. For example, AI technologies such as deep neural networks cannot be used to explain their own decision-making processes. Deep neural networks are a type of AI software that mimic the neural networks in the brain. There is limited understanding of how these software neural networks make particular decisions (Müller et al., 2016). Support vector machines and random forest techniques are other machine learning technologies that can find patterns in datasets. A support vector machine is software that divides data points into two groups. Random forest techniques use a number of decision trees; each tree uses a slightly different method, and the resulting pattern is an 'average' of all the trees. A decision tree is a flowchart-like structure, which looks a bit like a tree; the branches represent a set of rules for creating the dataset. Some branches are more likely or more represented in the dataset than others. The branches of a decision tree provide a pattern for understanding a dataset because it shows the main relationships between information in the dataset. Each tree is a guess at how the data was produced. Each decision tree is trained on a different part of the dataset and is trained slightly differently. Then the patterns of all the trees are 'averaged'. The thing that makes it impossible to interpret how support vector machines and random forest techniques arrived at their results is their internal operational complexity. We know how they function in principle, but they are too complex to understand when they do so. The same is true of the operation of deep neural network AI software. The operation of the code can be analysed on the minutest level but how multitudes of individual software operations combine to build up into higher level patterns is far too complex for humans to understand.

Whether they can be evaluated or not, the danger of biases is that they alter the data that we look for patterns in, or they alter how we look for patterns. And most importantly, biases can do this without us being aware of them doing it, or how they do it, which leads to the errors and unfair practices mentioned above. A related example is using heuristics. Heuristics are 'rules of thumb', 'short cuts', or methods of working that are easier, quicker or cheaper than the perfect approach, like an 'educated guess'. Heuristics make information processing easier, whereas biases are the cognitive performance gap between using a heuristic and not using it. Heuristics work well enough in many cases but sometimes they do not. For example, cases that deal with outliers, situations that are thought unlikely or impossible but when they do happen, they cause a problem. 'Black Swan' events are situations that are thought to be impossible because they have never occurred, like when Europeans thought all swans had white feathers, then they travelled to Australia where they saw black feathered swans for the first time (Taleb, 2007).

Any mathematical or software tool for collecting, preparing or finding pattens in data uses clever heuristics. As with biases, it is crucial to know the limits of the heuristics that the tools are based on. For example, many statistical analysis methods assume that what is being analysed is arranged in a normal distribution (Figure 10.1a), like the curve of the pupils' heights in a class of children is shaped into a 'bell curve' (Taleb et al., 2009). But what if the distribution is another shape, such as a bi-modal distribution (two bell shapes, side by side) (Figure 10.1b), or a skewed distribution (an off-centre bell shape) (Figure 10.1c and d), or something else? Take an analysis of customer buying data. If a normal distribution was assumed, but customers actually bought in two very different ways, then the distribution would be bimodal. There would be two bell curves not one (like Figure 10.1b), and the analysis might miss out a whole group. Analysts should be aware of the many biases and heuristics within their options for how they design the project, and how these relate to the purpose of the project.

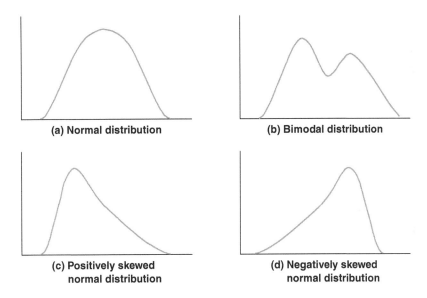

Figure 10.1   Drawings of simple distributions of 'Things' that data describes

Many data analysis software tools hold similar dangers and they all come from the underlying assumptions in the mathematics and data transformation operations that the tools are based on. For example, the 'deflated p-value' problem highlights the difference between statistical significance and practical significance. P-values are commonly used to establish significance. But modern datasets are so large that there can be many statistically significant patterns on a dataset (Lin et al., 2013). So which pattern should be the one to guide the decisions? The software that manipulates datasets to prepare them for analysis and to automate pattern searching also hides potential dangers, which come from clever heuristics that the software is based on. But these powerful tools are relatively new and still developing, and the effects of the heuristics that underlie standard industry research tools can be unclear. Tools such as Qlik Sense, Power

BI, Tableau, SPSS and MATLAB. The ultimate effects of combining different tools or combining off the shelf code from open repositories such as GitHub are also unclear.

In addition to the concerns around choosing and using datasets and analysis tools, emerging data technologies also present organisations with novel dangers that come from the new types of insights that they enable. Big data datasets can be used to produce insights that have never been possible before; possibilities such as personalised insurance and personalised drug treatment. The abilities that these insights enable are not something that organisations are used to. The implications of this for business ethics, legislation, public awareness and company strategy are not fully understood.

The lesson here is that modern data analytics projects depend on a host of new types of data and new analytical tools that are still being developed. The way they interact and the applications that they are being put to are also new and may not have been fully and systematically assessed. It is important to understand the context of how these technologies are used and critically evaluate any findings.

How qualitative data science helps in data analysis projects

In general, a qualitative approach to using emerging data technologies helps by providing context to data analysis projects; it helps people to see the 'big picture'. Data science depends heavily on coding and software development skills as well as mathematic and statistical knowledge, but these are of little use without a deep understanding of the organisation that is being analysed. Real life business context is the start and the end of each data analysis project. The strategy of the organisation, its business model and the organisational issues that need analysing are what initiates each data analysis project, and they also hold the means of evaluating the findings of the project. Qualitative data science is the link between data science and business strategy. It helps us to understand the capabilities of the people and technologies enough to suggest new business models to analyse. It helps us to understand our customers enough to ask the right questions of the data. Fundamentally, when we use qualitative skills, like those in this book, we are analysing what to count and what to measure, which in data analysis projects means deciding what data to use and how to use it.

Qualitative data science uses systems thinking ideas to consider organisational problems as systems of interrelated elements rather than isolated islands of problems (Checkland, 1999). Systems thinking provides us with a 'big picture' view of organisational problems and opportunities as well as views of each of the levels below the level of a whole system. It helps to avoid errors that come from missing out parts of the system, system levels or particular perspectives (Allen and Starr, 1982). We can see this with business model analyses that must function as value creation systems for all their stakeholders, not just a few. It also helps us to see new opportunities that build new system levels on the top of existing systems, like IT and business model platforms, and digital ecosystems.

Qualitative data science also uses a process perspective to consider organisational problems as a series of stages that are separated by decisions made by a stakeholder whose journey is being analysed. The customer journey ideas in Chapter 4 are based on a sequential view of organisational problems, and sequential views help with understanding cause and effect (Salthe, 1985; Hammer and Champy, 1993; Rescher, 2000; Styhre, 2002). We can see this with analyses of the sequences of activities that organisations use to produce products and services (Chapter 9). Lastly, qualitative data science uses ideas from value theory and service theory to provide a subjective decision-making view (Ramirez, 1999; Vargo and Lusch, 2004; Lepak et al., 2007). Understanding why different people value different things helps with understanding how they evaluate products and services, and how to better design them.

The quantitative tools of hard data science are complemented by the qualitative tools in this book. Every data analysis project has interlinked qualitative and quantitative cycles. It is very important to be systematic and aware of the qualitative cycles as well as the quantitative cycles. This helps organisations to avoid the dangers described here. In this book, Journey-based Thinking tools like VFA (Chapter 2) and customer journey mapping (Chapter 4) help to define the context of data analyses by providing system-wide and processual views of all stakeholders, not just customers. This context enables a systematic understanding of who and what capabilities and resources are available, and when they should be employed. At the same time, these tools help to get the best out of stakeholders and even devices because they give us a subjective view of them.

Elements of a data and decision-making strategy

This section is about what it takes to be data driven. It describes the strategic thinking behind the data analysis projects that improve customers' life journeys, and the production journeys that provide the products and services that they rely on.

Using data starts with asking the right Analysis Question

All analyses need a focus, that is their 'Analysis Question'. If you do not focus, then you will get lost in the vast amounts of data, software, devices and technological tools that organisations have access to, either internally or just a browser click away in the cloud. Let's take the example of analysing customer journeys because most business problems can be set out in terms of the journeys that they affect. Individual customers move along many different journeys all at the same time: shopping journeys, healthcare journeys, social life journeys, education journeys and many more. So, start by thinking about how your job and the business processes you work in help your customers progress along their customer journeys. These might be internal customers, colleagues who work in the same organisation, or external people who you rely on to get your job done. Porter's (1985) Value Chain provides an overview of all the different job functions in an organisation, for example:

- Sales and marketing jobs help customers with the journey of looking for products that they need, finding out about products and comparing them before finally choosing which to buy.
- Customer service jobs help customers with the journey of dealing with problems and questions that come up as they search for, purchase and then use products and services.
- Service production jobs help customers do what they need to do to progress along their life journeys, like retail sales staff or call centre staff.
- Product design, manufacturing and logistics jobs produce the products that also help customers to progress along their different life journeys. If you think of a product as a sort of 'frozen service', the product itself is the service 'generator'. For example, an umbrella provides a keep-dry or keep-in-the-shade service.
- Many other jobs help customers to progress along their journeys by providing information and advice. For example, jobs that build and maintain websites, mobile apps and other customer communication channels, like email newsletters, blog posts as well as those that use print and

online media. They include jobs that produce videos, images, text and other content for these communication channels.

- Many jobs do not interact with customers directly, or directly work on manufactured products. Their purpose is to help the progress of internal customers, colleagues, along their production journeys. These include finance and human resources staff, or they include the IT jobs and other technical jobs that maintain the communication channels (Porter, 1985).

Ask yourself 'which journey is my work helping people with?'. If you don't have a job right now, then think about the sort of job you want next or think about the people whose jobs help you get the products and services that you use all the time.

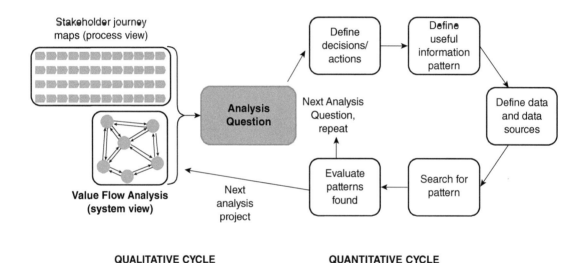

QUALITATIVE CYCLE   QUANTITATIVE CYCLE

Figure 10.2   Qualitative tools help to define the Analysis Question, which in turn defines each data analysis project

Qualitative tools like stakeholder journey maps and VFA help to specify the Analysis Question, which is the focus of a data analysis project. The decisions and actions that are required to answer an Analysis Question tell us the shape of the information pattern that is required, which tells us the information needed to build it and hence the data and the data sources that might come from it. The project can be evaluated by checking if the Analysis Question is answered. This might lead to further Analysis Questions or initiate another qualitative cycle to 'step back' and consider the context of the analysis.

Try to make the objective of your analysis into a single specific Analysis Question. It is common in many research methodologies and creative problem-solving systems to start with a question (Rickards and Moger, 1999; Silverman, 2000; Robson, 2002). Doing this focuses your mind and provides a sort of compass for navigating through all the stages of your analysis. In a complicated and lengthy analysis, it is easy to get diverted, but you can return to your Analysis Question at any time to check if you are on track. You can also use your Analysis Question to evaluate how well the project is going at any time, or its final outcomes.

An Analysis Question is a way of framing the specific problem that needs tackling. A precisely defined and agreed Analysis Question helps to focus a data analytics project and provides a 'compass' for navigating through the twists and turns of implementing the project. Usually, the Analysis Question is about helping an organisation with the decisions and actions it needs to take to improve customer journeys because every stakeholder is a type of customer. These decisions include which products to recommend to a customer and actions such as making specific recommendations. It also helps with decisions about how to improve the flows of resources between stakeholders in an organisation's business model (Figure 10.2).

However, the most useful thing about phrasing the aims and objectives of your analysis as an Analysis Question is that as soon as you write the question down your brain will start to try and answer it. Some example Analysis Questions include:

- How can late deliveries be reduced for pre-paying customers?
- How can customer satisfaction be improved for customers in Manchester?
- What do customers dislike about our hotel rooms?

Notice how these examples use qualifications like 'pre-paying customers', 'in Manchester' and 'hotel rooms' to make the Analysis Question more specific. Making the Analysis Question more specific will help you manage the scope of the analysis so that it fits the time and resources that you have available. Bigger projects with wider Analysis Questions take more time and it is usually best to focus your analysis project. Writing down the Analysis Question also helps you to agree it with whoever will use the outputs of the analysis. Your Analysis Question strongly depends on who the analysis is for. It might be for an internal customer, like your boss, or an external consultancy client. The analysis project is a service to that person and different people value different things. Analysing customer journeys should benefit customers but only so it can support the business model of the organisation in which the customers belong. Some ways you find to improve customer journeys will be too expensive, or they will not be something your boss or client is responsible for. So, the wording of your Analysis Question needs to be quite precise.

Analysis Questions also lead to deeper analysis questions. The initial ones might start with words like 'how', 'what', 'who', 'when', 'where' and 'why'. They can be used in more than one analysis cycle, so a general Analysis Question can lead to deeper Analysis Questions. A good way to begin is with a general Analysis Question that starts with 'how' and 'what'. Then you might follow up with deeper Analysis Questions that start with 'who', 'when' and 'where'. Finally, if you want to find causes you will need to ask Analysis Questions that start with 'why'.

Example Analysis Questions

How to improve the customer experience for holiday guests in a resort hotel in southern Portugal.

How to reduce the amount of water used in the paper recycling centres in Scotland.

(Continued)

Why do customers complain about the help they get from our call centre?

Notice how all these examples include specific stakeholders and the specific life journey that they are on. For example, customers who visit the resort for recreational purposes rather than business people on a conference. Stakeholders are not always people. In the paper recycling example, the journey is that made by waste paper as it is recycled.

These Analysis Questions illustrate how phrasing the objective of an analysis project as a specific question focuses efforts on what the question is about. Using a question format also starts the process of answering the question and it provides a way to evaluate the findings of the project – was the Analysis Question fully answered?

Looking for patterns in data

Patterns are what we look for when we analyse data. They are parts of a bigger dataset that has been arranged in a specific way that is useful for answering questions or for making decisions. The role of AI systems, machine learning algorithms and human data scientists is to search for those patterns. Patterns are like 'cheat sheets' or short cuts, they are useful summaries of information. They arrange the 'Things' that the data describes in ways that help us to answer our Analysis Questions.

Patterns are how humans deal with complexity. For example, customer data could include recordings of anything that happens with customers as they use products and services, and travel along their life journeys. This includes anything about them like age, name, address and other profile data. But analysing data to find a pattern is complex because of the sheer amount and variety of it, and the many different ways that it can be rearranged to look for useful patterns. There are many potential ways of summarising and arranging any dataset, but only some could be useful. The individual pieces of data in a dataset can be grouped and divided, and aggregated and transformed, in an infinite number of ways. Useful patterns are arrangements of the data that are simple enough for humans to cope with. But they also need to be complicated enough to be a close enough record of whatever the dataset describes, and at the same time avoid too many omissions. So, they cannot be too simplified; there needs to be a balance. Each pattern is a subset of the total dataset. Not as complicated as the whole dataset, but it needs to hold enough information to help to answer the Analysis Question.

Using different patterns of information in a customer dataset is like looking at customers from many different 'angles'. Like looking at them by age, or by gender, or by arranging them in a diagram according to where they last shopped. The objective of any data analysis is to look for patterns of information that are helpful for making decisions and taking actions. So, if you look at data from lots of different angles then you might spot a useful pattern. Information patterns inhabit the middle of the Big Data Information Value Chain model (BDIVC) in Figure 10.3. For an introduction to the BDIVC model please see Chapter 8. In the two boxes on the right, the information pattern helps with decision-making because it links the options to choose from with the likely results of those choices. For example, linking types of customers with products that they would probably like to buy. In the two boxes on the left, component parts of the information pattern can be used to make a list of what information is required to build the pattern and therefore, which data sources might provide that information.

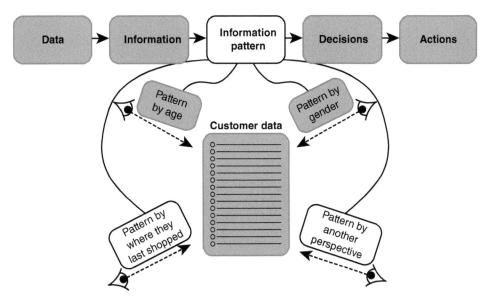

Figure 10.3   Searching for different patterns of data in a dataset is like looking at it from different perspectives

Table 10.1   Examples of information patterns that might help to answer some Analysis Questions

Analysis Questions	Examples of patterns
How to improve the customer experience for holiday guests in a resort hotel in southern Portugal	Types of guests linked with high guest satisfaction scores
	Types of guests linked with low guest satisfaction scores
How to reduce the amount of water used in the paper recycling centres in Scotland	Amount of water used linked to different recycling process stages
	Amount of water not reused linked to different recycling process stages
	Amount of water not reused in total linked to the reason why it was not recycled
Why do customers complain about the help they get from our call centre?	Types of complaints linked to their frequency
	Types of complaints linked to their seriousness
	Types of complaints linked to their root cause

In Table 10.1, notice how these patterns can be used to start the next analysis cycle. For example, if you understand the types of hotel guests that give high satisfaction scores then you can ask guests like that, and hotel staff, why this happens. The answers might lead to decisions and actions that the hotel management can take to improve overall satisfaction scores. Many of the first patterns to look for are at the whole system level, then you can 'drill' down to find priority areas for investigation, like investigating how the total amount of water that is used for recycling paper was divided up between the different recycling process stages. The stages that consumed the most water would be the ones to investigate next. Also, if the Analysis Question is 'How to reduce the total amount of water used', then the stages that did not consume much water should also be considered to see if they did not consume much water because they recycled most of it.

Data patterns help to answer Analysis Questions

Patterns help us to answer an Analysis Question in three ways:

1   They help us to find differences between the 'Things' that we analyse.
2   They help us to understand why there are such differences.
3   They help us to use this understanding to develop useful tools for making decisions and taking actions.

'Things' are customers, products, staff, suppliers, machines, events or whatever it is in the Analysis Question that is being analysed. To study the differences between them we must find a way of ranking them. Ranking puts them in an order, like when children in a class are ranked in order of their heights by lining them up with the tallest at one end and the shortest at the other. As with any quantitative analysis you first must decide what to rank the Things by. For example, customers could be ranked by variables like profitability, spend per year or average number of website visits per month. It depends on the focus of your Analysis Question. Ranking helps us to separate out the extremes so we can study them more closely to understand why they are at one end of the ranking. If you know who the most profitable and the least profitable customers are then you can look for reasons why they are ranked in this way. Maybe some types of customers return most of their purchases, or maybe they take up lots of staff time and never buy much? If all customers are grouped together without ranking, then it is difficult to see what causes the differences.

When you understand why there are differences between the two ends of a ranking, you may be able to make decisions and actions that cause more of the outcomes at the positive end of the ranking. For example, ranking sales staff by sales per week will show you which staff you might learn from, and which staff this learning might help the most. The worst performing staff might need some other support, which you can understand better by highlighting who they are and having a supportive chat. Over the years, ranking students by exam marks or class participation has helped me to learn the techniques that the best performers use and suggest them to the ones most in need of support. You may not be able to get to the root cause of some ranking differences but understanding how to recognise different extremes of customers, or whatever you are analysing, is helpful for replicating or avoiding most of them.

Information patterns in datasets are made up of not just one ranking of a variable but many rankings of many variables. In Figure 10.4 each of the columns represents a ranking of 'Things' according to a different variable. For example, the Things could be nine sales people a to i and the columns could be how they ranked according to different measures of their performance. Sales person c did the best at selling product units, but sales person b earned the most revenue, and sales person a earned the most in June. Sales person a had the least sick days and e had the most. The blank columns could be variables that examine profitability or other interesting information in the dataset.

One pattern in the dataset is the pattern of how sales performance varies with days taken off sick. As expected, the people with the highest number of days off performed the worst. It is important to define the variables very carefully. Notice that in Figure 10.4 the 'best' number of sick days means the highest number not the lowest, which was not 'best' for the organisation, nor for person e. Individual variables can be ranked to find sales people who performed especially well or especially badly. This could then be further investigated, maybe just by asking them about their performance. Variables can be examined together, like sales performance and sickness, to suggest possible reasons or even associations before investigating more deeply. For example, when high numbers of sick days seem to be associated with lower performance.

How organisations look for data patterns

Broadly speaking, data patterns are found in two different ways: the first is by grouping Things together that have similar characteristics, and the second is by quantifying the relationships between characteristics. Analyses that group Things together look for clustering and association patterns, and analyses that study the relationships between characteristics look for regression and classification patterns. Clustering and association methods decide how to group Things together and then how to identify which group an individual Thing belongs to. The pattern that they look for will be an algorithm, a set of instructions, that describes how one group of Things are separated from another, like a line separating two sets of points.

Regression and classification methods predict relations – the quantity of some characteristics based on the quantity of other characteristics. The pattern that they look for will be an algorithm that describes how one variable changes in relation to other variables, like a curve on a two-dimensional graph describes how X values can be changed into Y values.

Clustering and association data patterns

Clustering and association patterns group similar Things in a dataset together, like arranging similar customers into customer segments. They are useful for understanding the overall structure of whatever you are analysing, like a market or a set of related problems. The analyst must choose how the Things that are being analysed are grouped, what characteristics make members of the same group similar. For example, customers could be grouped by age, musical tastes, the size of their clothes, or a multitude of other characteristics. The Things that are being analysed could be customers, staff, products, projects, machines retail stores or whatever your Analysis Question is focused on.

Clustering patterns are very useful for deciding where to focus resources. For example, dividing a market into customer segments helps with prioritising which customers to target with marketing resources. Part of the process of clustering Things into groups involves deciding how many groups to have in total because different criteria for dividing up the groups generates different numbers of groups. Dividing a class of students by height into groups that are separated by ten centimetres will give you less groups than if you separated them by five centimetres. Deciding how many groups to have in your clustering pattern helps with deciding how to use your available resources. For example, if you are dividing customers into groups for customer support activities then the maximum number of groups might be limited by how many customer support staff members you have. If you have two staff members, then you might want a group pattern that divides customers into two groups. If you have ten staff, then you might have more groups but not necessarily ten of them. In both cases there is

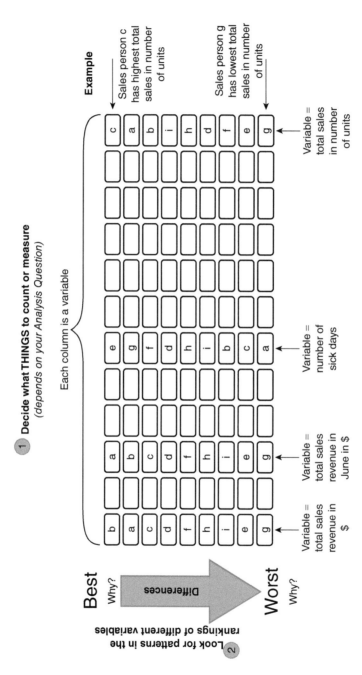

Figure 10.4   Columns representing the ranking of 'Things' by different variables in a dataset

no point in having one hundred groups because that would be too many different groups for the people whose job it would be to deal with groups. The number of groups in the clustering pattern is based on how you are going to treat the groups, which in turn depends on the capacity of your resources. If the clustering pattern is used by some software to automatically generate a digital service, then the number of groups can be much larger because the capacity to treat groups differently is much greater. For example, online video streaming services like Netflix and Amazon Prime Video can automatically suggest personalised viewing options based on patterns that match many different viewers' taste characteristics with hundreds of potential video choices. Knowing the pattern of which Things generally go with which other Things is used in image recognition systems, like Google's Vison service, to link images with descriptive labels (Cloud Vision API, 2021). It is also used in speech to text conversion systems like Google's Speech-to-Text service and many other machine learning systems, to link audio sounds to text (Cloud Speech-to-Text, 2021).

Regression and classification data patterns

Regression and classification patterns describe the relationships between variables, which describe the 'Things' in a dataset like a pattern that shows which people with certain characteristics will usually buy certain products. They are useful for understanding which Things' characteristics are associated with other characteristics. These patterns can describe relationships that act in parallel like when certain products will be bought together in a single store visit. Or they can describe relationships that act in a series over time, for example when certain customer behaviours lead to problems later on. Again, the Things that are being analysed are whatever your Analysis Question is focused on: customers, staff, products, projects, machines or stores. The difference between regression and classification patterns is that regression techniques produce a continuous output, like the equation of a straight line can be used to calculate all values of Y if you know the X value. Classification techniques just say which group or class something is in.

Regression and classification patterns are used in recommendation engines to give personalised recommendations to shoppers based on data such as their profile, past and current purchases and which pages they have looked at. These patterns are used to personalise all aspects of customer journeys (Boudet et al., 2019). It is important to note that even though some regression patterns might link past and future events they only provide correlations, they do not prove cause and effect. Correlations are patterns of association. They only show that two or more Things are associated with each other in some way. They do not prove that one Thing caused any other or that this will happen again in the future. But these associations are good enough for Amazon and many other online firms to predict the demand for goods and then ship them to a nearby warehouse so that they are ready to deliver to your door when you order them (Freshwater, 2019).

Machine learning and AI systems

Machine learning is an automated method for searching for patterns in data. It is one type of AI technology; the AI system learns patterns from the data. Machine learning software automates the process of finding patterns so more data can be searched, the data can be searched faster, and more complex patterns can be found.

Supervised machine learning methods

Regression and classification methods use supervised machine learning techniques to 'learn' patterns from training data (Brynjolfsson and Mcafee, 2017). Training data is data that has been tagged by humans with descriptive labels that describe what the pieces of data are. For example, image data might be labelled as faces, legs, cars, arms or whatever they are images of. Training data needs to be tagged by humans because what it signifies can be interpreted in many different ways. Pictures of trees can be tagged to point out species, the colours of leaves, trees' heights, the texture of the bark, or something about their backgrounds. Speech recordings can be tagged with a written transcript, the type of accent used, or what the emotions of the speaker are as they speak. Deciding on what to tag in the training data and how it should be tagged depends on what the Analysis Question is trying to answer. Supervised machine learning techniques automate the process of finding patterns of relationships between the training data and the tags. Some of the training data is not used to look for patterns, instead it is used to evaluate the patterns that are found. Then the best pattern can be used to interpret new data that was not part of the training data. For example, hundreds of hand drawings of birds that are tagged with the word 'bird' can be used to create a pattern that represents how people sketch a bird, then this pattern can be used to recognise sketches of birds (Quick Draw, 2021). Or a person's voice can be imitated by training an AI system using a recording of that person's voice (Palmai, 2021). The idea is that whatever the AI has to deal with after training should be similar enough for the training data to represent it. Like newly drawn bird sketches or new sentences to speak when imitating a person.

Specific supervised machine learning methods include:

- Least squares regression – which finds a best fit line through a set of data points.
- Decision trees – which find the optimal flow path of yes/no decisions.
- Support vector machines – which find the line or hyper plane, which separates separate groups of data points.
- Deep belief learning – which uses neural network software to link inputs with outputs in training data.

Unsupervised machine learning methods

Clustering and association methods use unsupervised machine learning techniques. The techniques are unsupervised in the sense that the data is not tagged or labelled. With supervised machine learning techniques, the data is individually tagged with descriptive labels. Unsupervised machine learning techniques automate the process of looking for patterns by grouping the Things that the data describes. They sift through huge numbers of customer records, fault reports, production reports or other data recordings of Things and automatically put them into similar groups according to the groups' definitions and number of groups that they are told to use. Clustering and association methods include Principal Component Analysis. The principal component in effect 'summarises' the dataset by describing most of the statistical information contained in it whilst using much fewer variables.

Reinforcement machine learning methods

Reinforcement machine learning methods are different to both supervised methods and unsupervised methods. Reinforcement methods use cycles of trial and error where the software learns from feedback about how well it did in a task. Good performance results in a reward and bad performance results in a penalty, and over many cycles, this feedback helps the software to improve by reinforcing good behaviours and weakening bad behaviours (Bhatt, 2018).

Reinforcement methods use training data like supervised learning methods, but their data is produced as feedback from testing the patterns they have found, rather than from a pre-prepared training dataset. Reinforcement methods produce their own training data in a similar way to A/B testing methods (see Chapter 9). They automate the process of searching for optimal chains of decisions by trying out many combinations. For example, Google's DeepMind team used reinforcement learning techniques to train an AI system to play the old video game Breakout. The objective of Breakout is to use a simple paddle at the bottom of the screen to bat a ball back up towards a horizontal wall of bricks at the top. Each time the ball hits a brick, the brick disappears, the ball rebounds and points are scored. The idea is to stop the ball moving through the bottom of the screen. After hundreds of training episodes, Google's AI system learned an important Breakout tactic. If the AI hit the ball so it flew behind the wall of bricks then the ball would bounce around between the top of the screen and the wall, gaining points without the need to save it from moving through the bottom of the screen (Silver, 2016).

Chapter summary

Emerging data technologies are very new, and they are still developing. The many ways that data is gathered and used present a range of dangers for organisations. A qualitative approach that uses systems and processes perspectives reduces these dangers by providing context. They help us to see the 'big picture' of a problem and its alternative solutions. We can also think subjectively about how using these technologies will affect different stakeholders.

Data analytics projects look for patterns in data and they all start by asking an Analysis Question. This helps to focus the project and it provides a way to evaluate its outputs. Patterns are arrangements of information, which help to answer the Analysis Question. These patterns show us the differences between the 'Things' that we analyse. 'Things' are customers, products, staff, suppliers, machines, events or whatever is being analysed. Patterns help us to understand why there are such differences between 'Things', and they help us to develop tools to make use of them.

Data analytics projects find patterns by grouping similar Things together (clustering and association) and by quantifying the relationships between the characteristics of Things (regression and classification). Machine learning automates the process of looking for patterns in datasets and its techniques include supervised, unsupervised and reinforcement learning methods.

Further reading

There are many sources for learning more about the quantitative side of data science, for example www.kdnuggets.com.

For ongoing developments in how businesses use emerging data technologies, I would also recommend the following sources:

Andreessen Horowitz's Future (https://future.a16z.com).

Mckinsey Quarterly (https://www.mckinsey.com/quarterly/overview).

PWC's *Strategy+Business* (https://www.strategy-business.com).

GLOSSARY

A/B testing   experimental comparisons of two or more similar things with a slight difference between them to check if the slight difference is an improvement. For example, used for testing small changes to competing versions of the same web page.

Accommodation   where an organisation adjusts its business model over time to turn what another organisation does from a negative to a positive, or to a neutral effect. For example, if competitors decide to form a joint venture.

Agile management techniques   see **Agile working**.

Agile working   collaborative method, where self-organising and cross-functional teams work closely with customers to solve their problems in a highly flexible manner.

AI   see **Artificial intelligence technologies**.

Analysis Question   a way of framing the specific problem that needs tackling in an analysis project.

Analytics translator   a person who links the data scientists on a data analytics team with the rest of the business. The analytics translator understands how data science technologies and capabilities can help an organisation, and they help to communicate this before, during and after a project.

Artificial intelligence (AI) technologies   a group of automation technologies that greatly increase the speed of finding patterns in very large digital datasets.

Attribution   linking a specific customer's act of buying a product to the specific advert or promotion that persuaded the customer to buy it.

Availability   the proportion of time that a machine or any other organisational capability is available to be used in normal operations, i.e., it is not broken or unavailable because of planned maintenance purposes.

Big data   a name for the huge increases in the scale and types of digital data that organisations capture and analyse after the start of the 21st century.

Blockchain   an encrypted distributed ledger technology, e.g. bitcoin. A distributed ledger records a series of transactions in 'blocks' on a database, and then distributes multiple copies and updates them securely with new blocks. Multiple ledger copies of a series of transactions provides proof of who did what, or who owes what to whom. Encryption stops the growing record from being tampered with.

Business model   a description of how the capabilities of organisational stakeholders transform resources from those stakeholders into what other stakeholders value. This is a **positive feedback loop**. When stakeholders get what they value they contribute more resources and capabilities, which produces more of what they value, and so on. See Chapter 2.

Business model rebalancing   a change to elements of a business model to compensate for changes already forced upon other elements, so that the stakeholders continue to mutually satisfy each other and support the purpose of the organisation, e.g., replacing staff or suppliers; changing capabilities to fit new customer requirements.

Business process models   the stage-by-stage activities that people and machines in organisations do. Every stage has inputs and outputs; in each stage people and machines change the inputs into outputs. Higher level stages contain sub-stages, which contain even smaller sub-sub stages.

Business Process Reengineering (BPR)   the systematic and significant redesign of business processes to better support an organisation's aims.

Call To Action (CTA)   an order or recommendation to an audience to provoke them to do something useful for whoever made the CTA.

Capability   the ability to change inputs into outputs.

Chatbot   software that simulates a text or text-to-speech conversation between a customer and a human staff member.

Churn   the continuous replacement of stakeholders by similar ones as some leave, e.g., attrition, customer churn or staff churn.

Closed system   a system with no external input flows or output flows.

Cloud computing   the outsourcing of digital storage and computer processing power to third party providers that is accessed using the Internet.

Co-creation   the two-way flow of resources between stakeholders as they create value together, e.g., customers give information about their needs as well as cash payments; they do not just take a product or service.

Competition   where different business models try to use the same but limited stakeholders, stakeholders' values, capabilities, or resources. Similar to competition between animal species with the same genome.

Consideration set   a short list of possible options to choose from, e.g., when making a purchase.

Continuous improvement   repeatedly changing aspects of an organisation to improve them, e.g., improving business processes.

Customer Buying Process model   a Journey-based Thinking model by Philip Kotler that charts the stages of shoppers before and after they make a purchase. Also known by other names including the Customer Funnel, the Marketing Funnel and the Conversion Funnel.

Customer Decision Journey model   a Journey-based Thinking model by McKinsey, which charts the stages of shoppers' journeys before and after they make a purchase, and where stages are separated by decisions that retailers can influence.

Customer experience   the individual and subjective feelings that customers experience at every stage of their customer journey. Each customer will feel differently: you cannot guess, you must ask them.

Customer journey   the stages that a customer goes through, from realising that they have a problem or need, to looking for solutions, to comparing solutions and then choosing one. The customer then buys the product or service. But the journey continues afterwards as the customer uses the product for their own purpose. Product manufacturers or service providers must focus on all journey stages after the buying stage.

Customer sentiment   customers' feelings and attitudes towards brands and products.

Cybernetic loop   a feedback loop used to control a process.

Data   a recording of something that happens in words, graphs, charts or pictures; in pencil, pen, paint, in photos or digitally.

Database   a collection of data organised in a specific way and stored on an IT system.

Data analytics   analysing digital data.

Data-driven organisations   data-driven organisations use data to make their decision-making much more systematic and much more detailed (see Chapter 6).

Data exhaust   customer data that is needed to let a transaction happen plus the data that is created during the transaction.

Data science   the use of software coding and mathematical tools for generating digital data, analysing it and then using insights to make decisions that help organisations and people.

Data scientist   someone who is skilled in software coding and mathematical analysis but who also understands the business being analysed.

Dataset   a collection of data in a database.

Data strategy   the overall strategy of how an organisation makes strategic and operational decisions using digital data. Includes the process of getting data, analysing it and using the resulting insights. Starts with the decisions to be made and works backwards to choosing the data.

Digital channels   digitally enabled communications channels, like email, mobile phones, social media, direct messaging or any online or electronic communications medium.

Digital ecosystem   a general term for separate organisations and individuals working together to mutually benefit each other. Digital technologies, like the World Wide Web and cloud computing enable these collaborations. Also called a 'business ecosystem' (see Chapter 7).

Flywheel business model   a way of describing a business model to emphasise ideas of creating and storing value as well as a **business model**'s strong **positive feedback loop**s.

IMEI number   the International Mobile Equipment Identity number is a 15-digit ID number for every mobile phone. Includes information on the phone's country of origin, manufacturer and model number.

Industry 4.0   the 'fourth industrial revolution': the use of data sensing, networking, analytics, simulation and automation to improve manufacturing and other industries.

Interference   a way to picture the interlocking patchwork pattern of how successful a business model is across an area, a timescale, or another continuum, like different waves interfering on a lake. For example, the pattern of convenience stores across a large city, or the performance of different business models across economic cycles.

Internet   the globally linked system of computer networks that enables computers and other devices to communicate with each other.

Internet of Things   a collection of electronic devices linked by the Internet.

Journey-based Thinking an approach to problem solving and data strategy, which analyses stakeholders and the serial stages of their life. The aim is to understand their goals and values and plan backwards to help them realise these goals. The aim is also to plan forwards to suggest better goals using information from other stakeholders. Any stakeholder, device or time-based entity is on a journey through time, which is made up of stages.

Learning journeys based on the ideas of a customer journey, the stages that a learner goes through as they progress to their learning goal.

Machine learning techniques automated methods for finding patterns in data, a type of AI.

Minimum Viable Product (MVP) approach where a product is initially just good enough to get feedback from users, which starts a continuous improvement loop.

Mutualism where interactions between two business models affect them both. Based on mutualism between animal species. Common in business outsourcing relationships.

Negative feedback loop a repeating process where the output of the process feeds back as an input to the same process. Each cycle through the loop decreases whatever the process produces, and again and so on. For example, if your boss always criticises your ideas then you will gradually stop suggesting them. Opposite to a **positive feedback loop**.

Network effect a **positive feedback loop** where the more people there are in a network then the more valuable the network is to them, e.g., social networks or mobile phone networks.

No-code tools online software applications that enable users to make complex changes to how software operates without writing any code. Users can choose from and customise templates to build websites, social media management tools, mobile apps and whatever else the tool is for. Many of them are also free to use for low levels of use or for introductory periods.

Open system a system with external input flows and output flows.

Platform strategy constructing a digital platform to connect a business model's stakeholders together so they can share information, e.g., when social media organisations construct an online network and gather data from users, whilst allowing advertisers to target users. See Chapter 7.

Positive feedback loop a repeating process where the output of the process feeds back as an input to the process, which increases whatever the process produces. For example, putting a microphone near a loud speaker, any sound is quickly amplified into a loud shriek. Opposite to a **negative feedback loop**.

to redesign them to be faster, cheaper or with higher quality outputs.

Productivity a measure of process outputs divided by inputs, like the number of cars manufactured divided by their time and cost. Productivity data is a key measure for improving the use of resources.

Quantum computing an experimental computing technology that uses quantum phenomena such as quantum superposition and quantum entanglement. It uses quantum bits, 'qubits', rather than the bits used in classical computing. Quantum computers use subatomic particles like electrons or photons as qubits. A classical computing bit has two states, it can either be 1 or 0; quantum superposition enables the quantum states of several qubits to be added together so that they represent many different 1s and

0s at once. The same computing process can potentially work on many different versions of the same calculation at once. Quantum entanglement is where a pair of subatomic particles, the qubits, have the same quantum state. If the state of one of the pair is changed then in an instant, so is the state of the other, even over great distances. There are many hurdles to overcome before quantum computing leaves the experimental stage.

Real-time data   a live stream of data that is used straight after it is recorded, rather than being recorded and used later.

Recommendation engines   software that makes recommendations or suggestions to users based on the behaviours of similar users, e.g., 'customers who bought your book also bought these books'.

Reusable capabilities and resources   capabilities and resources that are already provided by a business model's stakeholders and that can also be supplied to other stakeholders.

Robot Process Automation (RPA)   uses rules and AI to mimic repetitive and routine tasks that are carried out by people. RPA learns how staff operate an organisation's normal software by analysing what happens on users' screens. This allows RPA technologies to operate the same software using the user interfaces rather than by connecting different software applications directly together, which is more technically complicated.

Self-service   an automated service, where users of the service can use it without human help, e.g., an ATM or a website.

Service-needs   the exact thing that a well-designed product or service satisfies.

Software-as-a-service (SaaS)   software that runs on the cloud and is accessed through a Web browser.

Start-up   new organisation started up by its founders. Usually, the product or service is still forming, and the organisation is small. An Internet start-up makes much use of the Internet for providing its main service, as well as for marketing and customer relationships.

Stakeholder   anyone with a stake in an organisation: customers, staff, suppliers, investors, partner organisations, government regulators. Any person or other organisation with some connection to the organisation.

Sustaining innovation strategy   when incumbent firms make current products better to satisfy a core group of key customers rather than improving them in ways that satisfy all customers. Allows new entrant firms to grow a market based on neglected non-core customers.

Technology   technologies are 'know-how', ways of getting things done. They can be electrical, mechanical, chemical, or involve materials, painting, singing or any other sophisticated knowledge that is used to accomplish a task.

Time series data   data that has been recorded over time and includes a time stamp for data value in the **dataset**.

Touchpoints   events where a customer interacts with an organisation; information from that interaction can be stored digitally.

Truth table   a method used in Boolean algebra to set out all the possible combinations of several binary variables.

Unmet needs   anything that a stakeholder values but that they do not currently get, e.g., additional products or services, or small changes to the products or services that they get already.

Value Flow Analysis (VFA) diagram   a diagram made of circles and arrowed lines. The circles represent stakeholders in a business model, and the arrows represent the flows of any resources and capabilities they contribute to each other. Stakeholders can be at any level – the individual, team, department, organisation, ecosystem or higher. It is best to focus VFAs on as low a level as possible so that the flows from and to them are as specific as they can be. A VFA has a very simple architecture, but each diagram can be very complicated. They are normally used to put information from many people and organisations on a single large display for information sharing and analysis purposes. A VFA can be used to reengineer a business model by looking for unmet needs of stakeholders, and reusable resources and capabilities. This is done by looking for opportunities to 'rewire' the stakeholders and flows in the diagram, or to add more.

VFA   see **Value Flow Analysis**.

World Wide Web   the globally linked system of web pages that we see when we go online using Web browsers.

Yield   the measure of outputs for a fixed set of inputs, like the number of car products in a fixed time or a fixed cost. Related to productivity, but the inputs are fixed so the outputs can be focused on more easily.

REFERENCES

Abbasi, A., Sarker, S. and Chiang, R.H.L. (2016) 'Big data research in information systems: toward an inclusive research agenda', *Journal of the Association for Information Systems*, *17*(2). DOI: 10.17705/1jais.00423.

Agarwal, R. and Dhar, V. (2014) 'Editorial: big data, data science, and analytics: the opportunity and challenge for IS research', *Information Systems Research*, *25*(3): 443–448. https://doi.org/10.1287/isre.2014.0546 (accessed 3 April 2022).

Ahl, V. and Allen, T.F.H. (1996) *Hierarchy Theory*. New York: Columbia University Press.

Akakura, Y., Ono, K., Watanabe, T. and Kawamura, H. (2015) 'Estimation of alternative ports for container transport after large-scale disasters – estimation method and application to port-BCPs', *Journal of Integrated Disaster Risk Management*, *5*(2): 135–152.

Allen, T.F.H. and Hoekstra, T.W. (2015) *Toward a Unified Ecology*, 2nd edn. New York: Columbia University Press.

Allen, T.F.H. and Starr, T.B. (1982) *Hierarchy: Perspectives for Ecological Complexity*. Chicago: University of Chicago Press.

Allen, T.F.H. and Starr, T.B. (2017) *Hierarchy: Perspectives for Ecological Complexity*, 2nd edn. Chicago: University of Chicago Press.

Amazon (2021) 'Connect Smart Home devices to Alexa', Amazon. https://www.amazon.co.uk/gp/help/customer/display.html?nodeId=201749240 (accessed 3 April 2022).

Anderson, C. (2015) 'Creating a data-driven organization', O'Reilly Media. https://www.oreilly.com/library/view/creating-a-data-driven/9781491916902/ch01.html (accessed 3 April 2022).

Andreessen, M. (2011) 'Why software is eating the world', *The Wall Street Journal*, C2.

Arnott, D. (2006) 'Cognitive biases and decision support systems development: a design science approach', *Information Systems Journal*, *16*(1): 55–78. https://doi.org/10.1111/j.1365-2575.2006.00208.x (accessed 3 April 2022).

Atasu, A., Duran, S., and Van Wassenhove, L. (2021) 'The circular business model', *Harvard Business Review*, July–August.

Atluri, V., Dietz, M. and Henke, N. (2017) 'Competing in a world of sectors without borders', *McKinsey Quarterly*, June. www.mckinsey.com/business-functions/mckinsey-analytics/our-insights/competing-in-a-world-of-sectors-without-borders (accessed 3 April 2022).

Azevedo, M.A. (2020) 'Apple's 2020 buying spree: tech giant reportedly acquiring NextVR for about $100M', Crunchbase News. https://news.crunchbase.com/news/apples-2020-buying-spree-tech-giant-reportedly-acquiring-nextvr-for-about-100m (accessed 5 April 2022).

Bain (2020) 'Next-best-action model', Bain and Company. https://www.bain.com/insights/customer-experience-tools-next-best-action-model/# (accessed 5 April 2022).

Barney (1991) 'Firm resources and sustained competitive advantage', *Journal of Management*, *17*, 99–120. https://doi.org/10.1177%2F014920639101700108 (accessed 5 April 2022).

BBC (2019) 'CES 2019: IBM's hourly weather reports will cover entire Earth', BBC. https://www.bbc.co.uk/news/technology-46790221 (accessed 5 April 2022).

BCorp (2021) 'About B Corps'. https://bcorporation.net/about-b-corps (accessed 5 April 2022).

Beauchamp, T.L. and Childress, J.F. (2001) *Principles of Biomedical Ethics*. New York: Oxford University Press.

Beebee, H. (2016) 'Hume and the problem of causation', in P. Russell (ed.) *The Oxford Handbook of Hume*. New York: Oxford University Press.

Beer, S. (1979) *The Heart of Enterprise*. New Jersey: John Wiley & Sons Ltd.

Begum, T. (2020) 'Microplastics: what they are and how you can reduce them', Natural History Museum. https://www.nhm.ac.uk/discover/what-are-microplastics.html (accessed 5 April 2022).

Bhatt, S. (2018) '5 things you need to know about reinforcement learning', KDnuggets. https://www.k.dnuggets.com/2018/03/5-things-reinforcement-learning.html (accessed 5 April 2022).

Birkinshaw, J. (2019) 'Ecosystem businesses are changing the rules of strategy', *Harvard Business Review*, 8. https://hbr.org/2019/08/ecosystem-businesses-are-changing-the-rules-of-strategy (accessed 5 April 2022).

Birkinshaw, J. and Foss, N.J. and Lindenberg, S. (2014) 'Combining purpose with profits', *MIT Sloan Management Review*, *55*: 49–56. https://www.researchgate.net/profile/Siegwart_Lindenberg/publication/279324286_Combining_Purpose_With_Profits/links/56a8d38308ae997e22be0287.pdf (accessed 5 April 2022).

Blank, S. (2013) 'Why the lean start-up changes everything', *Harvard Business Review*, *91*(5): 63–72.

Boudet, J., Gregg, B., Rathje, K., Stein, E. and Vollhardt, K. (2019) 'The future of personalization – and how to get ready for it', Mckinsey. https://www.mckinsey.com/business-functions/marketing-and-sales/our-insights/the-future-of-personalization-and-how-to-get-ready-for-it (accessed 5 April 2022).

Boulton, C. (2018) 'What is RPA? A revolution in business process automation', CIO.com. https://www.cio.com/article/3236451/what-is-rpa-robotic-process-automation-explained.html (accessed 5 April 2022).

Bourguignon, D. (2015) 'EU biofuels policy: dealing with indirect land use change', European Parliamentary Research Service. https://www.europarl.europa.eu/RegData/etudes/BRIE/2015/548993/EPRS_BRI(2015)548993_REV1_EN.pdf (accessed 5 April 2022).

Bower, J.L. and Christensen, C.M. (1995) 'Disruptive technologies: catching the wave', *Harvard Business Review*, January–February. https://hbr.org/1995/01/disruptive-technologies-catching-the-wave (accessed 5 April 2022).

Bowne-Anderson, H. (2018) 'What data scientists really do, according to 35 data scientists', *Harvard Business Review*, August. https://hbr.org/2018/08/what-data-scientists-really-do-according-to-35-data-scientists (accessed 5 April 2022).

Bradt, G. (2016) 'Wanamaker was wrong: the vast majority of advertising is wasted', Forbes. https://www.forbes.com/sites/georgebradt/2016/09/14/wanamaker-was-wrong-the-vast-majority-of-advertising-is-wasted (accessed 22 April 2022).

Brandenburger, A. and Nalebuff, B. (1996) *Co-opetition: A Revolution Mindset that Combines Competition and Cooperation*. New York: Doubleday.

Bronstein, J.L. (2012) 'Mutualism and symbiosis', in S.A. Levin, S.R. Carpenter, H.C. Godfray, A.P. Kinzig, M. Loreau, J.B. Losos, B. Walker and D.S. Wilcove (eds.) (2012) *The Princeton Guide to Ecology*. New Jersey: Princeton University Press, Part II Section 11.

Bronstein, J.L. (ed.) (2015) *Mutualism*. New York: Oxford University Press.

Brown, A., Fishenden, J., Thompson, M., Venters, W. (2017) 'Appraising the impact and role of platform models and Government as a Platform (GaaP) in UK Government public service reform: Towards a Platform Assessment Framework (PAF)', *Government Information Quarterly*, *34*: 167–182. https://doi.org/10.1016/j.giq.2017.03.003 (accessed 5 April 2022).

Brynjolfsson, E. and Mcafee, A. (2017) 'The business of artificial intelligence', *Harvard Business Review*, July. https://hbr.org/cover-story/2017/07/the-business-of-artificial-intelligence (accessed 5 April 2022).

Brynjolfsson, E. and Mcelheran, K. (2016) 'The rapid adoption of data-driven decision-making', *American Economic Review*, *106*(5): 133–139. DOI: 10.1257/aer.p20161016.

Buchanan, L. and O'Connell, A. (2006) 'A brief history of decision making', *Harvard Business Review*, *84*(1): 32. https://hbr.org/2006/01/a-brief-history-of-decision-making (accessed 5 April 2022).

Cellan-Jones, R. (2016) 'Amazon Dash – who wants to live in a push-button world?', BBC. http://www.bbc.co.uk/news/technology-37224691 (accessed 5 April 2022).

Cellan-Jones, R. (2018) 'Facebook hires former deputy PM Sir Nick Clegg', BBC Technology. https://www.bbc.co.uk/news/technology-45913587 (accessed 5 April 2022).

Chaffey, D. and Smith, P.R. (2017) *Digital Marketing Excellence: Planning, Optimizing and Integrating Online Marketing*. Oxfordshire Taylor & Francis.

Chan, C. (2019) 'Four trends in consumer tech', Andreessen Horowitz. https://a16z.com/2020/01/23/four-trends-in-consumer-tech/ (accessed 5 April 2022).

Chan, C. (2020) 'Four trends in consumer tech', Andreessen Horowitz. https://a16z.com/2020/01/23/four-trends-in-consumer-tech (accessed 5 April 2022).

Checkland, P. (1999) *Systems Thinking, Systems Practice.* Chichester: John Wiley & Sons.

Chesbrough, H.W. (2006) *Open Business Models: How to Thrive in the New Innovation Landscape.* Boston, MA: Harvard Business School Press.

Chesbrough, H.W. (2007) 'Why companies should have open business models', *MIT Sloan Management Review, 48*(2): 22. https://sloanreview.mit.edu/article/why-companies-should-have-open-business-models (accessed 5 April 2022).

Christensen, C.M. (1992) 'Exploring the limits of the technology S-Curve'. *Part I: Component Technologies, Production and Operations Management, 1*(4): 334–357.

Christensen, C.M. (2000) *The Innovator's Dilemma: When New Technologies Cause Great Firms to Fail.* Harvard Business Review Press.

Christensen, C.M., Raynor, M.E. and McDonald, R. (2015) 'What is disruptive innovation?', *Harvard Business Review*, December. https://hbr.org/2015/12/what-is-disruptive-innovation (accessed 5 April 2022).

CIPD (2021) 'HR shared services', CIPD. https://www.cipd.co.uk/knowledge/fundamentals/people/hr/shared-services-factsheet#gref (accessed 5 April 2022).

Cloud Speech-to-Text (2021) 'Speech-to-Text', Google. https://cloud.google.com/speech-to-text (accessed 5 April 2022).

Cloud Vision API (2021) 'Vision AI', Google. https://cloud.google.com/vision (accessed 5 April 2022).

CNBC (2020) 'Oil falls on oversupply fears and US inventory growth', Reuters. https://www.cnbc.com/2020/04/01/oil-markets-crude-output-in-focus.html (accessed 5 April 2022).

Cohen, A. (2020) 'Manufacturers are struggling to supply electric vehicles with batteries', Forbes. https://www.forbes.com/sites/arielcohen/2020/03/25/manufacturers-are-struggling-to-supply-electric-vehicles-with-batteries (accessed 22 April 2022).

Comfort, L.K., Sungu, Y., Johnson, D. and Dunn, M. (2001) 'Complex systems in crisis: anticipation and resilience in dynamic environments', *Journal of Contingencies and Crisis Management, 9*(3): 144–158. https://doi.org/10.1111/1468-5973.00164 (accessed 5 April 2022).

Coolican, D. and Jordan, J. (2020) '"Deep" job platforms and how to build them', Andreessen Horowitz. https://a16z.com/2020/09/23/deep-job-platforms (accessed 5 April 2022).

Courea, E. (2020) 'Facebook goes on PR hiring spree as parliament debates tougher rules', *The Times.* https://www.thetimes.co.uk/article/facebook-goes-on-pr-hiring-spree-as-parliament-debates-tougher-rules-g0gqqkrtc (accessed 5 April 2022).

Court, D., Elzinga, D., Mulder, S. and Vetvik, O.J. (2009) 'The consumer decision journey'. *McKinsey Quarterly.* https://www.mckinsey.com/business-functions/marketing-and-sales/our-insights/the-consumer-decision-journey (accessed 5 April 2022).

Curtis, B., Kellner, M.I. and Over, J. (1992) 'Process modelling', *Communications of the ACM, 35*(9): 75–90. https://doi.org/10.1145/130994.130998 (accessed 5 April 2022).

Cuthbertson, A. (2016) 'Robot lawyer overturns $4 million in parking tickets', *Newsweek.* https://www.newsweek.com/robot-lawyer-chatbor-donotpay-parking-tickets-475751 (accessed 7 April 2022).

Dasgupta, P. (2021) 'The economics of biodiversity: the Dasgupta Review'. *MH Treasury.* https://www.gov.uk/government/publications/final-report-the-economics-of-biodiversity-the-dasgupta-review (accessed 7 April 2022).

Davenport, T. (2015) 'In praise of "light quants" and "analytical translators"'. *Deloitte Insights.* https://www2.deloitte.com/us/en/insights/topics/analytics/new-big-data-analytics-skills.html (accessed 7 April 2022).

Davenport, T.H. (2009) 'How to design smart business experiments', *Harvard Business Review*, 68–76. https://hbr.org/2009/02/how-to-design-smart-business-experiments (accessed 7 April 2022).

Davis, B. (2014) '10 implications of AmazonFresh and Amazon Dash', *econsultancy*. https://econsultancy.com/blog/64723-10-implications-of-amazonfresh-and-amazon-dash (accessed 7 April 2022).

Day One Team (2021) 'AmazonFresh', Amazon. https://www.aboutamazon.eu/innovation/amazonfresh (accessed 7 April 2022).

de Reuver, M., Sørensen, C. and Basole, R.C. (2017) 'The digital platform: a research agenda', *Journal of Information Technology*, 1–12. https://doi.org/10.1057%2Fs41265-016-0033-3 (accessed 7 April 2022).

Dell (2020) 'Winning worldwide and on the web', Dell Technologies. https://www.dell.com/learn/aw/en/awcorp1/winning-on-the-worldwide-web (accessed 7 April 2022).

Denning, S. (2017) 'Moving to Blue Ocean Strategy: a five-step process to make the shift', Forbes. https://www.forbes.com/sites/stevedenning/2017/09/24/moving-to-blue-ocean-strategy-a-five-step-process-to-make-the-shift (accessed 7 April 2022).

Desouza, K. (2006) *Agile Information Systems*. Oxfordshire: Routledge.

Dhanaraj, C. and Parkhe, A. (2006) 'Orchestrating innovation networks', *Academy of Management Review*, 31(3), 659–669. https://doi.org/10.2307/20159234 (accessed 7 April 2022).

Divol, R., Edelman, D. and Sarrazin, H. (2012) 'Demystifying social media', *Mckinsey Quarterly*, April.

Dyson, R.G. (2004) 'Strategic development and SWOT analysis at the University of Warwick', *European Journal of Operational Research*, 152(3), 631–640. https://doi.org/10.1016/S0377-2217(03)00062-6 (accessed 7 April 2022).

EC (2020) 'A European Green Deal', European Commission. https://ec.europa.eu/info/strategy/priorities-2019-2024/european-green-deal_en (accessed 7 April 2022).

Ecover (2021) Home page. https://www.ecover.com (accessed 7 April 2022).

Edlich, A. and Sohoni, V. (2017) 'Burned by the bots: why robotic automation is stumbling', McKinsey. https://www.mckinsey.com/business-functions/mckinsey-digital/our-insights/digital-blog/burned-by-the-bots-why-robotic-automation-is-stumbling (accessed 7 April 2022).

EIA (2020) 'Annual Coal Report', US Energy Information Administration. https://www.eia.gov/todayinenergy/detail.php?id=46096 (accessed 7 April 2022).

EMF (2021) 'What is the circular economy?'. Ellen Macarthur Foundation. https://www.ellenmacarthurfoundation.org/circular-economy/what-is-the-circular-economy (accessed 7 April 2022).

Ferrar, J. and Green, G. (2021) *Excellence in People Analytics: How to Use Workforce Data to Create Business Value*. London: Kogan Page.

Fitzgerald, B. and Howcroft, D. (1998) 'Towards dissolution of the IS research debate: from polarization to polarity', *Journal of Information Technology*, 13(4): 313–326. https://doi.org/10.1177%2F026839629801300409 (accessed 7 April 2022).

Frenkel, S. and Barnes, J.E. (2020) 'Russians again targeting Americans with disinformation, Facebook and Twitter say', *New York Times*. https://www.nytimes.com/2020/09/01/technology/facebook-russia-disinformation-election.html (accessed 7 April 2022).

Freshwater, J. (2019) 'Keynote presentation by Amazon's director of forecasting', Amazon Science. https://www.amazon.science/re-mars-2019-jenny-freshwater-director-forecasting-presentation (accessed 7 April 2022).

Galliers, R.D., Newell, S., Shanks, G. and Topid, H. (2017) 'Datification and its human, organizational and societal effects: the strategic opportunities and challenges of algorithmic decision making', *Journal of Strategic Information Systems*, 26, 185–190. https://doi.org/10.1016/j.jsis.2017.08.002 (accessed 7 April 2022).

Gartenberg, C. (2019) 'Amazon will stop taking orders from Dash buttons at the end of August', The Verge. https://www.theverge.com/2019/8/1/20750814/amazon-dash-buttons-discontinued-orders-august-31st (accessed 7 April 2022).

Gartner (2020) 'Gartner says worldwide semiconductor revenue declined 11.9% in 2019', Newsroom. https://www.gartner.com/en/newsroom/press-releases/2020-01-14-gartner-says-worldwide-semi-conductor-revenue-declined-11-point-9-percent-in-2019 (accessed 7 April 2022).

Gartner (2021) 'Robotic process automation software reviews and ratings', Gartner. https://www.gartner.com/reviews/market/robotic-process-automation-software (accessed 7 April 2022).

Geller, L.W. (2017) 'Howard Yu disrupts disruptive innovation, strategy & business', PWC. https://www.strategy-business.com/article/Howard-Yu-Disrupts-Disruptive-Innovation (accessed 7 April 2022).

Ghose, S. (2020) 'Are you ready for the quantum computing revolution?', *Harvard Business Review*, September. https://hbr.org/2020/09/are-you-ready-for-the-quantum-computing-revolution (accessed 7 April 2022).

Giles, M. (2019a) 'Explainer: what is quantum communication?', *MIT Technology Review*. https://www.technologyreview.com/2019/02/14/103409/what-is-quantum-communications (accessed 7 April 2022).

Giles, M. (2019b) 'Explainer: what is a quantum computer?' *MIT Technology Review*. https://www.technologyreview.com/2019/01/29/66141/what-is-quantum-computing (accessed 7 April 2022).

Gilliland, N. (2021) 'Octopus energy's head of digital on creating "outrageously good customer experiences"', *econsultancy*. https://econsultancy.com/octopus-energys-head-of-digital-on-creating-outrageously-good-customer-experiences (accessed 7 April 2022).

Goerzen, A. (2005) 'Managing alliance networks: emerging practices of multinational corporations'. *The Academy of Management Executive*, 9(2): 94–107.

Goldratt, E.M. and Cox, J. (2004) *The Goal: A Process of Ongoing Improvement*, 3rd edn. Great Barrington, MA: North River Press.

Green, G. (2021) 'The four responsibilities for people analytics in the consumerisation of HR'. *LinkedIn Pulse*. https://www.linkedin.com/pulse/four-responsibilities-people-analytics-hr-david-green (accessed 7 April 2022).

Gregor, S. (2006) 'The nature of theory in information systems', *MIS Quarterly*, 30(3): 611–642. https://doi.org/10.2307/25148742 (accessed 7 April 2022).

Grigoroudis, E. and Siskos, Y. (2009) 'Customer satisfaction evaluation: methods for measuring and implementing service quality'. Vol. *139*. Springer Science & Business Media.

Gross, D. (2019) 'Making automation easy', *Strategy + Business*. https://www.strategy-business.com/article/Making-automation-easy (accessed 7 April 2022).

Grothaus, M. (2018) 'Facebook is hiring more Washington lobbyists as privacy scandal continues', Fastcompany. https://www.fastcompany.com/40550156/facebook-is-hiring-more-washington-lob-byists-as-privacy-scandal-continues (accessed 7 April 2022).

Ha, A. (2014) 'Amazon tests Dash barcode scanner for ordering AmazonFresh groceries', TechCrunch. https://techcrunch.com/2014/04/04/amazon-dash/ (accessed 7 April 2022).

Haeckel, S.H. and Nolan, R.L. (1993) 'Managing by wire'. *Harvard Business Review*, 71(5): 122–132. https://hbr.org/1993/09/managing-by-wire (accessed 7 April 2022).

Hagel III, J. (2002) 'Leveraged growth: expanding sales without sacrificing profits', *Harvard Busines Review*, 10(80): 69–77. https://hbr.org/2002/10/leveraged-growth-expanding-sales-without-sacrificing-profits (accessed 7 April 2022).

Hall, A., Towers, N. and Shaw, D.R. (2017) 'Understanding how Millennial shoppers decide what to buy: digitally connected unseen journeys', *International Journal of Retail and Distribution Management*, 45(2): 498–517.

Hammer, M. and Champy, J. (1993) *Reengineering the Corporation: A Manifesto for Business Revolution*. New York: Harper Business.

Harrabin, R. (2018) 'Should we burn or bury waste plastic?', BBC. https://www.bbc.co.uk/news/science-environment-43120041 (accessed 7 April 2022).

Harrabin, R. (2020) 'Hydrogen power: Firms join forces in bid to lower costs', BBC. https://www.bbc.co.uk/news/business-55218573 (accessed 7 April 2022).

Harris, J.G. and Davenport, T.H. (2017) *Competing on Analytics: The New Science of Winning*. Brighton, MA: Harvard Business School Press.

Harvey, F. (2020) 'China pledges to become carbon neutral before 2060', *The Guardian*. https://www.theguardian.com/environment/2020/sep/22/china-pledges-to-reach-carbon-neutrality-before-2060 (accessed 7 April 2022).

Hedman, J. and Kalling, T. (2003) 'The business model concept: theoretical underpinnings and empirical illustrations', *European Journal of Information Systems*, *12*: 49–59.

Helm, B. (2020) 'Credit card companies are tracking shoppers like never before: Inside the next phase of surveillance capitalism', Fast Company. https://www.fastcompany.com/90490923/credit-card-companies-are-tracking-shoppers-like-never-before-inside-the-next-phase-of-surveillance-capitalism (accessed 7 April 2022).

Henfridsson, O., Nandhakumar, J., Scarbrough, H. and Panourgias, N. (2018) 'Recombination in the open-ended value landscape of digital innovation'. *Information and Organization*, *28*(2): 89–100. DOI: http://dx.doi.org/10.1016/j.infoandorg.2018.03.001 (accessed 7 April 2022).

Henke, N., Levine, J. and McInerney, P. (2018) 'Analytics translator: the new must-have role'. https://www.mckinsey.com/business-functions/mckinsey-analytics/our-insights/analytics-translator (accessed 7 April 2022).

Heracleous, L., Wirtz, J. and Pangarkar, N. (2009) *Flying High in a Competitive Industry*. Singapore: McGraw-Hill.

Herring, D. and Simmon, R. (1999) 'Evolving in the presence of fire'. *NASA Earth Observatory*. https://earthobservatory.nasa.gov/features/BOREASFire (accessed 7 April 2022).

Hicks, H.M., Gilcreast, A., Marais, H. and Manning, C. (2021) 'A CEO guide to today's value creation ecosystem', *Strategy+Business*. https://www.strategy-business.com/article/A-CEO-guide-to-todays-value-creation-ecosystem (accessed 7 April 2022).

Hodjat, B. (2015) 'The AI resurgence: why now?'. Wired. https://www.wired.com/insights/2015/03/ai-resurgence-now (accessed 7 April 2022).

Hsieh, C.-H., Tai, H.-H. and Lee, Y.-N. (2014) 'Port vulnerability assessment from the perspective of critical infrastructure interdependency'. *Maritime Policy & Management*, *41*(6): 589–606. DOI:10.1080/03088839.2013.856523.

Huston, L. and Sakkab, N. (2006) 'Inside Procter & Gamble's new model for innovation'. *Harvard Business Review*, *84*(3): 58–66. https://hbr.org/2006/03/connect-and-develop-inside-procter-gambles-new-model-for-innovation (accessed 7 April 2022).

IDEO (2021) 'Design thinking', IDEO. https://www.ideou.com/pages/design-thinking (accessed 7 April 2022).

IEA (2020) 'World energy outlook 2020', IEA. https://webstore.iea.org/world-energy-outlook-2020 (accessed 7 April 2022).

IKEA (2021) Billy bookcase product page, IKEA. https://www.ikea.com/gb/en/p/billy-bookcase-white-00263850/ (accessed 7 April 2022).

IPCC (2014) 'Climate change 2014 synthesis report summary for policymakers', IPCC. https://www.ipcc.ch/site/assets/uploads/2018/02/AR5_SYR_FINAL_SPM.pdf (accessed 7 April 2022).

Iyengar, S. and Agrawal, K. (2010) 'A better choosing experience'. *Strategy+Business*, *61*: Winter. Booze & Co. https://www.strategy-business.com/article/00046 (accessed 7 April 2022).

Iyer, B. and Davenport, T.H. (2008) 'Reverse engineering Google's innovation machine', *Harvard Business Review*, *86*(4): 58–68.

Jacobides, M.G., Cennamo, C. and Gawer, A. (2018) 'Towards a theory of ecosystems', *Strategic Management Journal*, *39*(8): 2255–2276. https://doi.org/10.1002/smj.2904 (accessed 7 April 2022).

Janssen, M. and Estevez, E. (2013) 'Lean government and platform-based governance: doing more with less', *Government Information Quarterly*, *30*: S1–S8. https://doi.org/10.1016/j.giq.2012.11.003 (accessed 7 April 2022).

Janssen, M. and van der Voort, H. (2016) 'Editorial: adaptive governance: towards a stable, accountable and responsive government', *Government Information Quarterly*, *33*: 1–5.

Janssen, M. and Helbig, N. (2018) 'Innovating and changing the policy-cycle: policy-makers be prepared!', *Government Information Quarterly*, *35*(4): S99–S105. https://doi.org/10.1016/j.giq.2015.11.009 (accessed 7 April 2022).

Kaplan, R.S. and Norton, D.P. (1992) 'The balanced scorecard: measures that drive performance'. *Harvard Business Review*, January–February. https://hbr.org/1992/01/the-balanced-scorecard-measures-that-drive-performance-2 (accessed 7 April 2022).

Kelion, L. (2020) 'Why Amazon knows so much about you'. BBC. https://www.bbc.co.uk/news/extra/CLQYZENMBI/amazon-data (accessed 7 April 2022).

Khemani, R.S. and Shapiro, D.M. (1993) *Glossary of Industrial Organisation Economics and Competition Law*, commissioned by the Directorate for Financial, Fiscal and Enterprise Affairs, OECD.

Kinni, T. (2020) 'What people like you like'. *Strategy+Business*, *61*: Winter. https://www.strategy-business.com/article/What-people-like-you-like (accessed 7 April 2022).

Kitchin, R. (2014) 'Big data, new epistemologies and paradigm shifts'. *Big Data and Society*, *1*(1): 1–12. https://doi.org/10.1177%2F2053951714528481 (accessed 7 April 2022).

Kobie, N. (2020) 'As electric car sales soar, the industry faces a cobalt crisis', Wired. https://www.wired.co.uk/article/cobalt-battery-evs-shortage (accessed 7 April 2022).

Kohavi, R. and Thomke, S. (2017) 'The surprising power of online experiments', *Harvard Business Review*, *95*(5): 74–82. https://hbr.org/2017/09/the-surprising-power-of-online-experiments (accessed 7 April 2022).

Kotler, P. (1991) *Marketing Management*, 7th edn. Englewood Cliffs, NJ: Prentice-Hall.

Kotler, P., Keller, K.L., Brady, M., Goodman, M. and Hansen, T. (2009) *Marketing Management*. England: Harlow.

KPMG (2020) 'Super app or super disrupt'. KPMG. https://home.kpmg/xx/en/home/insights/2019/06/super-app-or-super-disruption.html (accessed 7 April 2022).

Lamarre, E. and May, B. (2019) 'Ten trends shaping the Internet of Things business landscape'. *McKinsey*. https://www.mckinsey.com/business-functions/mckinsey-digital/our-insights/ten-trends-shaping-the-internet-of-things-business-landscape (accessed 7 April 2022).

Lemon, K.N. and Verhoef, P.C. (2016) 'Understanding customer experience throughout the customer journey', *Journal of Marketing*, *80*(6): 69–96 (especially table on p. 86). https://doi.org/10.1509%2Fjm.15.0420.

Lepak, D.P., Smith, K.G. and Taylor, M.S. (2007) 'Value creation and value capture: a multilevel perspective', *Academy of Management Review*, *32*(1): 180–194.

LF (2021) 'What we do', Fung Group. https://funggroup.com/en/about/what_we_do (accessed 7 April 2022).

Lhuer, X. (2016) 'The next acronym you need to know about: RPA (robotic process automation)', McKinsey. https://www.mckinsey.com/business-functions/mckinsey-digital/our-insights/the-next-acronym-you-need-to-know-about-rpa (accessed 7 April 2022).

Lin, M., Lucas, H.C. and Shmueli, G. (2013) 'Too big to fail: large samples and the P-value problem', *Information Systems Research*, *24*(4): 906–917. https://psycnet.apa.org/doi/10.1287/isre.2013.0480 (accessed 7 April 2022).

LOC (2013) 'Japan: legal responses to the Great East Japan Earthquake of 2011', Library of Congress. https://www.loc.gov/law/help/japan-earthquake/index.php (accessed 7 April 2022).

Lorenzoni, G. and Lipparini, A. (1999) 'The leveraging of interfirm relationships as a distinctive organizational capability: a longitudinal study', *Strategic Management Journal*, *20*: 317–338.

Lynch, R. (2021) *Strategic Management*. London: Sage.

Maechler, N., Neher, K. and Park, R. (2016) 'From touchpoints to journeys: seeing the world as customers do'. https://www.mckinsey.com/business-functions/marketing-and-sales/our-insights/from-touchpoints-to-journeys-seeing-the-world-as-customers-do (accessed 7 April 2022).

March, J.G. (1994) *Primer on Decision Making: How Decisions Happen*. New York: Simon and Schuster.

Markman, A. (2015) 'How do people's values change as they get older?', *Psychology Today*, September. https://www.psychologytoday.com/gb/blog/ulterior-motives/201509/how-do-people-s-values-change-they-get-older (accessed 7 April 2022).

Markus, M.L. and Robey, D. (1988) 'Information technology and organizational change: causal structure in theory and research', *Management Science*, 34(5): 583–599.

Marr, B. (2020) 'The future of jobs and education', *Forbes*, December. https://www.forbes.com/sites/bernardmarr/2020/12/11/the-future-of-jobs-and-education (accessed 7 April 2022).

Mars, M.M., Bronstein, J.L. and Lusch, R.F. (2012) 'The value of a metaphor: organizations and ecosystems', *Organizational Dynamics*, 41(4): 271–280. https://doi.org/10.1016/j.orgdyn.2012.08.002 (accessed 7 April 2022).

Mattioli, D. (2020) 'Amazon scooped up data from its own sellers to launch competing products', *The Wall Street Journal*. https://www.wsj.com/articles/amazon-scooped-up-data-from-its-own-sellers-to-launch-competing-products-11587650015 (accessed 7 April 2022).

Mayhew, H., Saleh, T. and Williams, S. (2016) 'Making data analytics work for you—instead of the other way around', *McKinsey Quarterly*, October. https://www.mckinsey.com/business-functions/digital-mckinsey/our-insights/making-data-analytics-work-for-you-instead-of-the-other-way-around (accessed 7 April 2022).

McLaughlin, D. (2020) 'Big Tech goes on shopping spree, brushing off antitrust scrutiny', Bloomberg. https://financialpost.com/technology/big-tech-goes-on-shopping-spree-brushing-off-antitrust-scrutiny (accessed 25 April 2022).

Mintzberg, H., Raisinghani, D. and Théorêt, A. (1976) 'The structure of "unstructured" decision processes', *Administrative Science Quarterly*, 21(2): 246–275.

Mintzberg, H. and Westley, F. (2001) 'Decision making: it's not what you think', in P.C. Nutt and D.C. Wilson (eds.) *Handbook of Decision Making* (2010). New Jersey: John Wiley & Sons.

Moller, K. and Svahn, S. (2006) 'Role of knowledge in value creation in business nets', *Journal of Management Studies*, 43(5): 985–1007.

Moller, K., Rajala, A. and Svahn, S. (2005) 'Strategic business nets – their type and management, *Journal of Business Research*, 58: 1274–1284. DOI: 10.1016/j.jbusres.2003.05.002.

Monday (2021) 'Our story', Monday. https://monday.com/p/about/ (accessed 7 April 2022).

Moritz, R.E. and Zahidi, S. (2021) 'Upskilling for shared prosperity: insight report', World Economic Forum and PWC https://www.pwc.com/gx/en/issues/upskilling/shared-prosperity/upskilling_for_shared_prosperity_final.pdf (accessed 7 April 2022).

MTO (2017) 'Trucks handbook', Ministry of Transportation, Ontario. http://www.mto.gov.on.ca/english/trucks/handbook/section1-7-4.shtml (accessed 7 April 2022).

Müller, O., Junglas, I., vom Brocke, J. and Debortoli, S. (2016) 'Utilizing big data analytics for information systems research: challenges, promises and guidelines', *European Journal of Information Systems*, 25: 289–302. https://doi.org/10.1057/ejis.2016.2 (accessed 7 April 2022).

NAO (2015) 'A short guide to regulation', National Audit Office, September. https://www.nao.org.uk/wp-content/uploads/2015/08/Regulation-short-guide.pdf (accessed 7 April 2022).

NAO (2020) 'The supply of personal protective equipment (PPE) during the COVID-19 pandemic', National Audit Office. https://www.nao.org.uk/wp-content/uploads/2020/11/The-supply-of-personal-protective-equipment-PPE-during-the-COVID-19-pandemic.pdf (accessed 7 April 2022).

Naous, J. (2019) 'Everyone is an analyst: opportunities in operational analytics', Andreessen Horowitz. https://a16z.com/2019/05/16/everyone-is-an-analyst-opportunities-in-operational-analytics/ (accessed 7 April 2022).

Neely, A. (2008) 'Exploring the financial consequences of the servitisation of manufacturing', *Operations Management Research*, *1*: 103–118.

Newell, S. and Marabelli, M. (2015) 'Strategic opportunities (and challenges) of algorithmic decision-making: a call for action on the long-term societal effects of "datification"', *Journal Strategic Information Systems*, *24* (1): 3–14.

NHS (2021) 'Overview – consent to treatment', NHS. https://www.nhs.uk/conditions/consent-to-treatment (accessed 7 April 2022).

Nix, N., House, B. and Allison, B. (2018) 'Facebook goes on a hiring spree for Washington lobbyists', Bloomberg. https://www.bloomberg.com/news/articles/2018-03-27/facebook-in-hiring-spree-for-washington-lobbyists-amid-scandal (accessed 25 April 2022).

Nunez, S. (2020) 'Your phone is now more powerful than your PC', Samsung. https://insights.samsung.com/2020/08/07/your-phone-is-now-more-powerful-than-your-pc-2 (accessed 7 April 2022).

Nunis, V. (2020) '"Price rises likely" due to UK shipping problems', BBC. https://www.bbc.co.uk/news/business-55237791 (accessed 7 April 2022).

Osborne, D. and Gaebler, T. (1993) *Reinventing Government: How the Entrepreneurial Spirit Is Transforming the Public Sector*. Reading, MA: Addison-Wesley.

Osterwalder, A. (2013) 'A better way to think about your business model', *Harvard Business Review*, May. https://hbr.org/2013/05/a-better-way-to-think-about-yo (accessed 7 April 2022).

Osterwalder, A., Pigneur, Y. and Tucci, C.L. (2005) 'Clarifying business models: origins, present, and future of the concept', *Communications of the AIS*, *16*(1).

Palmai, K. (2021) 'Voice cloning of growing interest to actors and cybercriminals', BBC. https://www.bbc.co.uk/news/business-57761873 (accessed 7 April 2022).

Partington, R. (2019) 'What is a free port? All you need to know about the free-trade zones', *The Guardian*. https://www.theguardian.com/politics/2019/jul/06/what-is-a-free-port-all-you-need-to-know-about-free-trade-zones-brexit (accessed 7 April 2022).

Polestar (2020) 'Designing smarter factories', Polestar Cisco case study, www.polestarinteractive.com (accessed 25 April 2022).

Polestar (2021) 'Carlsberg wi-fi project case study', www.polestarinteractive.com (accessed 25 April 2022).

Porter, M.E. (1985) *Competitive Advantage*. New York: The Free Press.

Porter, M.E. (2008) 'The five competitive forces that shape strategy', *Harvard Business Review*, *86*(1). https://hbr.org/2008/01/the-five-competitive-forces-that-shape-strategy (accessed 7 April 2022).

Porter, M.E. and Heppelmann, J.E. (2014) 'How smart, connected products are transforming competition', *Harvard Business Review*, November. https://hbr.org/2014/11/how-smart-connected-products-are-transforming-competition (accessed 7 April 2022).

Porter, M.E. and Heppelmann, J.E. (2015) 'How smart, connected products are transforming companies', *Harvard Business Review*, October. https://hbr.org/2015/10/how-smart-connected-products-are-transforming-companies (accessed 7 April 2022).

Press, G. (2016) 'A very short history of artificial intelligence (AI)', *Forbes*. https://www.forbes.com/sites/gilpress/2016/12/30/a-very-short-history-of-artificial-intelligence-ai (accessed 7 April 2022).

Priem, R.L. (2007) 'A consumer perspective on value creation', *The Academy of Management Review*, *32*(1): 219–235.

Punt, D. (2020) 'Sir David Attenborough breaks Instagram record for fastest time to reach one million followers'. https://www.guinnessworldrecords.com/news/2020/9/sir-david-attenborough-breaks-instagram-record-for-fastest-time-to-reach-one-mill-632391 (accessed 7 April 2022).

Quick Draw (2021) 'Quick, Draw! The data', Google. https://quickdraw.withgoogle.com/data (accessed 7 April 2022).

Ramirez, R. (1999) 'Value co-production: intellectual origins and implications for practice and research', *Strategic Management Journal*, *20*: 49–65.

Reis, E. (2011) *The Lean Startup*. New York: Crown Business.

Rescher, N. (2000) *Process Metaphysics: An Introduction to Process Philosophy*. New York: State University of New York Press.

Richardson, A. (2010) 'Using customer journey maps to improve customer experience', *Harvard Business Review*, November. https://hbr.org/2010/11/using-customer-journey-maps-to (accessed 8 April 2022).

Rickards, T. and Moger, S. (1999) *Handbook for Creative Team Leaders*. Aldershot: Gower Publishing.

Ribeiro, H. and Zhang, X. (2019) 'Lithium oversupply to continue in 2020', S&P Global, Commodity Insights. https://www.spglobal.com/commodityinsights/en/market-insights/latest-news/metals/121319-lithium-oversupply-to-continue-in-2020 (accessed 25 April 2022).

Robson, C. (2002) *Real World Research*, 2nd edn. Oxford: Blackwell.

Rodgers, P. (2011) 'Tesco cuts NatWest tie to link with Royal Bank', *The Independent*. https://www.independent.co.uk/news/business/tesco-cuts-natwest-tie-to-link-with-royal-bank-1278538.html (accessed 8 April 2022).

Rohwedder, C. (2006) 'No. 1 retailer in Britain uses "Clubcard" to thwart Wal-Mart', *The Wall Street Journal*, June. https://www.wsj.com/articles/SB114955981460172218 (accessed 8 April 2022).

Rolls-Royce (2012) 'Rolls-Royce celebrates 50th anniversary of Power-by-the-Hour', Rolls-Royce. https://www.rolls-royce.com/media/press-releases-archive/yr-2012/121030-the-hour.aspx (accessed 8 April 2022).

Rosenbaum, M.S., Otalora, M.L. and Ramírez, G.C. (2017) 'How to create a realistic customer journey map', *Business Horizons*, *60*(1): 143–150.

Rotman, D. (2020) 'We're not prepared for the end of Moore's Law', *Technology Review*, February 24. https://www.technologyreview.com/2020/02/24/905789/were-not-prepared-for-the-end-of-moores-law/ (accessed 25 April 2022).

Roth, W.D. and Mehta, J.D. (2002) 'The Rashomon Effect combining positivist and interpretivist approaches in the analysis of contested events', *Sociological Methods and Research*, *31*(2): 131–17. https://doi.org/10.1177%2F0049124102031002002 (accessed 8 April 2022).

Rusbridger, A. (2020) 'Why I'm joining Facebook's Oversight Board', Medium. https://onezero.medium.com/why-im-joining-facebook-s-oversight-committee-f5b0c30f2d14 (accessed 8 April 2022).

Ruz, C. (2011) 'The six natural resources most drained by our 7 billion people', *The Guardian*, October. https://www.theguardian.com/environment/blog/2011/oct/31/six-natural-resources-population (accessed 8 April 2022).

Saha, S., Egol, M. and Siegel, M. (2020) 'Enterprise agility and experience management efforts work best when they work together', *Strategy+Business*, Winter: 101. https://www.strategy-business.com/article/Enterprise-agility-and-experience-management-efforts-work-best-when-they-work-together (accessed 8 April 2022).

Salthe, S. (1985) *Evolving Hierarchical Systems: Their Structure and Representation*. New York: Columbia University Press.

SAS (2011) 'The translation layer: the role of analytic talent', SAS Institute. https://www.sas.com/en_id/whitepapers/translation-layer-role-of-analytic-talent-104171.html (accessed 8 April 2022).

Scheyder, E. (2019) 'Exclusive: Tesla expects global shortage of electric vehicle battery minerals', Reuters. https://www.reuters.com/article/us-usa-lithium-electric-tesla-exclusive-idUSKCN1S81QS (accessed 8 April 2022).

Shaw, D.R. (2007) 'Manchester United Football Club: developing a Network Orchestration Model', *European Journal of Information Systems*, *16*(5): 628–642. DOI: 10.1057/palgrave.ejis.3000702.

Shaw, D.R. (2009) 'A structure and process theory of network orchestration', unpublished PhD thesis.

Shaw, D.R. (2018) '"Analytics translator": a new job to link data scientists with the rest of the firm', LinkedIn, October. https://www.linkedin.com/pulse/analytics-translator-new-job-link-data-scientists-rest-duncan-r-shaw (accessed 8 April 2022).

Shaw, D.R. (2020) 'Super Apps: recycle your data exhaust to power a whole ecosystem, LinkedIn Pulse, September. https://www.linkedin.com/pulse/super-apps-recycle-your-data-exhaust-power-whole-ecosystem-shaw (accessed 8 April 2022).

Shaw, D., Achuthan, K., Sharma, A. and Grainger, A. (2019) 'Resilience orchestration and resilience facilitation: how government can orchestrate the whole UK ports market with limited resources – the case of UK ports resilience', *Government Information Quarterly*, 36(2): 252–263.

Shaw, D.R. and Allen, T.F.H. (2017) 'Studying innovation ecosystems using ecology theory', *Technological Forecasting and Social Change*, 136, 88–102. DOI: 10.1016/j.techfore.2016.11.030.

Shaw, D.R., Grainger, A. and Achuthan, K. (2017) 'Multi-level port resilience planning in the UK: how can information sharing be made easier?' *Technological Forecasting and Social Change*, Special issue on Disaster Resilience, *121*: 126–138.

Shaw, D.R., Holland, C.P., Kawalek, P., Snowdon, R. and Warboys, B. (2006) 'Electronic commerce strategy in the UK electricity industry: the case of Electric Co and Dataflow Software', *International Journal of Technology and Human Interaction*, 2(3): 38–60. DOI: 10.4018/jthi.2006070103.

Shaw, D.R., Holland, C.P., Kawalek, P., Snowdon, R. and Warboys, B. (2007) 'The elements of a business process management system: theory and practice', *Business Process Management Journal*, *13*(1): 91–107. https://doi.org/10.1108/14637150710721140 (accessed 8 April 2022).

Shaw, J. (2018) 'Reusable versus disposable nappies: the real story of their environmental impact', Baba+Boo. https://www.babaandboo.com/blogs/news/reusable-versus-disposable-nappies-the-real-story-of-their-environmental-impact (accessed 8 April 2022).

Shimokawa, S. (2015) 'Sustainable meat consumption in China', *Journal of Integrative Agriculture*, *14*(6): 1023–1032. https://doi.org/10.1016/S2095-3119(14)60986-2 (accessed 8 April 2022).

Silver, D. (2016) 'Deep reinforcement learning', Google Deepmind. https://deepmind.com/blog/deep-reinforcement-learning (accessed 8 April 2022).

Silverman, D. (2000) *Doing Qualitative Research*. Thousand Oaks, CA: Sage.

Smith, J. (2021) Interviews with Polestar CEO.

Stewart, T.A. and O'Connell, P. (2017) 'The art of customer delight', *Strategy+Business*. http://www.strategy-business.com/article/The-Art-of-Customer-Delight (accessed 8 April 2022).

Styhre, A. (2002) 'How process philosophy can contribute to strategic management', *Systems Research and Behavioral Science*, *19*(6): 577–587. https://doi.org/10.1002/sres.475 (accessed 8 April 2022).

Subramanian, S. and Rao, A. (2019) 'How to build disruptive strategic flywheels', *Strategy+Business*, 19. https://www.strategy-business.com/article/How-to-build-disruptive-strategic-flywheels (accessed 8 April 2022).

Sweney, M. (2021) 'Global shortage in computer chips "reaches crisis point"', *The Guardian*, March. https://www.theguardian.com/business/2021/mar/21/global-shortage-in-computer-chips-reaches-crisis-point (accessed 8 April 2022).

Taguchi, G. and Yokoyama, Y. (1994) *Taguchi Methods: Design of Experiments*. Dearborn MI: American Supplier Institute.

Tainter, J. and Patzak, T. (2012) *Drilling Down: The Gulf Oil Debacle and Our Energy Dilemma*. New York: Copernicus Books

Taleb, N.N. (2007) *The Black Swan: The Impact of the Highly Improbable*. New York: Random House.

Taleb, N.N., Goldstein, D.G. and Spitznagel, M.W. (2009) 'The six mistakes executives make in risk management', *Harvard Business Review*, 87(10): 78–81.

Teece, D.J., Pisano, G. and Shuen, A. (1997) 'Dynamic capabilities and strategic management', *Strategic Management Journal*, *18*(7): 509–533. https://doi.org/10.1002/(SICI)1097-0266(199708)18:7<509::AID-SMJ882>3.0.CO;2-Z (accessed 8 April 2022).

Terracycle (2021) 'Recycled products'. https://www.terracycle.com/en-GB/pages/recycled-products (accessed 8 April 2022).

Thomke, S. (2020) 'Building a culture of experimentation', *Harvard Business Review*, *98*(2): 40–47.

Tueanrat, Y., Papagiannidis, S. and Alamanos, E. (2021) 'Going on a journey: a review of the customer journey literature', *Journal of Business Research*, *125*: 336–353. DOI: 10.1016/j.jbusres.2020.12.028.

Uexküll, J.V. (1957) 'A stroll through the worlds of animals and men: a picture book of invisible worlds', in *Instinctive Behavior: The Development of a Modern Concept*, edited and translated by Claire H. Schiller.

van Heck, E. and Vervest, P. (2007) 'Smart business networks: how the network wins', *Communications of the ACM*, *50*(6): 28–37. DOI: 10.1145/1247001.1247002.

Vargo, S.L. and Lusch, R.F. (2004) 'Evolving to a new dominant logic for marketing', *Journal of Marketing* (*68*), 1–17. https://doi.org/10.1509%2Fjmkg.68.1.1.24036 (accessed 8 April 2022).

Varian, H.R. (2007) 'Kaizen, that continuous improvement strategy, finds its ideal environment', *New York Times*, 8 February.

Waller, D. (2020) 'Ten steps to creating a data-driven culture', *Harvard Business Review*, February. https://hbr.org/2020/02/10-steps-to-creating-a-data-driven-culture (accessed 8 April 2022).

Waymo (2021) 'Waymo Driver', Waymo. https://waymo.com/waymo-driver (accessed 8 April 2022).

Waze (2021a) 'About us', Waze. https://www.waze.com (accessed 8 April 2022).

Waze (2021b) 'Waze for cities', Waze. https://www.waze.com/wazeforcities (accessed 8 April 2022).

Webb, J. (2017) 'What is supplier development? Three levers to get the most from the supply base', Forbes. https://www.forbes.com/sites/jwebb/2017/04/27/what-is-supplier-development-three-levers-to-get-the-most-from-the-supply-base (accessed 8 April 2022).

Wedel, M. and Kannan, P.K. (2016) 'Marketing analytics for data-rich environments', *Journal of Marketing*, *80*(6): 97–121. https://doi.org/10.1509%2Fjm.15.0413 (accessed 8 April 2022).

Wells, G., Horwitz, J. and Seetharaman, D. (2021) 'Facebook knows Instagram is toxic for teen girls', *The Wall Street Journal*. https://www.wsj.com/articles/facebook-knows-instagram-is-toxic-for-teen-girls-company-documents-show-11631620739 (accessed 8 April 2022).

Welsh, M. (2014) 'Resilience and responsibility: governing uncertainty in a complex world', *The Geographical Journal*, *180*(1): 15–26. https://doi.org/10.1111/geoj.12012 (accessed 8 April 2022).

Weyler, R. (2018) 'A brief history of environmentalism', Greenpeace. https://www.greenpeace.org/international/story/11658/a-brief-history-of-environmentalism (accessed 8 April 2022).

Wiener, N. (1948) *Cybernetics: Or Control and Communication in the Animal and the Machine*. Cambridge, MA: MIT Press (2nd revised edn, 1961).

Yong, E. (2008) 'Immune snakes outrun toxic newts in evolutionary arms races', National Geographic. https://www.nationalgeographic.com/science/phenomena/2008/03/10/immune-snakes-outrun-toxic-newts-in-evolutionary-arms-races (accessed 8 April 2022).

Zanolli, L. and Oliver, M. (2019) 'Explained: the toxic threat in everyday products, from toys to plastic', *The Guardian*. https://www.theguardian.com/us-news/2019/may/22/toxic-chemicals-everyday-items-us-pesticides-bpa (accessed 8 April 2022).

Zapier (2021) 'Unlock a more efficient way to work', Zapier. https://zapier.com/how-it-works (accessed 8 April 2022).

Zoho (2021) 'Homepage'. https://www.zoho.com (accessed 8 April 2022).

INDEX

Note: page numbers in *italic* type refer to figures and tables.